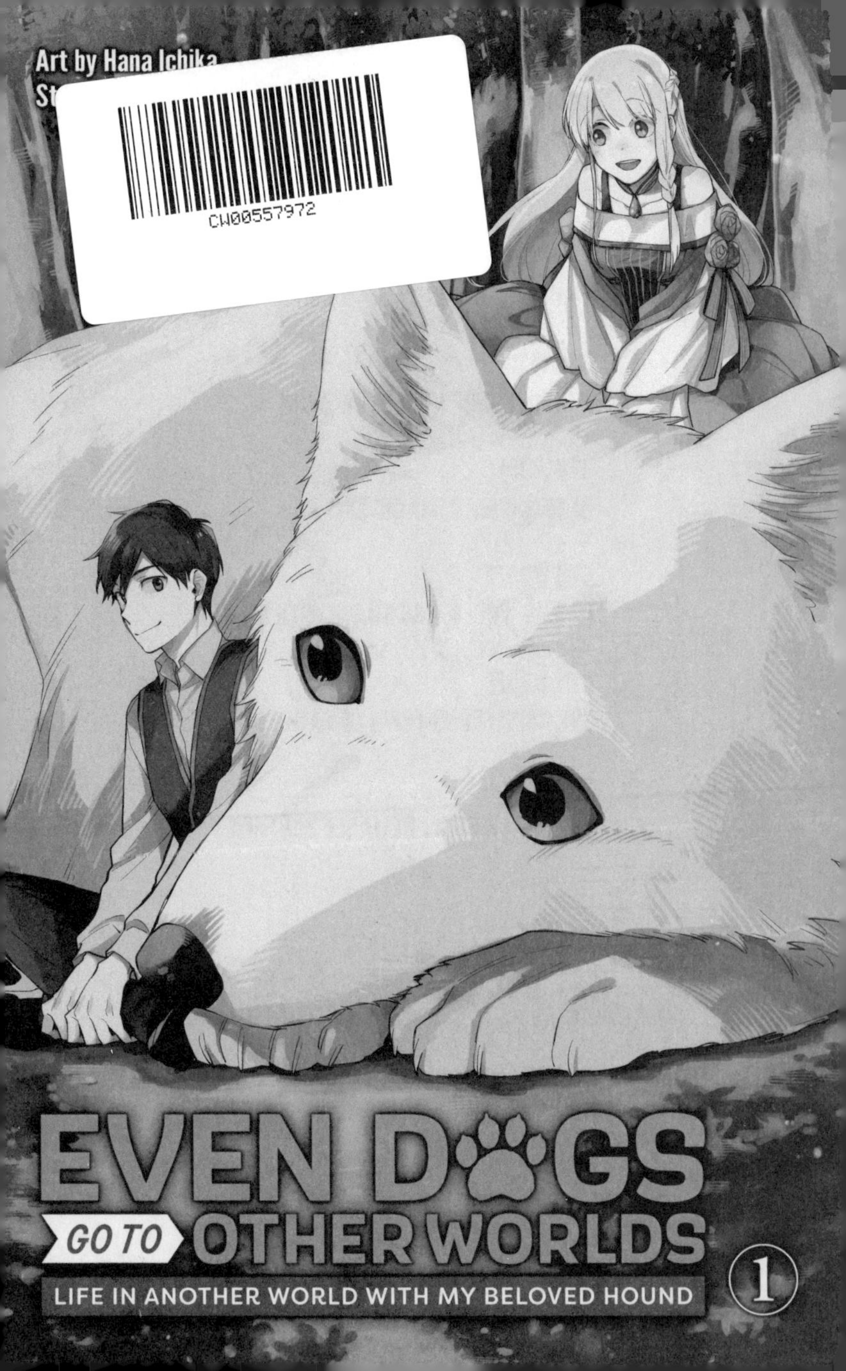
Art by Hana Ichika
EVEN DOGS GO TO OTHER WORLDS
LIFE IN ANOTHER WORLD WITH MY BELOVED HOUND
1

CONTENTS

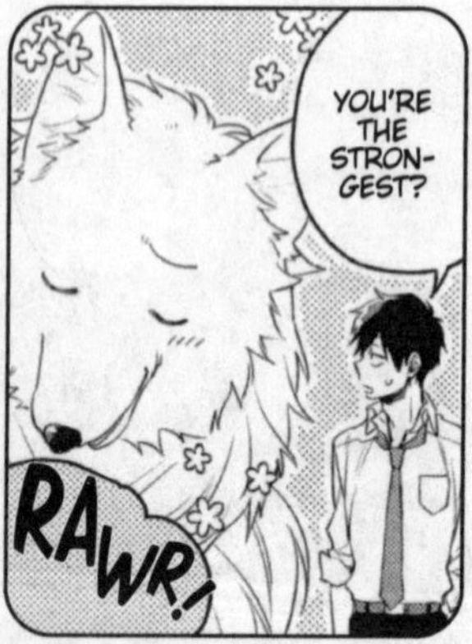

YOU'RE THE STRON-GEST?
RAWR!

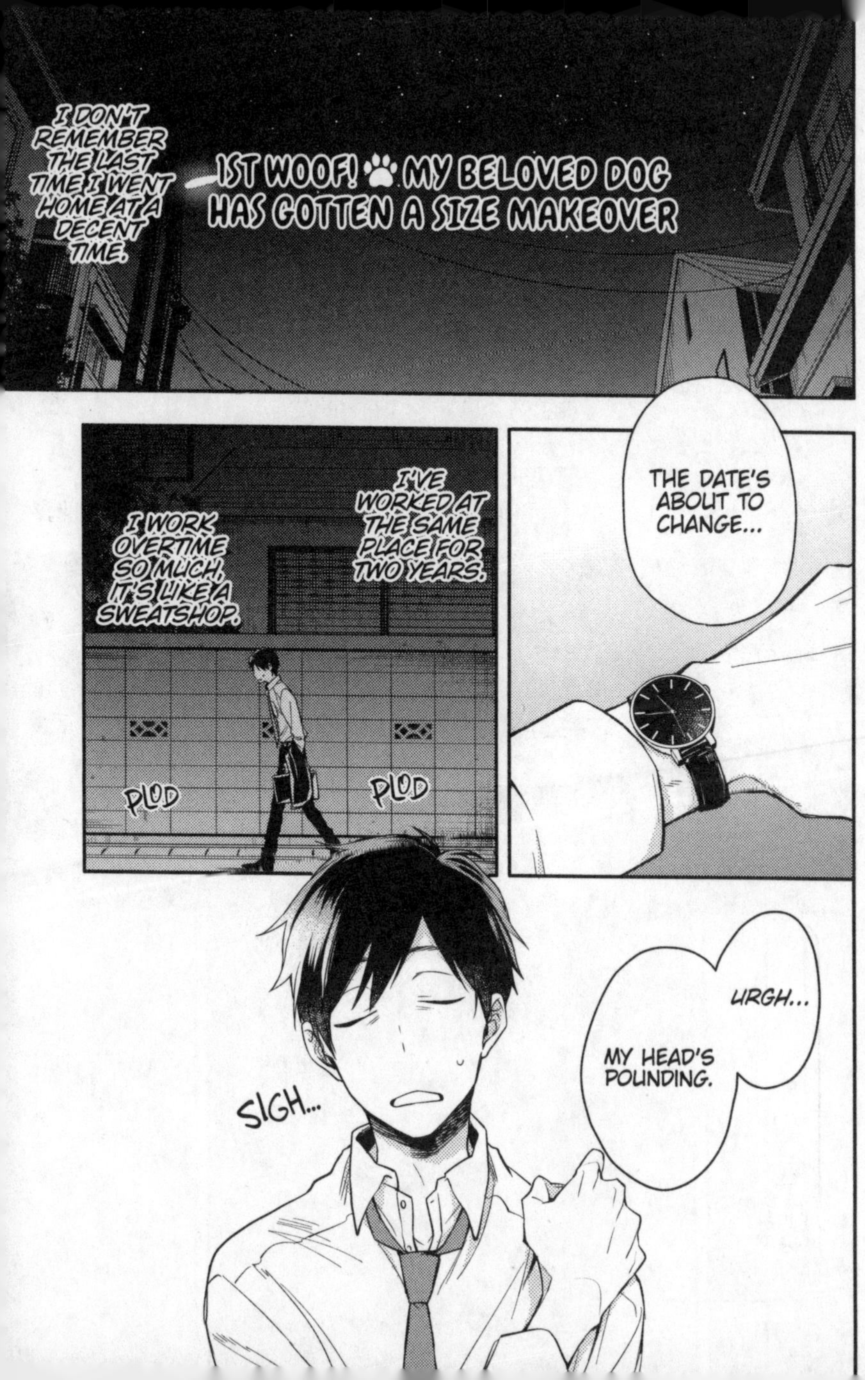
1ST WOOF! MY BELOVED DOG HAS GOTTEN A SIZE MAKEOVER
I DON'T REMEMBER THE LAST TIME I WENT HOME AT A DECENT TIME.
THE DATE'S ABOUT TO CHANGE...
I'VE WORKED AT THE SAME PLACE FOR TWO YEARS.
I WORK OVERTIME SO MUCH, IT'S LIKE A SWEATSHOP.
PLOD
PLOD
URGH...
MY HEAD'S POUNDING.
SIGH...

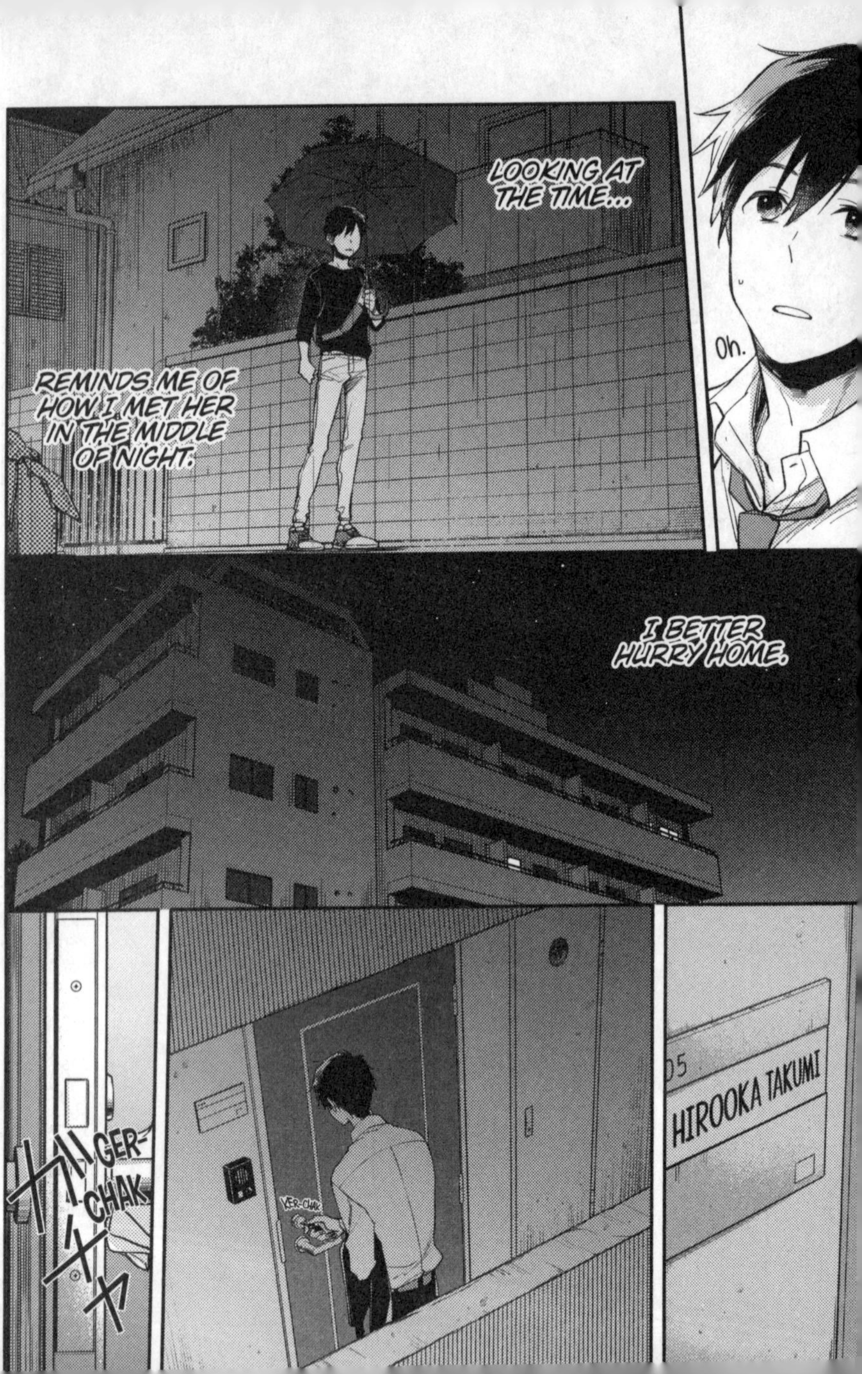
Oh.
LOOKING AT THE TIME...
REMINDS ME OF HOW I MET HER IN THE MIDDLE OF NIGHT.
I BETTER HURRY HOME.
HIROOKA TAKUMI
KER-CHAK
GER-CHAK

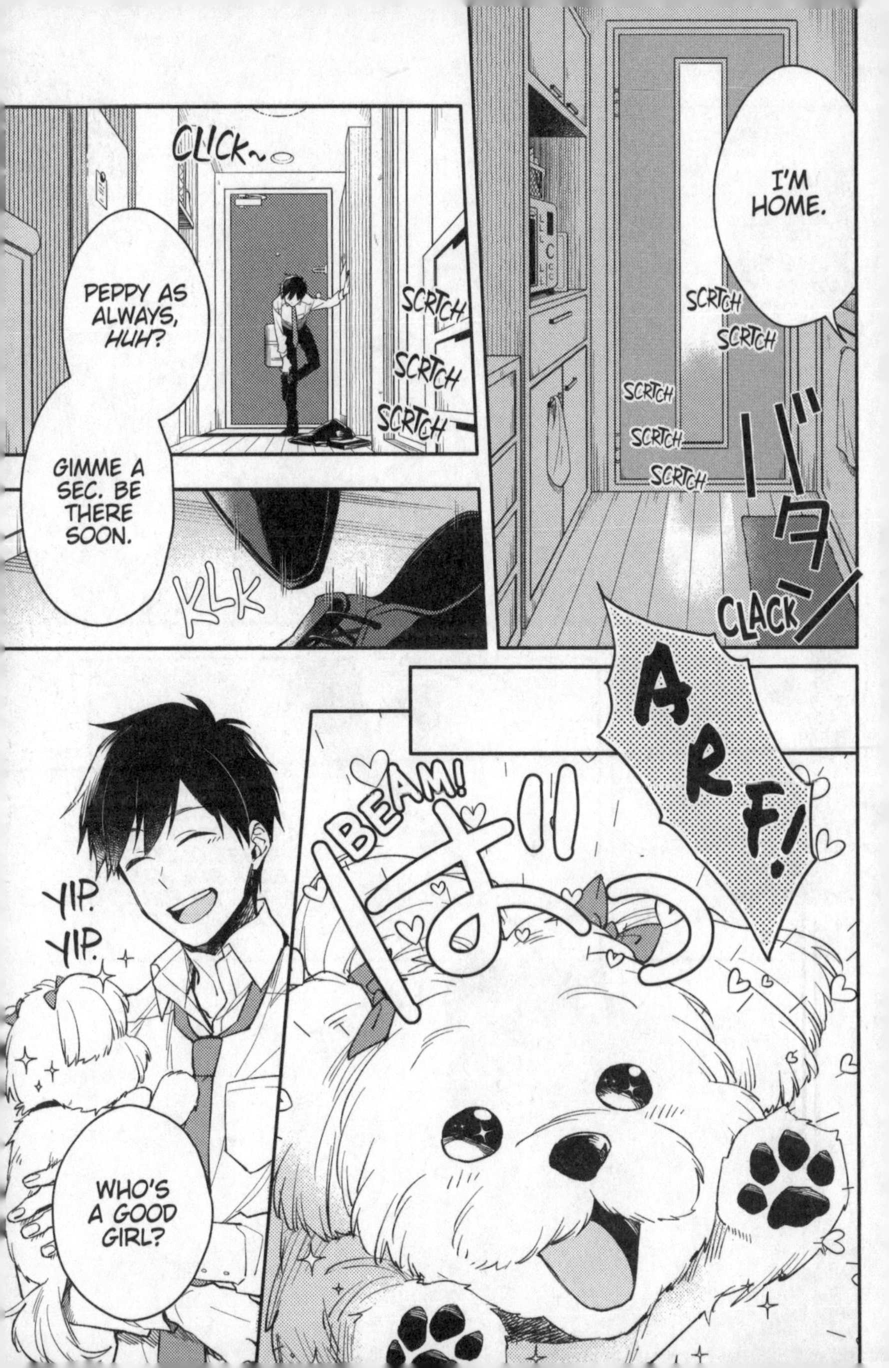

I'M HOME.
SCRTCH
SCRTCH
SCRTCH
SCRTCH
SCRTCH
バタ
CLACK
CLICK~
PEPPY AS ALWAYS, HUH?
SCRTCH
SCRTCH
SCRTCH
GIMME A SEC. BE THERE SOON.
KLK
ARF!
BEAM!
YIP.
YIP.
WHO'S A GOOD GIRL?

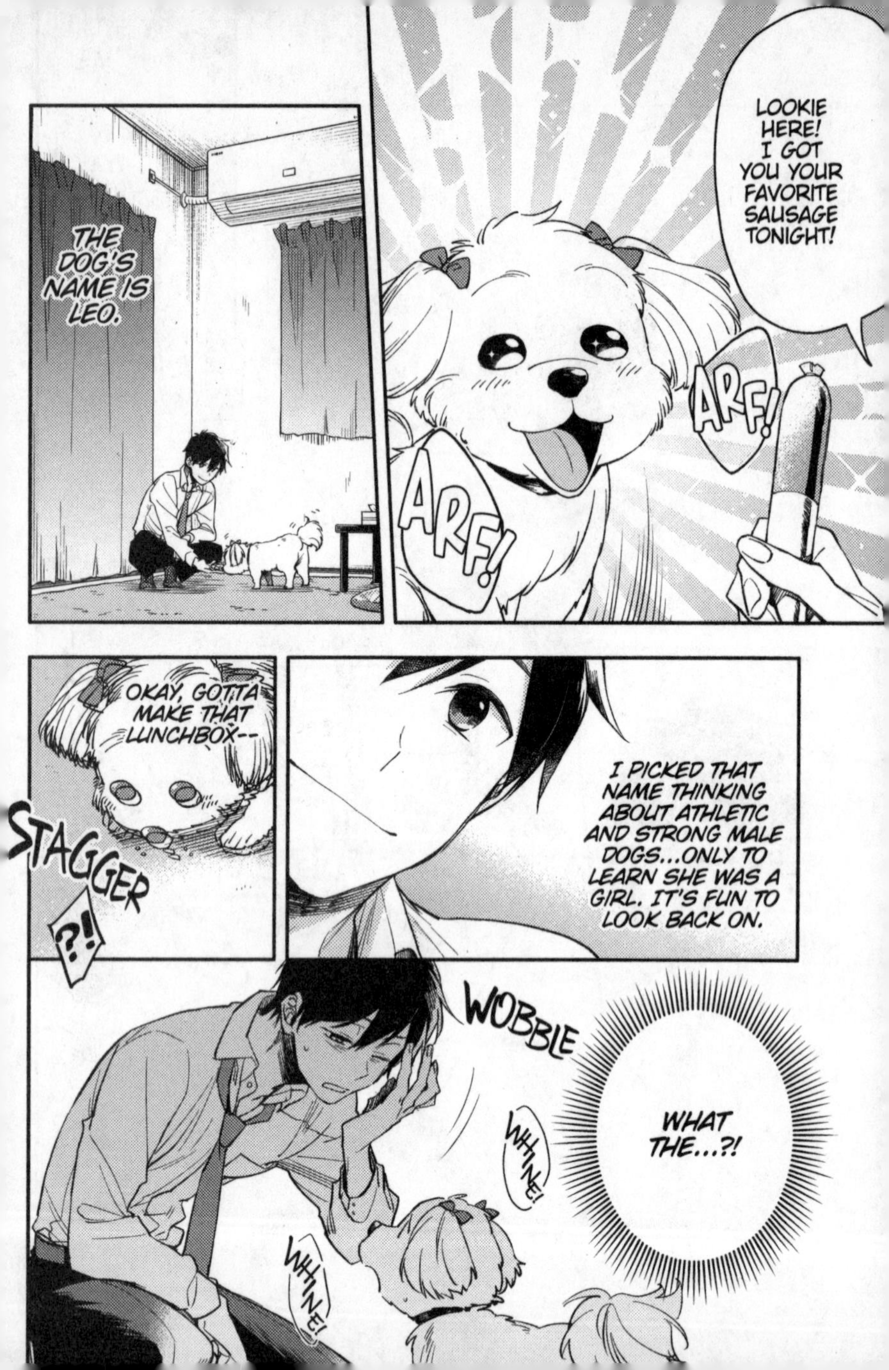
LOOKIE HERE! I GOT YOU YOUR FAVORITE SAUSAGE TONIGHT!
ARF!
ARF!
THE DOG'S NAME IS LEO.
I PICKED THAT NAME THINKING ABOUT ATHLETIC AND STRONG MALE DOGS...ONLY TO LEARN SHE WAS A GIRL. IT'S FUN TO LOOK BACK ON.
OKAY, GOTTA MAKE THAT LUNCHBOX--
STAGGER
?!
WOBBLE
WHAT THE...?!
WHINE!
WHINE!

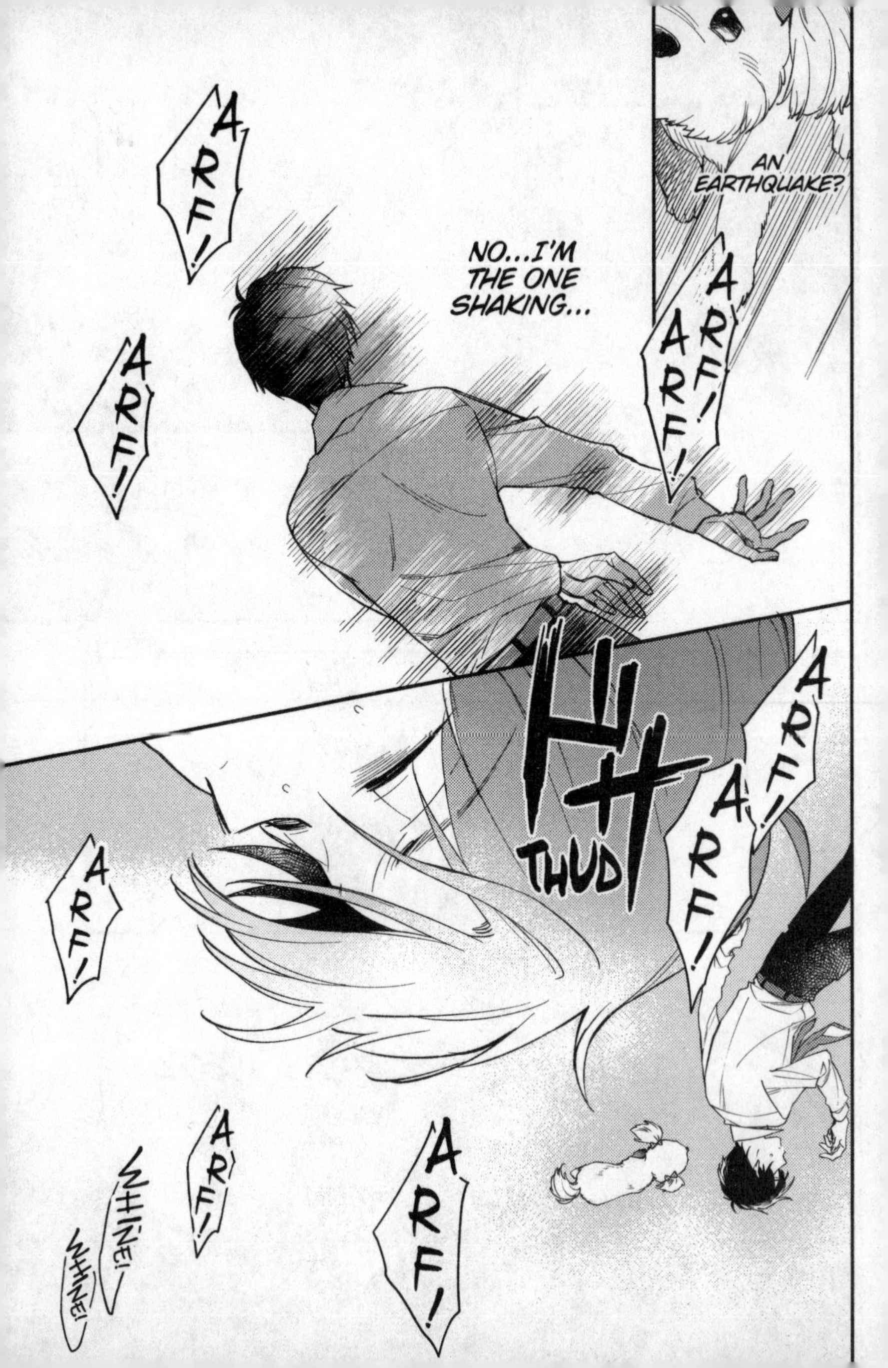
AN EARTHQUAKE?
ARF!
ARF!
NO...I'M THE ONE SHAKING...
ARF!
ARF!
THUD
ARF!
ARF!
ARF!
ARF!
ARF!
WHINE!
WHINE!

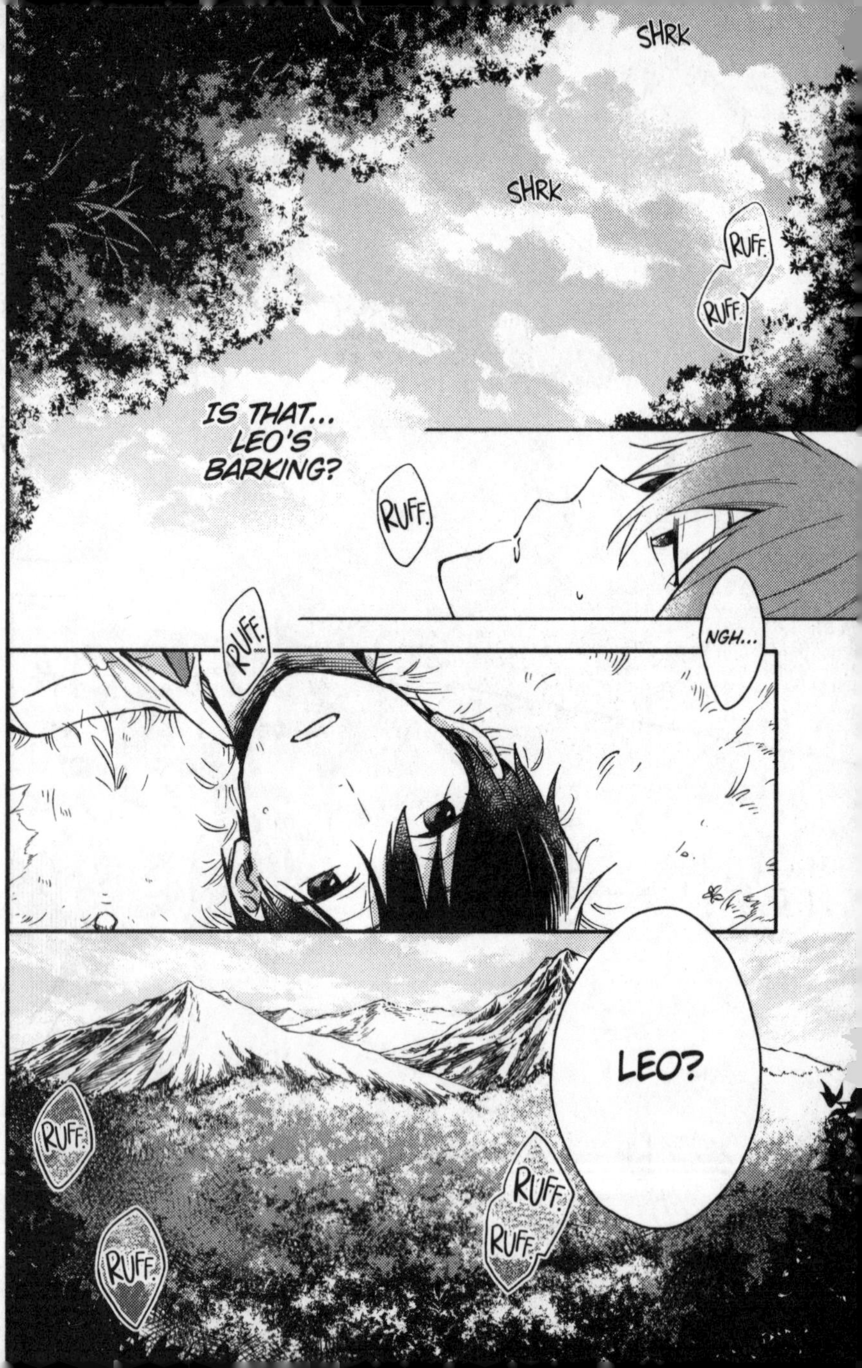
SHRK
SHRK
RUFF.
RUFF.
IS THAT... LEO'S BARKING?
NGH...
RUFF.
RUFF.
LEO?
RUFF.
RUFF.
RUFF.
RUFF.

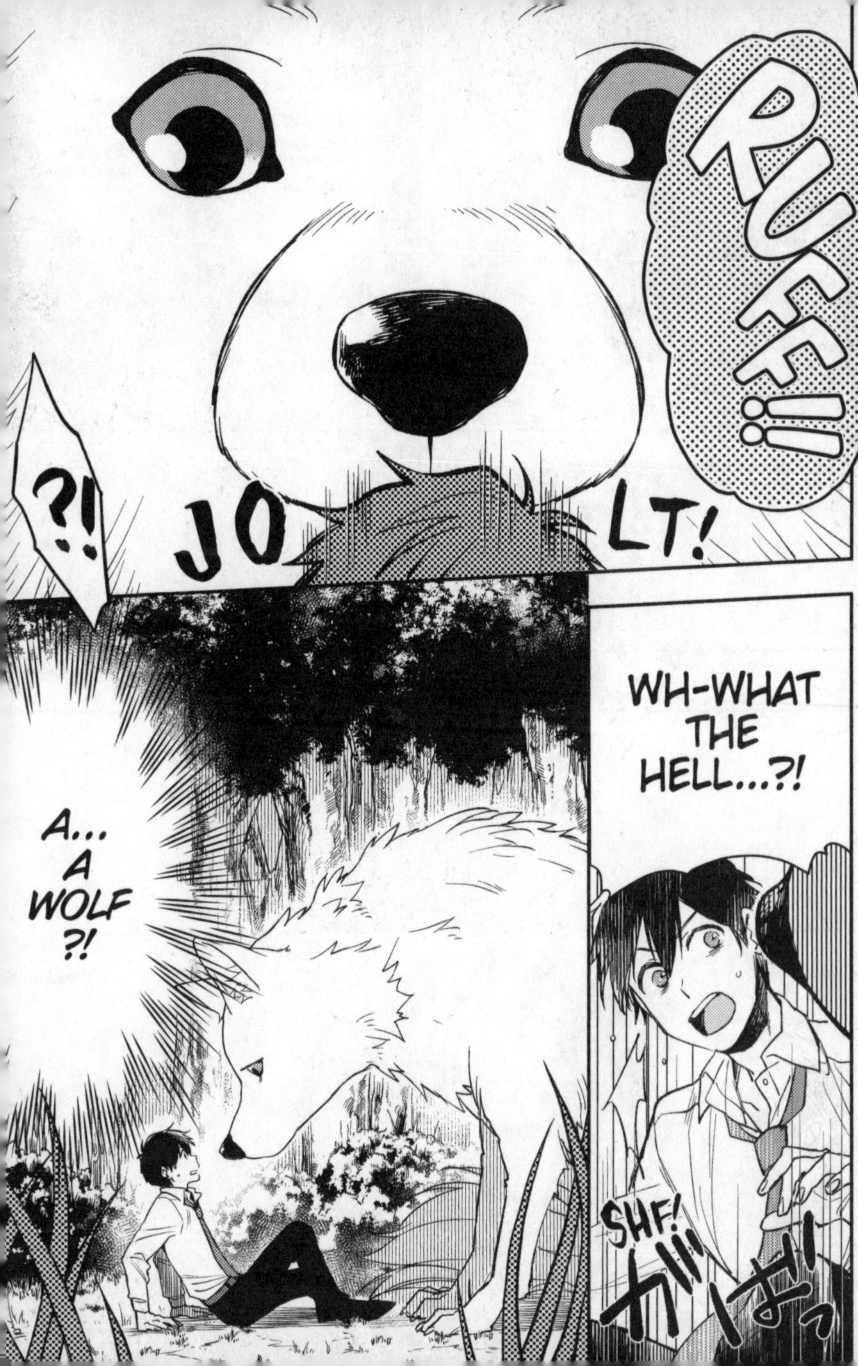
RUFF!!!
JOLT!
?!
WH-WHAT THE HELL...?!
SHF!
がばっ
A... A WOLF ?!

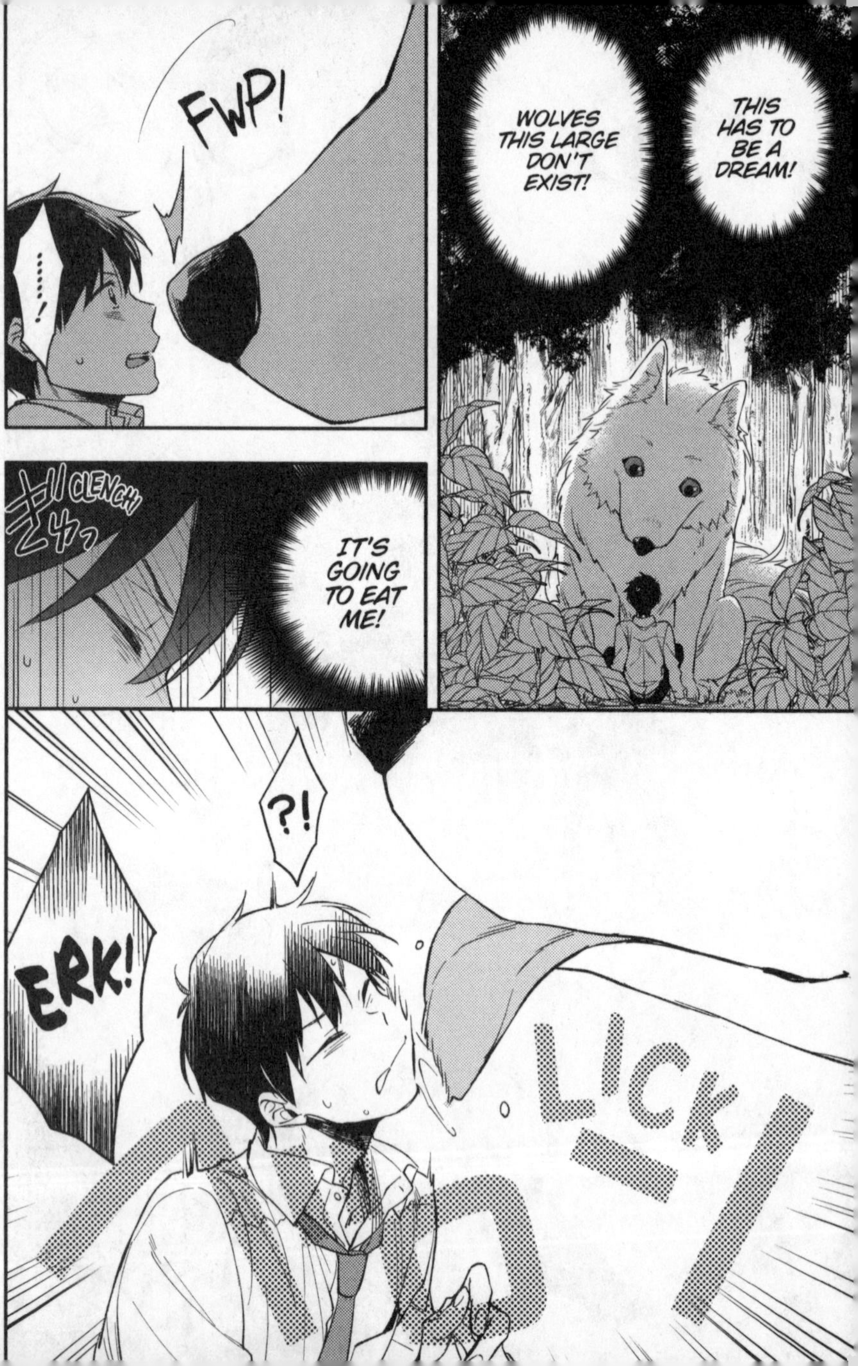
THIS HAS TO BE A DREAM!
WOLVES THIS LARGE DON'T EXIST!
FWP!
......!
IT'S GOING TO EAT ME!
ぎゅっ
CLENCH
?!
LICK!
ERK!

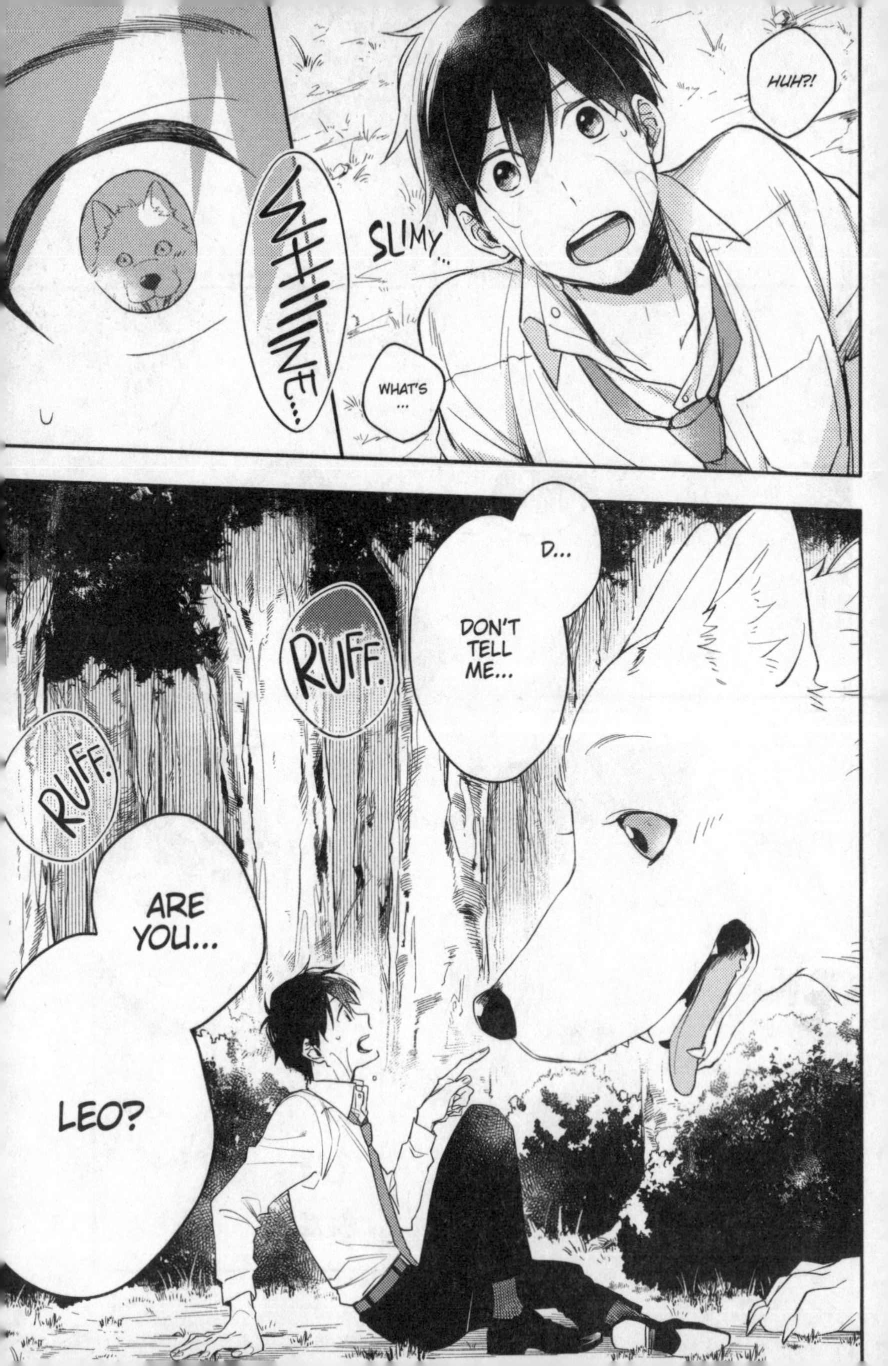
HUH?!
SLIMY...
WHAT'S ...
WHIIINE...
D...
DON'T TELL ME...
RUFF.
RUFF.
ARE YOU...
LEO?

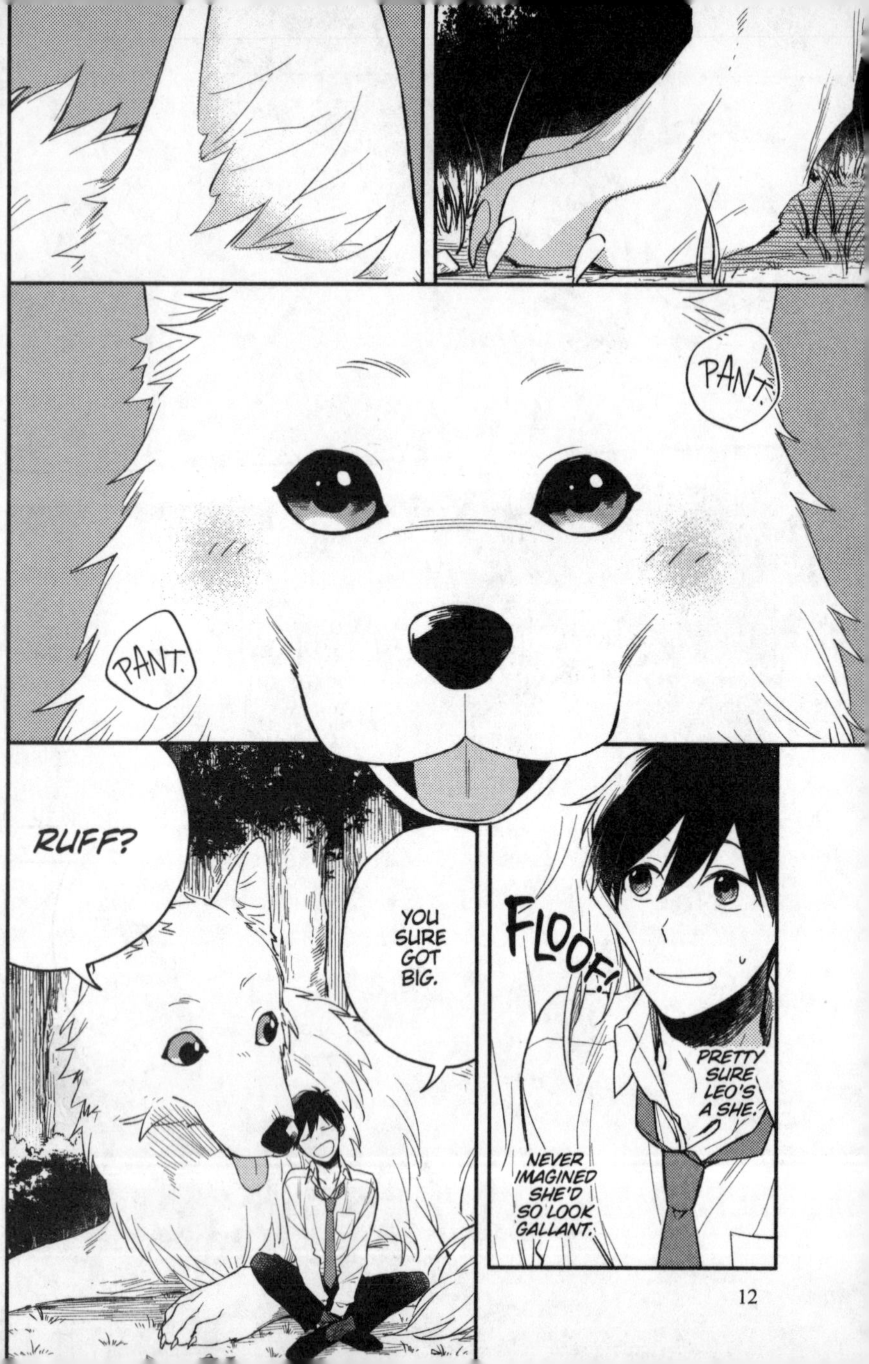
PANT.
PANT.
FLOOF!
PRETTY SURE LEO'S A SHE.
NEVER IMAGINED SHE'D SO LOOK GALLANT.
YOU SURE GOT BIG.
RUFF?

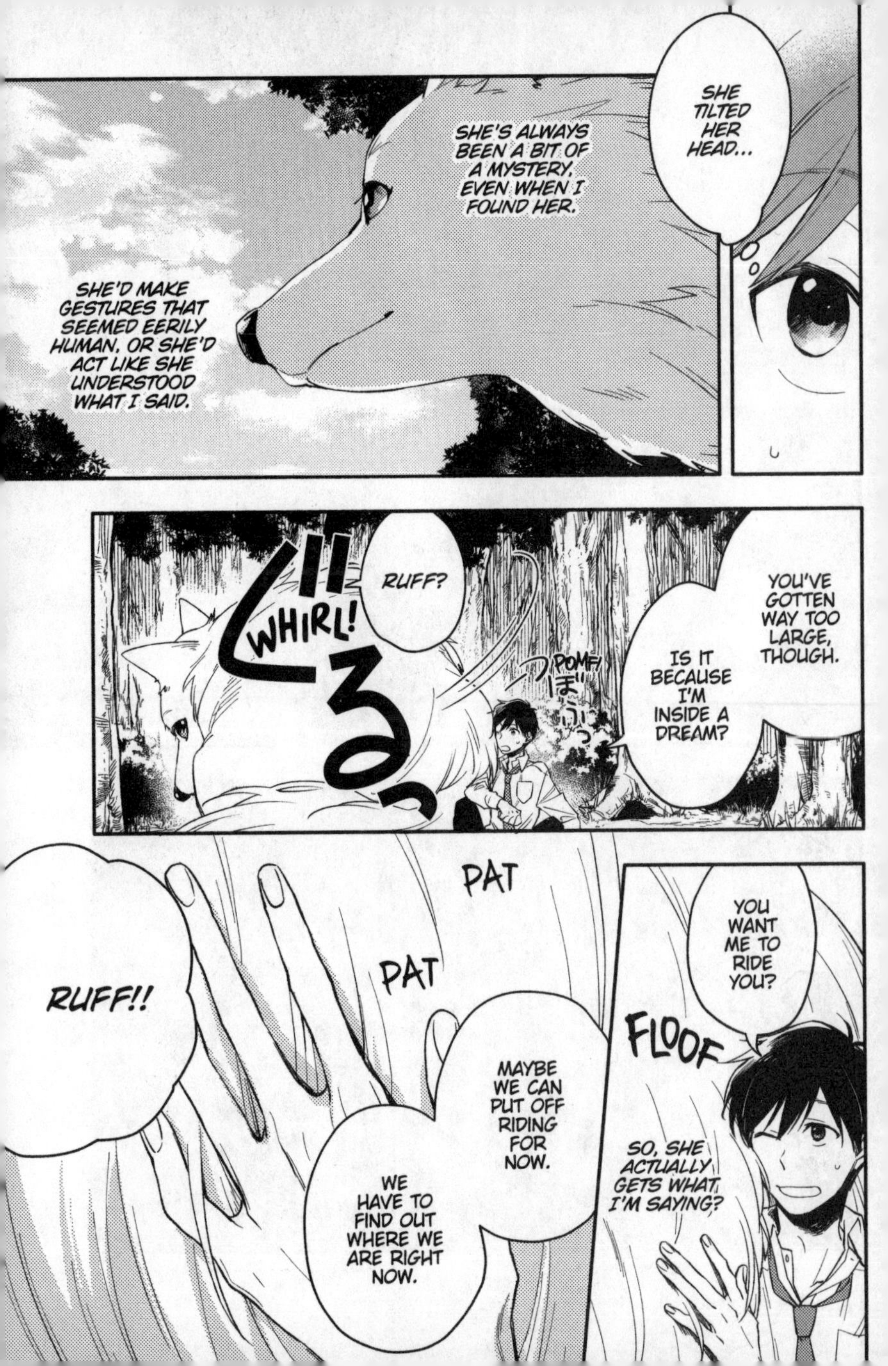
SHE TILTED HER HEAD...
SHE'S ALWAYS BEEN A BIT OF A MYSTERY, EVEN WHEN I FOUND HER.
SHE'D MAKE GESTURES THAT SEEMED EERILY HUMAN, OR SHE'D ACT LIKE SHE UNDERSTOOD WHAT I SAID.
YOU'VE GOTTEN WAY TOO LARGE, THOUGH.
IS IT BECAUSE I'M INSIDE A DREAM?
POMF
RUFF?
WHIRL!
YOU WANT ME TO RIDE YOU?
FLOOF
SO, SHE ACTUALLY GETS WHAT I'M SAYING?
PAT
PAT
MAYBE WE CAN PUT OFF RIDING FOR NOW.
WE HAVE TO FIND OUT WHERE WE ARE RIGHT NOW.
RUFF!!

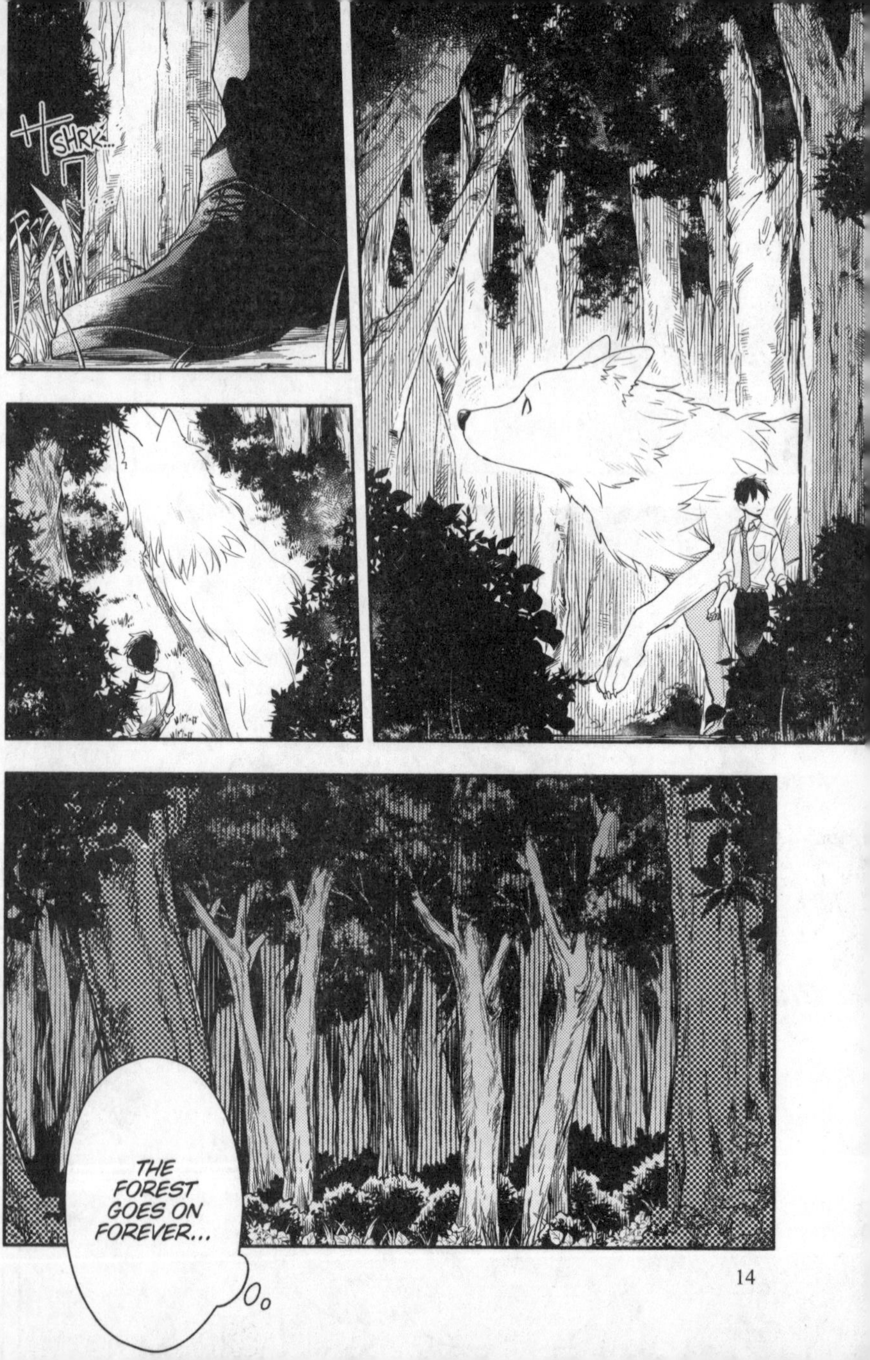
SHRK...
THE FOREST GOES ON FOREVER...

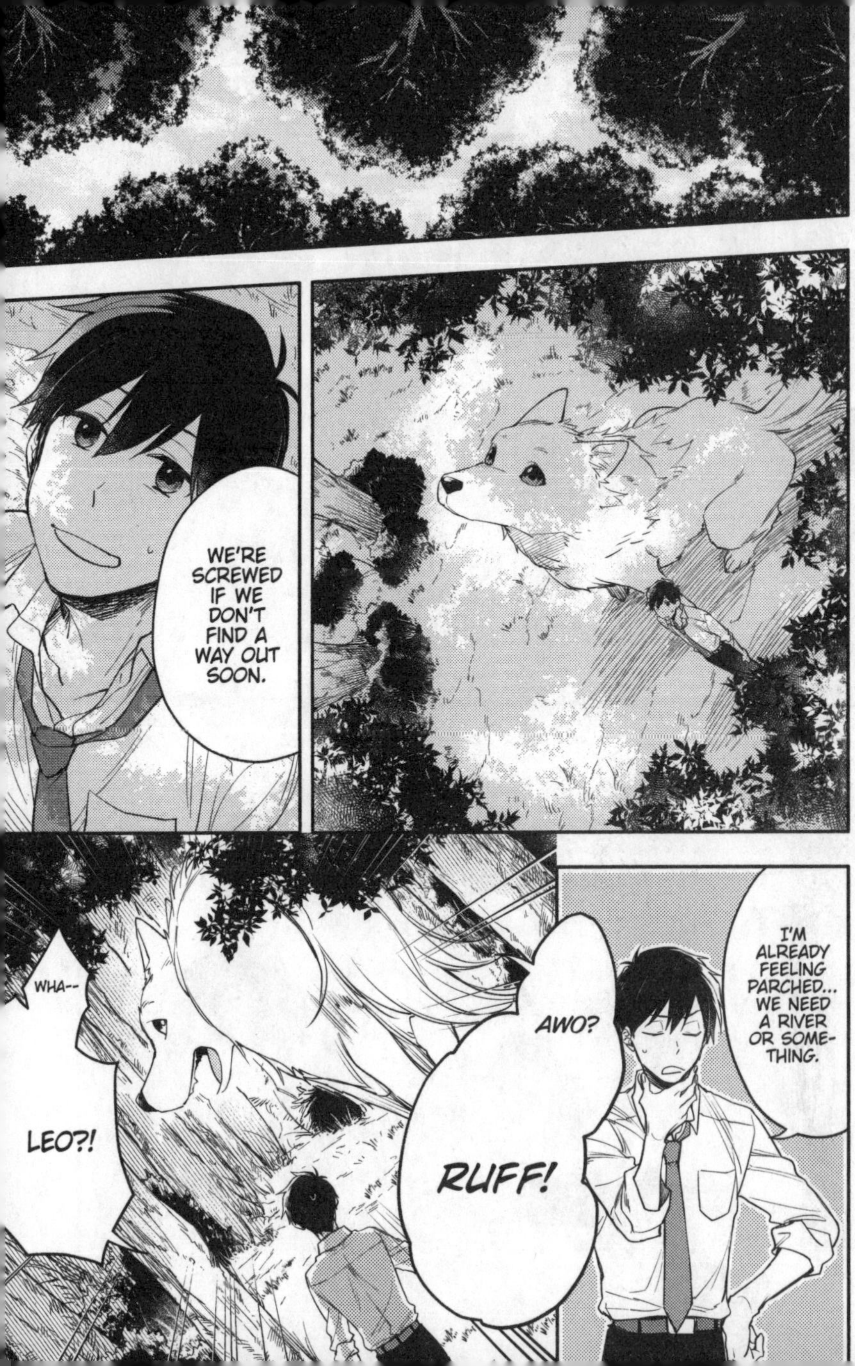
WE'RE SCREWED IF WE DON'T FIND A WAY OUT SOON.
I'M ALREADY FEELING PARCHED... WE NEED A RIVER OR SOME-THING.
AWO?
RUFF!
WHA--
LEO?!

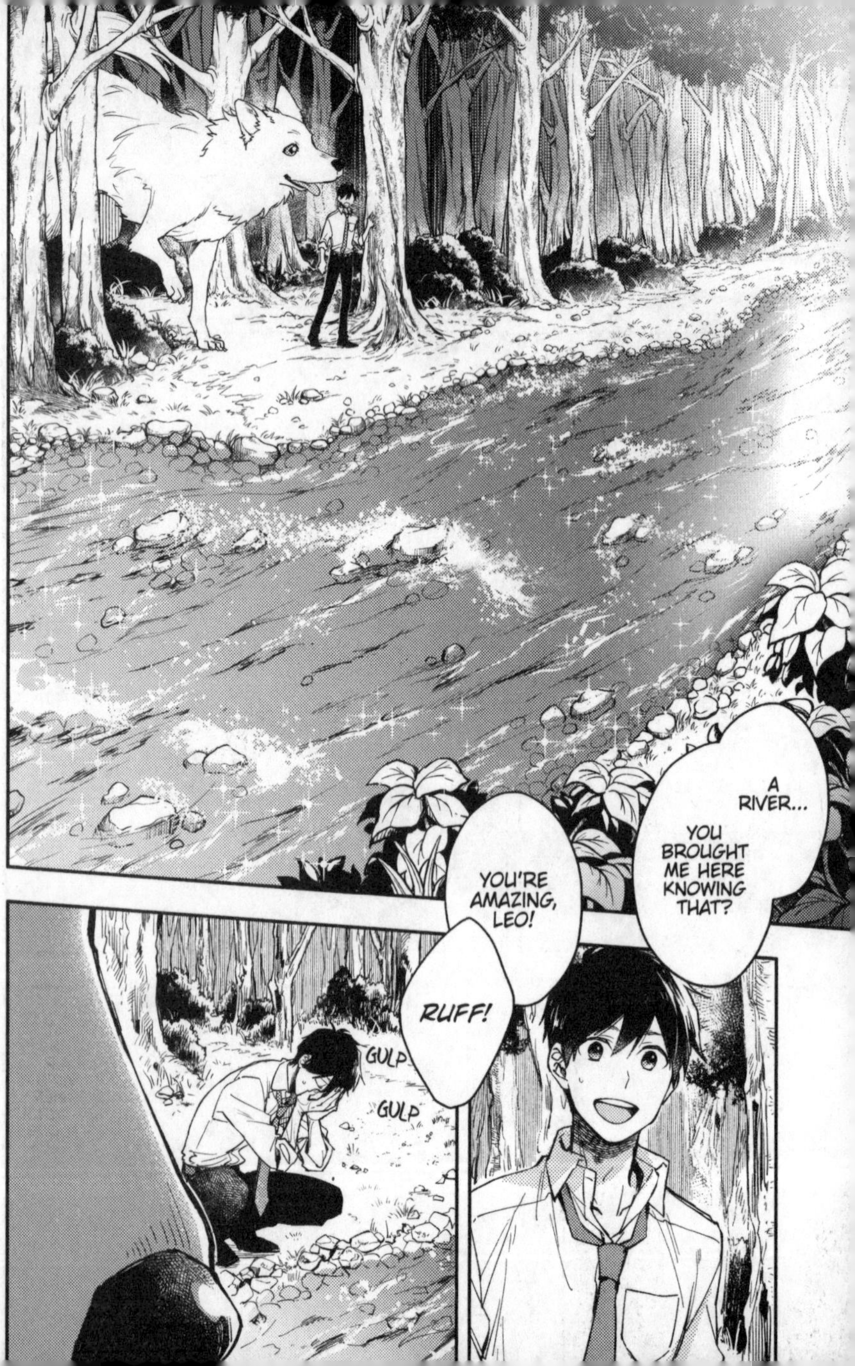
A RIVER...
YOU BROUGHT ME HERE KNOWING THAT?
YOU'RE AMAZING, LEO!
RUFF!
GULP
GULP

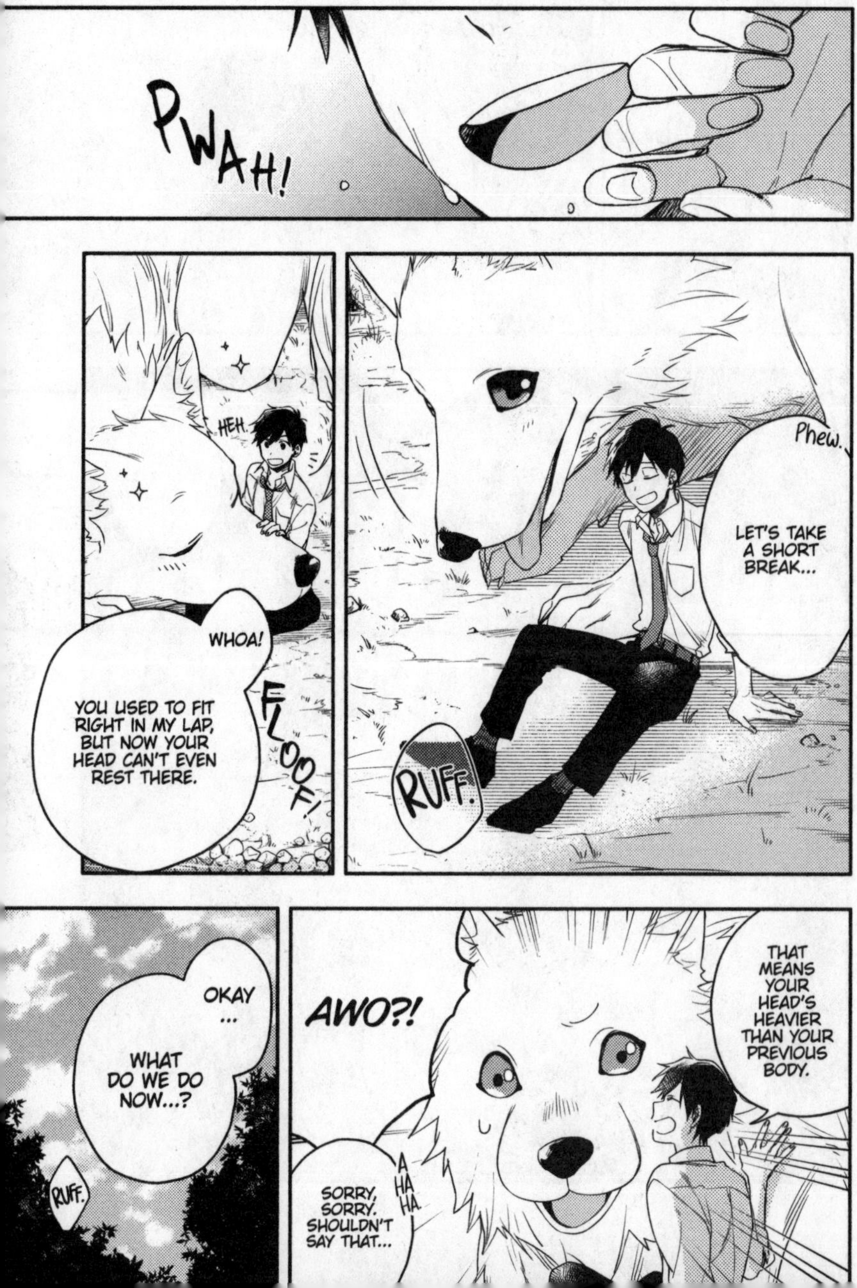
PWAH!
Phew.
LET'S TAKE A SHORT BREAK...
RUFF.
HEH.
WHOA!
YOU USED TO FIT RIGHT IN MY LAP, BUT NOW YOUR HEAD CAN'T EVEN REST THERE.
FLOOF!
THAT MEANS YOUR HEAD'S HEAVIER THAN YOUR PREVIOUS BODY.
AWO?!
A HA HA.
SORRY, SORRY. SHOULDN'T SAY THAT...
OKAY ... WHAT DO WE DO NOW...?
RUFF.

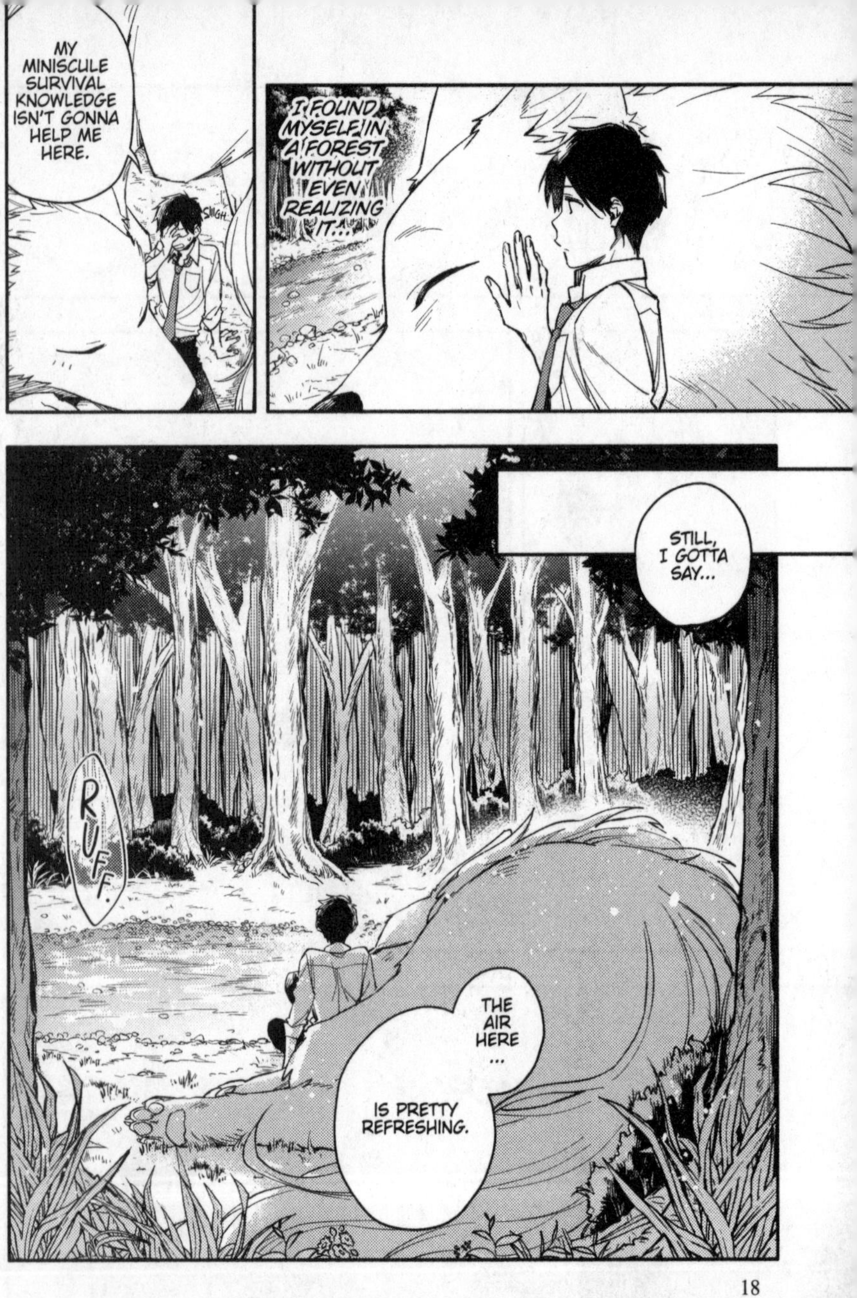
I FOUND MYSELF IN A FOREST WITHOUT EVEN REALIZING IT...
MY MINISCULE SURVIVAL KNOWLEDGE ISN'T GONNA HELP ME HERE.
SIIIGH...
STILL, I GOTTA SAY...
RUFF.
THE AIR HERE ...
IS PRETTY REFRESHING.

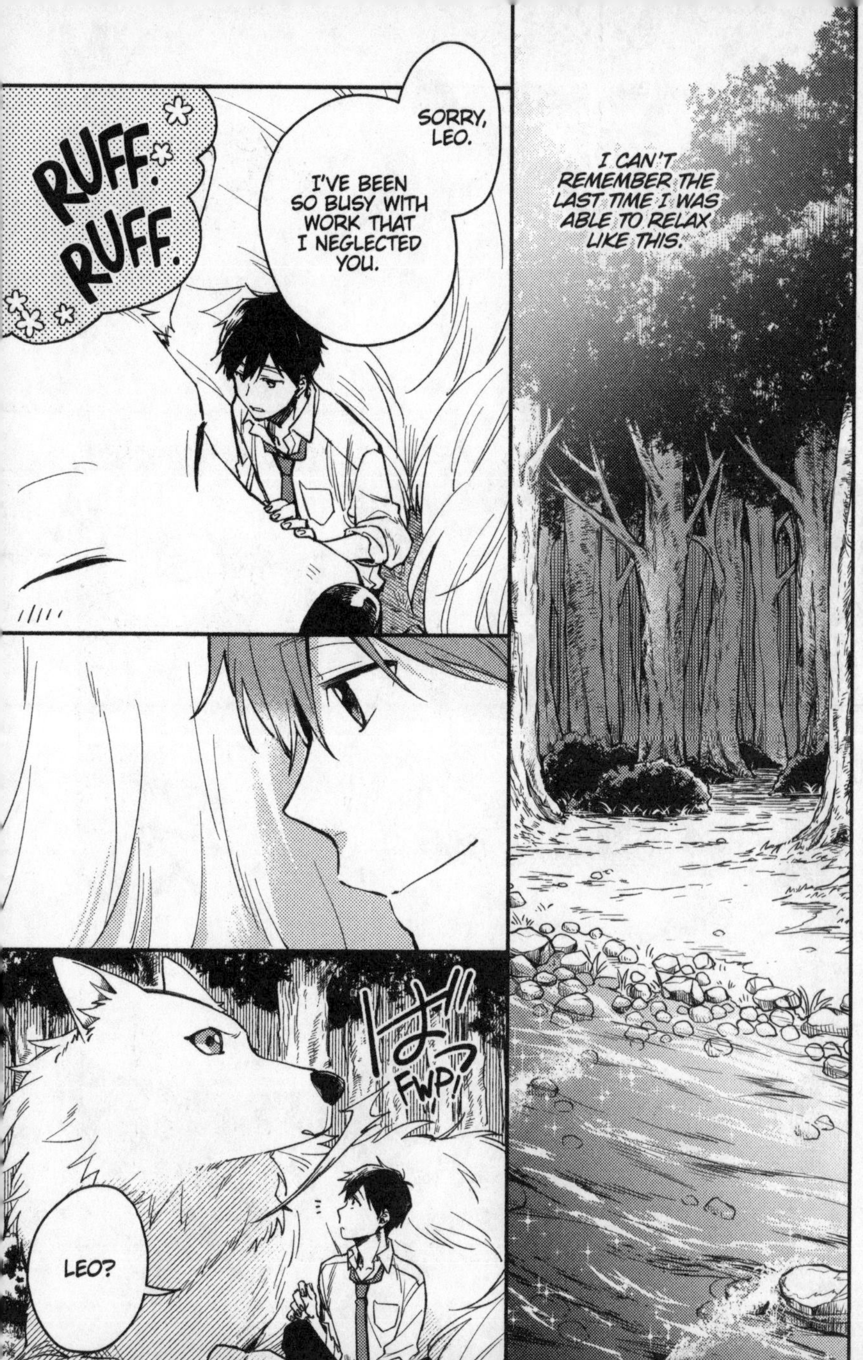
I CAN'T REMEMBER THE LAST TIME I WAS ABLE TO RELAX LIKE THIS.
SORRY, LEO.
I'VE BEEN SO BUSY WITH WORK THAT I NEGLECTED YOU.
RUFF. RUFF.
FWP!
LEO?

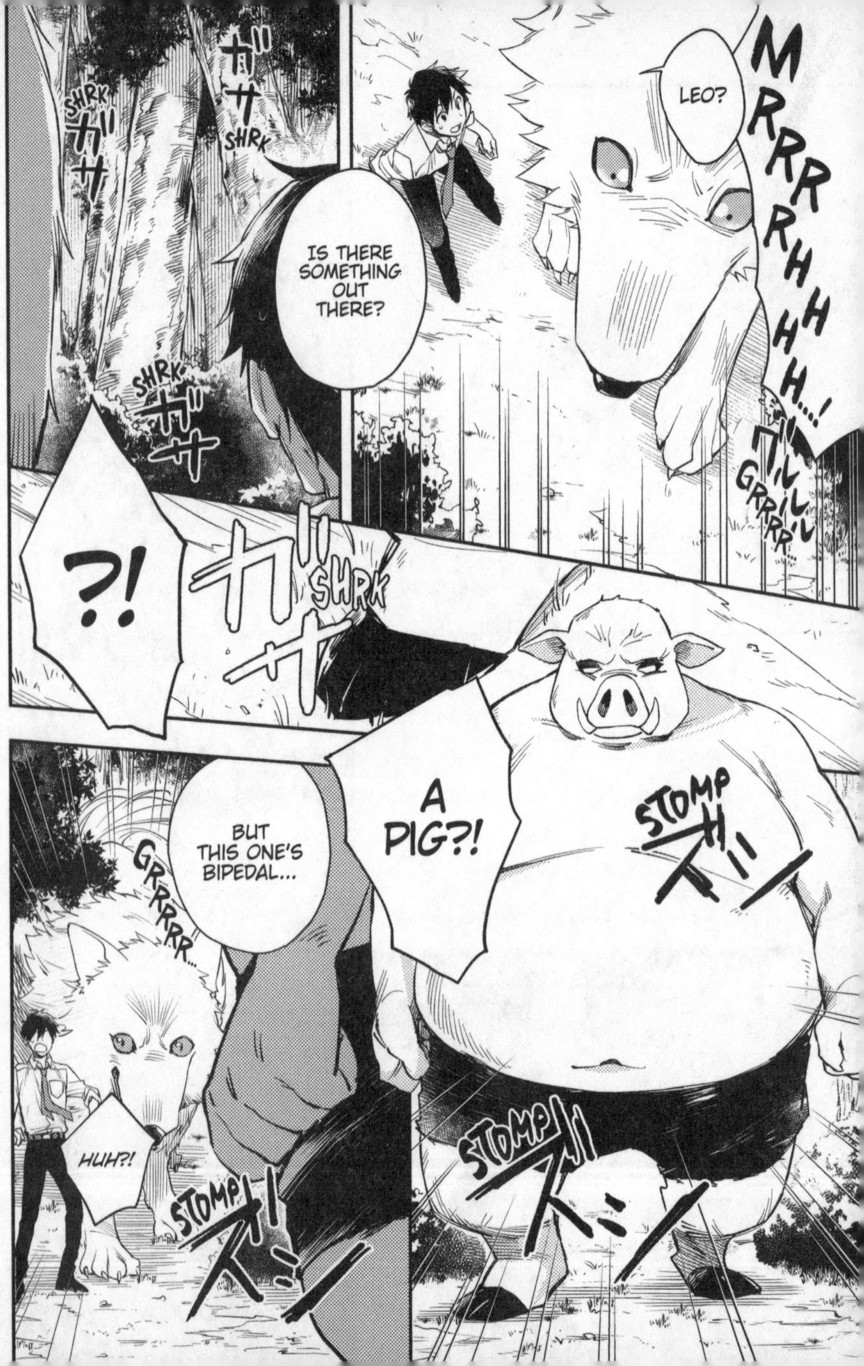

MRRRRHHHH...!
LEO?
グルルル
GRRRRR...
IS THERE SOMETHING OUT THERE?
ガサ
SHRK
SHRK
ガサ
SHRK
ガサ
SHRK
ガサ
?!
A PIG?!
STOMP
BUT THIS ONE'S BIPEDAL...
STOMP
GRRRRR...
HUH?!
STOMP

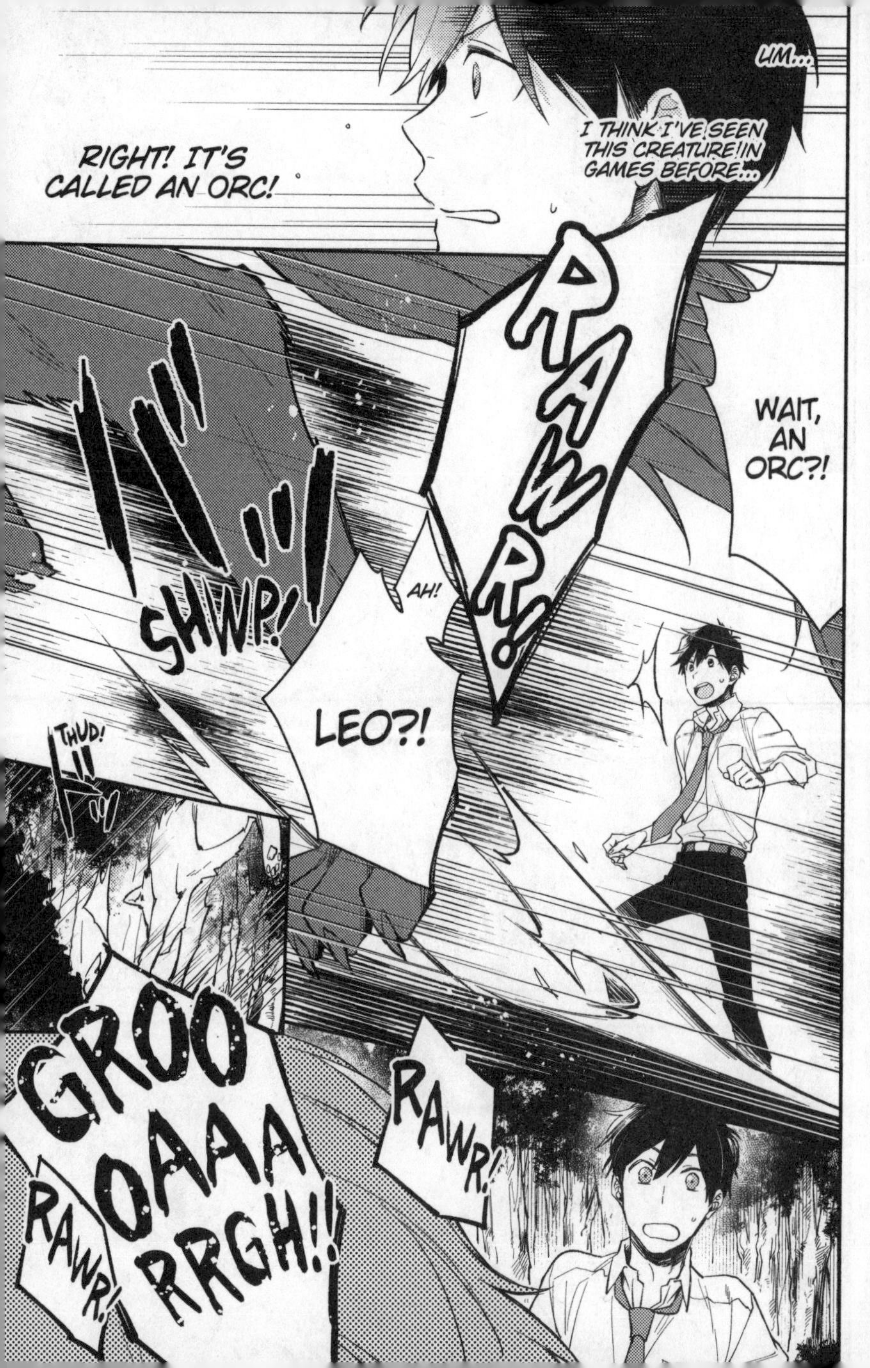
UM...
I THINK I'VE SEEN THIS CREATURE IN GAMES BEFORE...
RIGHT! IT'S CALLED AN ORC!
WAIT, AN ORC?!
RAWR!
SHWP!
AH!
LEO?!
THUD!
RAWR!
GROOOAAARRGH!!
RAWR!

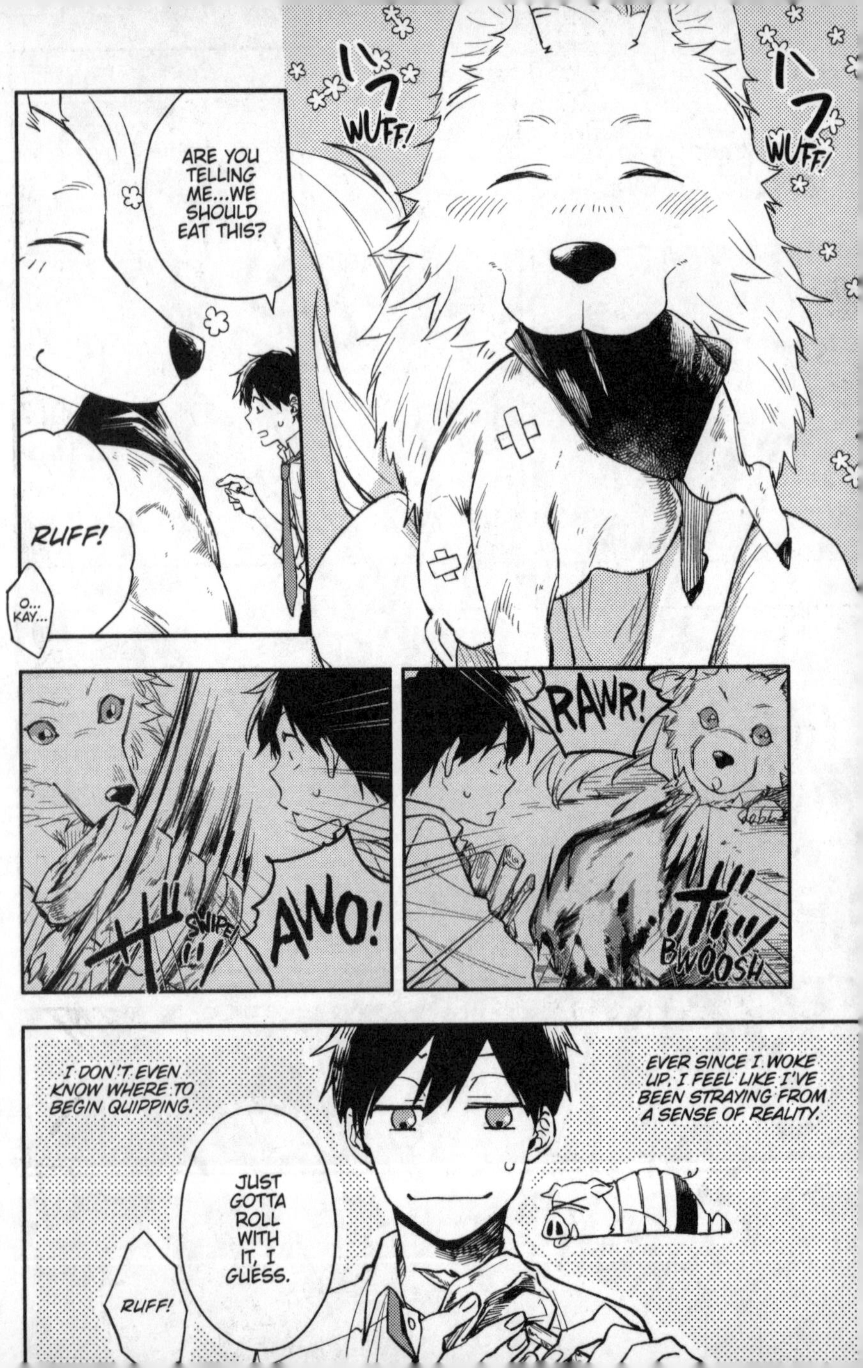
ハフ
WUFF!
ハフ
WUFF!
ARE YOU TELLING ME...WE SHOULD EAT THIS?
RUFF!
O... KAY...
RAWR!
BWOOSH
AWO!
SWIPE!
EVER SINCE I WOKE UP, I FEEL LIKE I'VE BEEN STRAYING FROM A SENSE OF REALITY.
I DON'T EVEN KNOW WHERE TO BEGIN QUIPPING.
JUST GOTTA ROLL WITH IT, I GUESS.
RUFF!

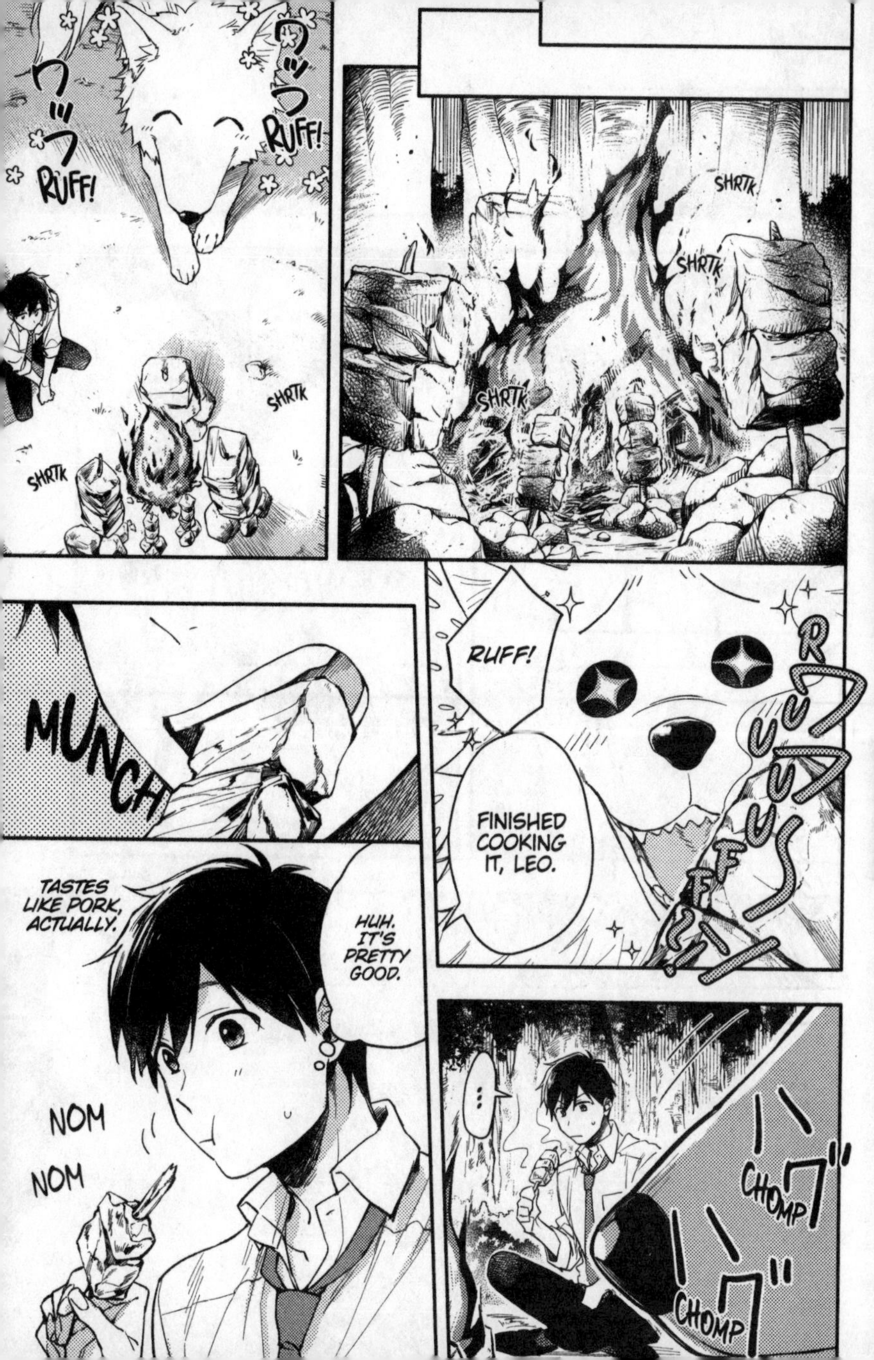
SHRTK
SHRTK
SHRTK
ワッフ
RUFF!
ワッフ
RUFF!
SHRTK
SHRTK
RUUUUFF
RUFF!
FINISHED COOKING IT, LEO.
MUNCH
...
CHOMP
CHOMP
HUH. IT'S PRETTY GOOD.
TASTES LIKE PORK, ACTUALLY.
NOM
NOM

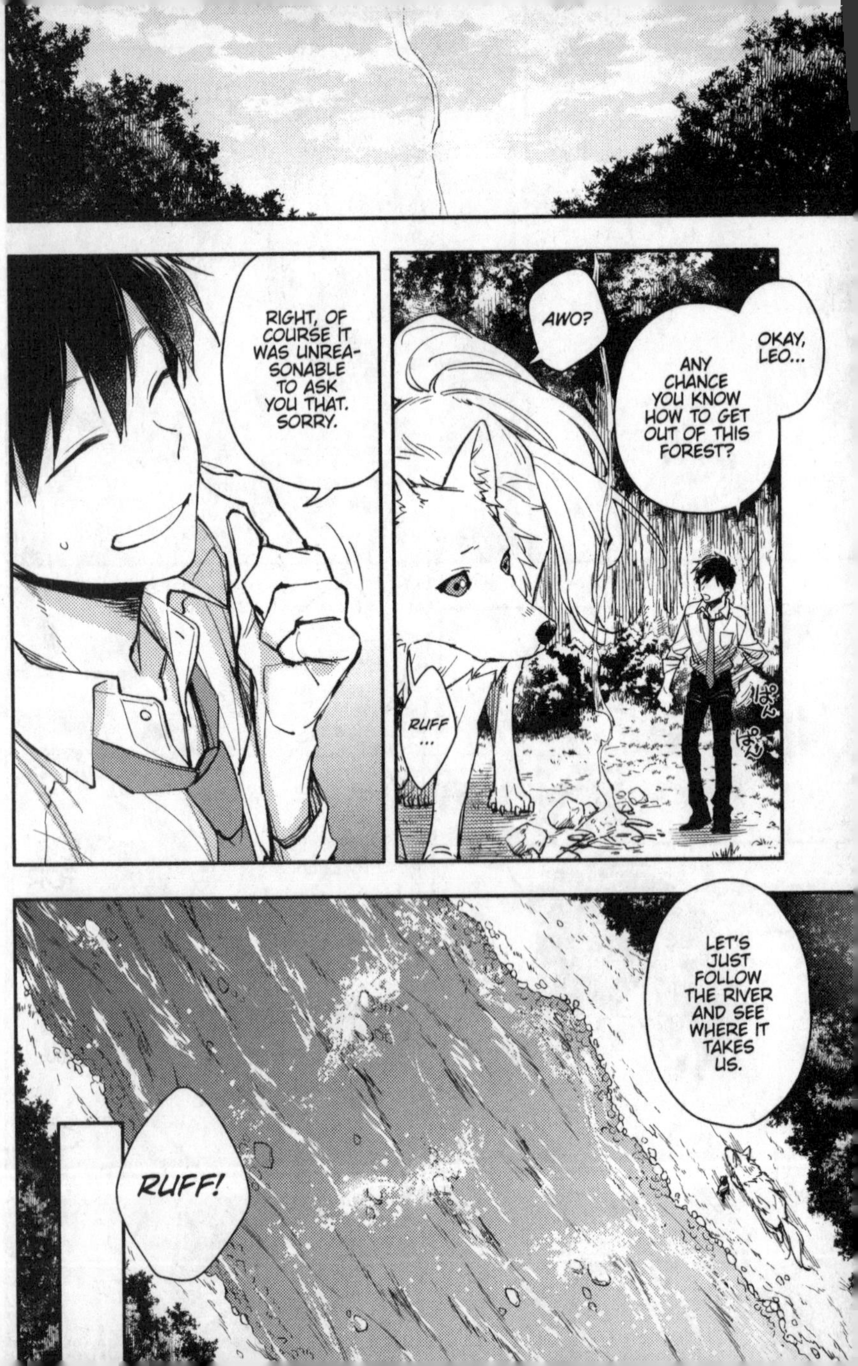
OKAY, LEO... ANY CHANCE YOU KNOW HOW TO GET OUT OF THIS FOREST?
AWO?
RUFF ...
ぱん
ぱん
RIGHT, OF COURSE IT WAS UNREASONABLE TO ASK YOU THAT. SORRY.
LET'S JUST FOLLOW THE RIVER AND SEE WHERE IT TAKES US.
RUFF!

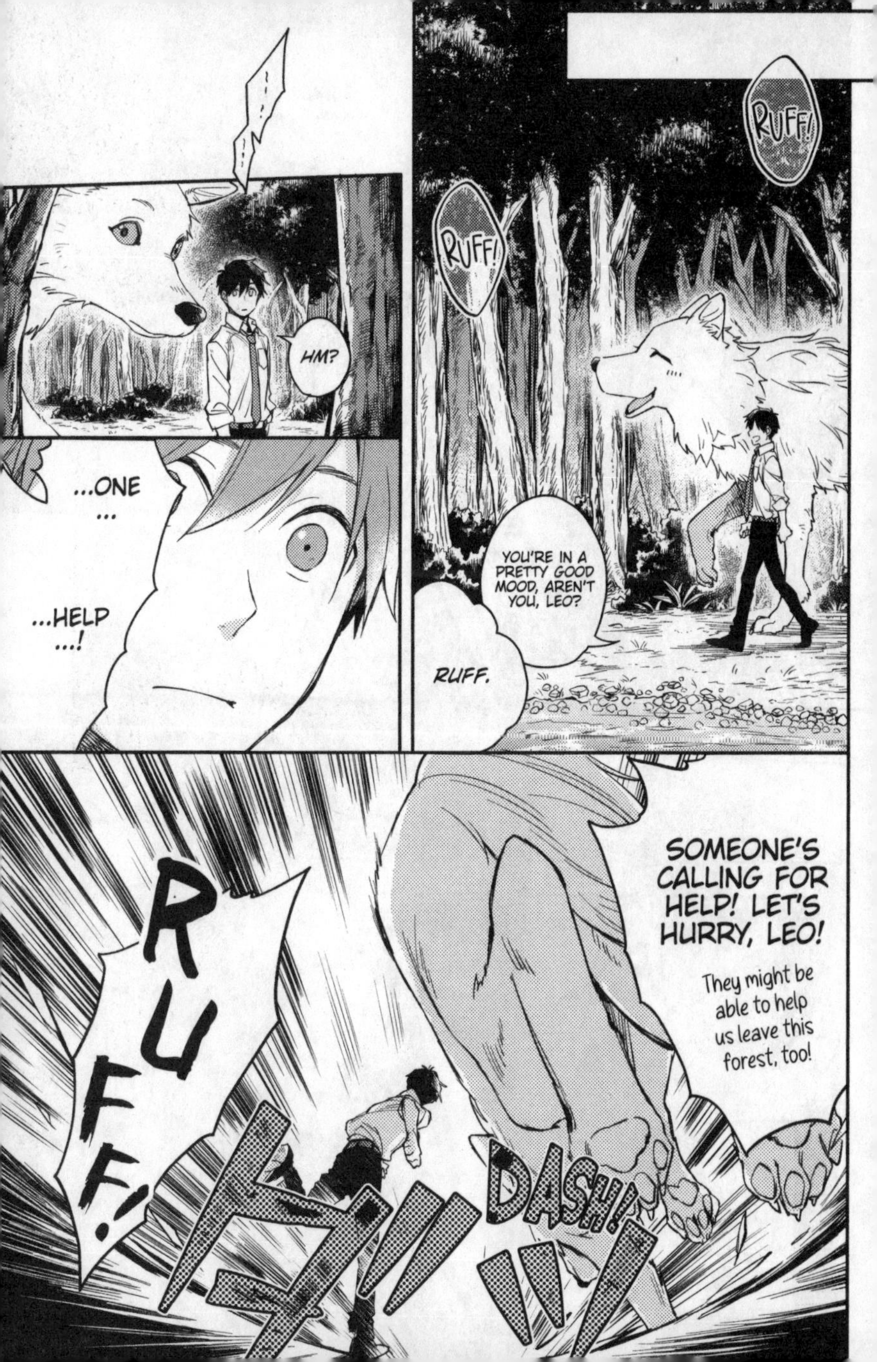
RUFF!
RUFF!
YOU'RE IN A PRETTY GOOD MOOD, AREN'T YOU, LEO?
RUFF.
HM?
...ONE ...
...HELP ...!
SOMEONE'S CALLING FOR HELP! LET'S HURRY, LEO!
They might be able to help us leave this forest, too!
DASH!
RUFF!

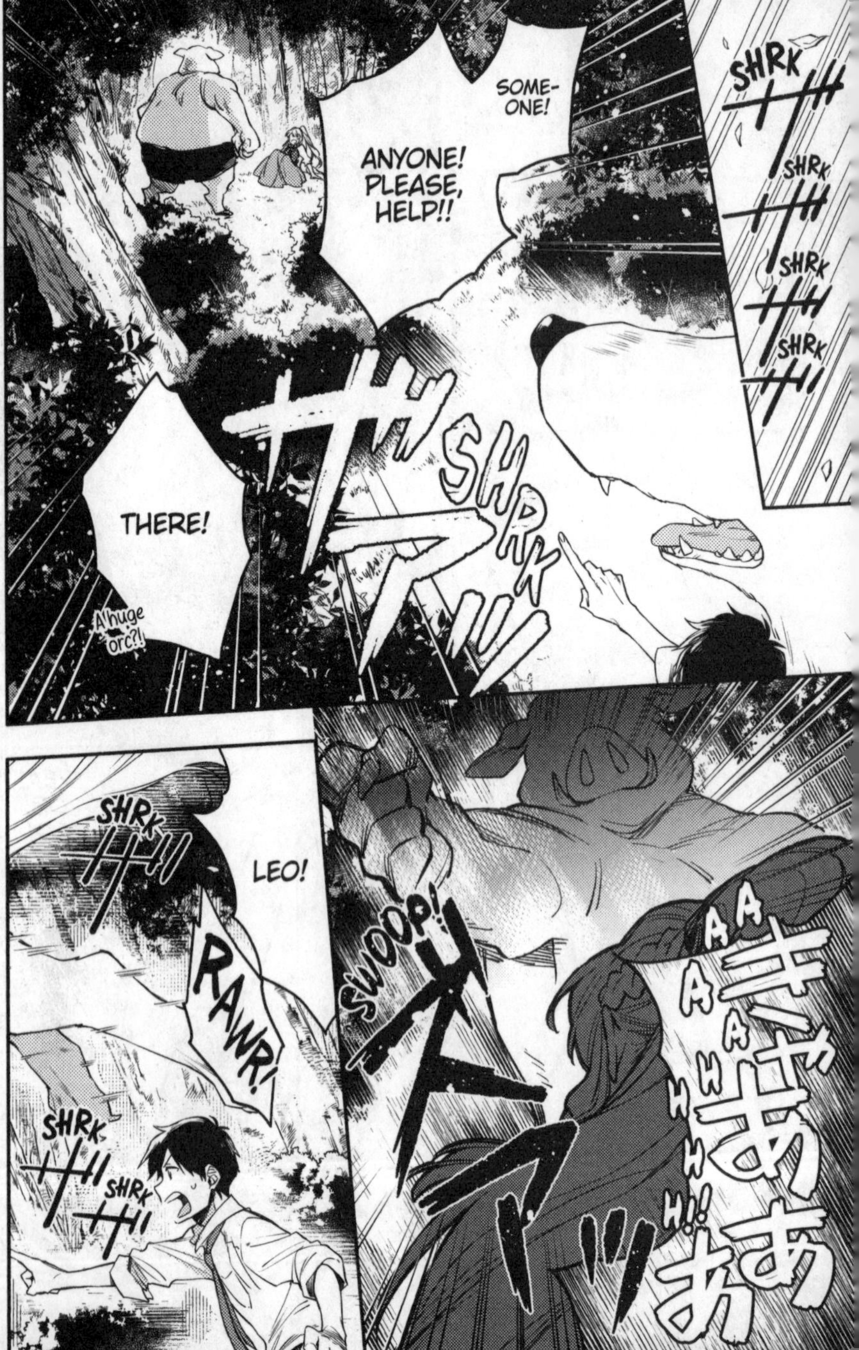
SHRK
SHRK
SHRK
SHRK
SOME-ONE!
ANYONE! PLEASE, HELP!!
SHRK
THERE!
A huge orc?!
AAAAHHHH!!
きゃあああ
SWOOP!
SHRK
LEO!
RAWR!
SHRK
SHRK

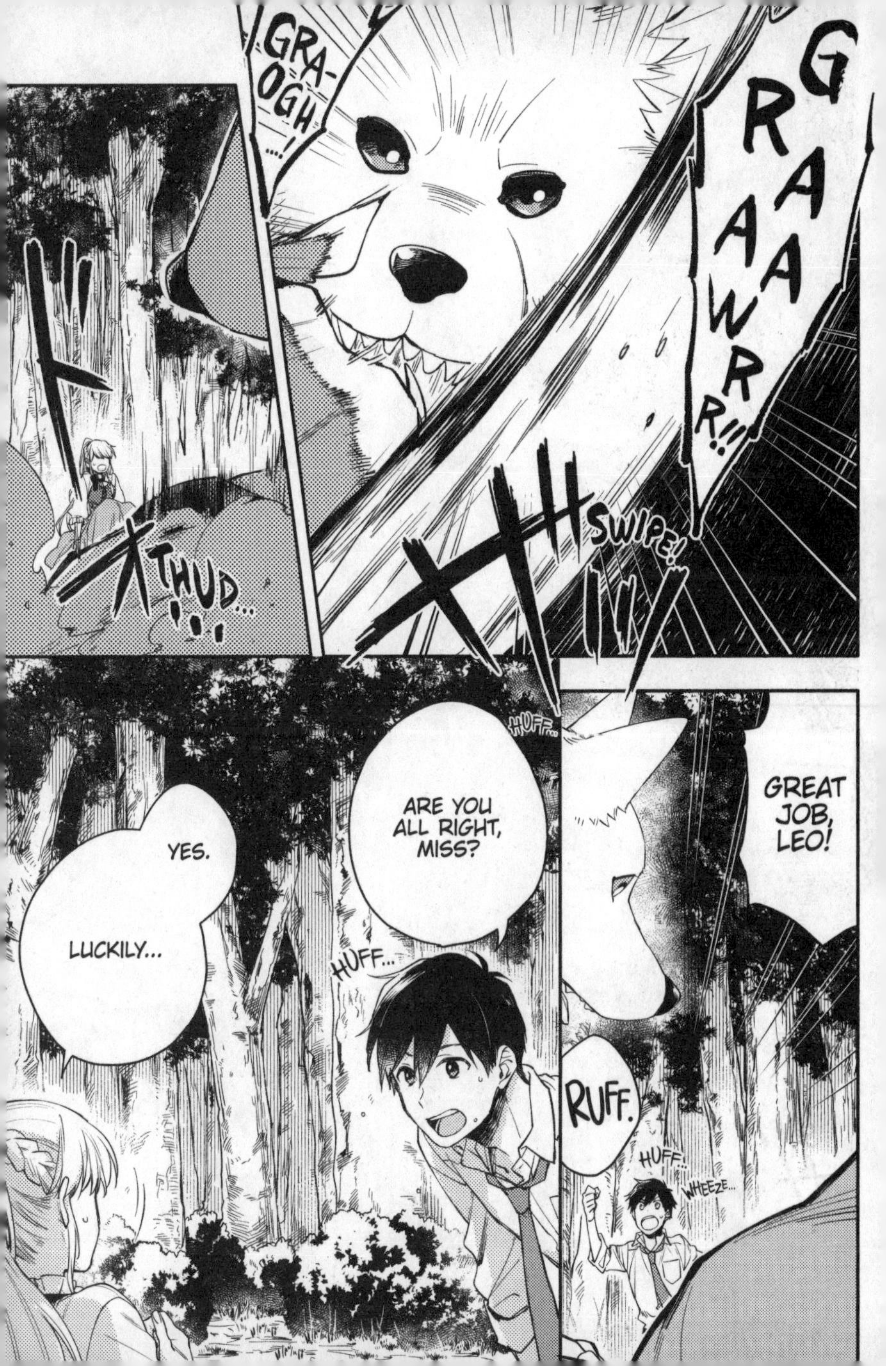
GRAAAWRR!!
GRA-OGH...!
SWIPE!
THUD...
GREAT JOB, LEO!
RUFF.
HUFF...
WHEEZE...
HUFF...
ARE YOU ALL RIGHT, MISS?
HUFF...
YES.
LUCKILY...

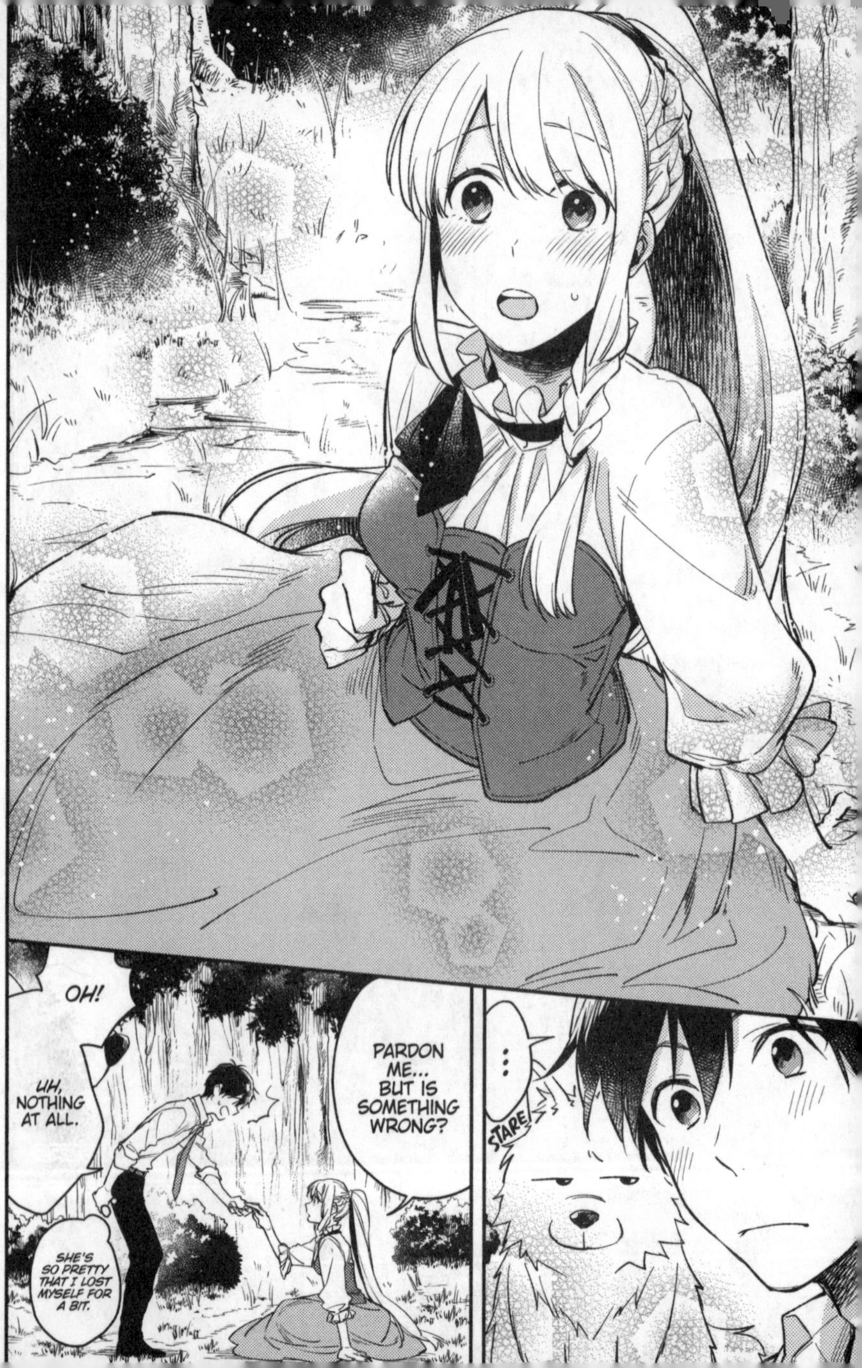
...
STARE
PARDON ME... BUT IS SOMETHING WRONG?
OH!
UH, NOTHING AT ALL.
SHE'S SO PRETTY THAT I LOST MYSELF FOR A BIT.

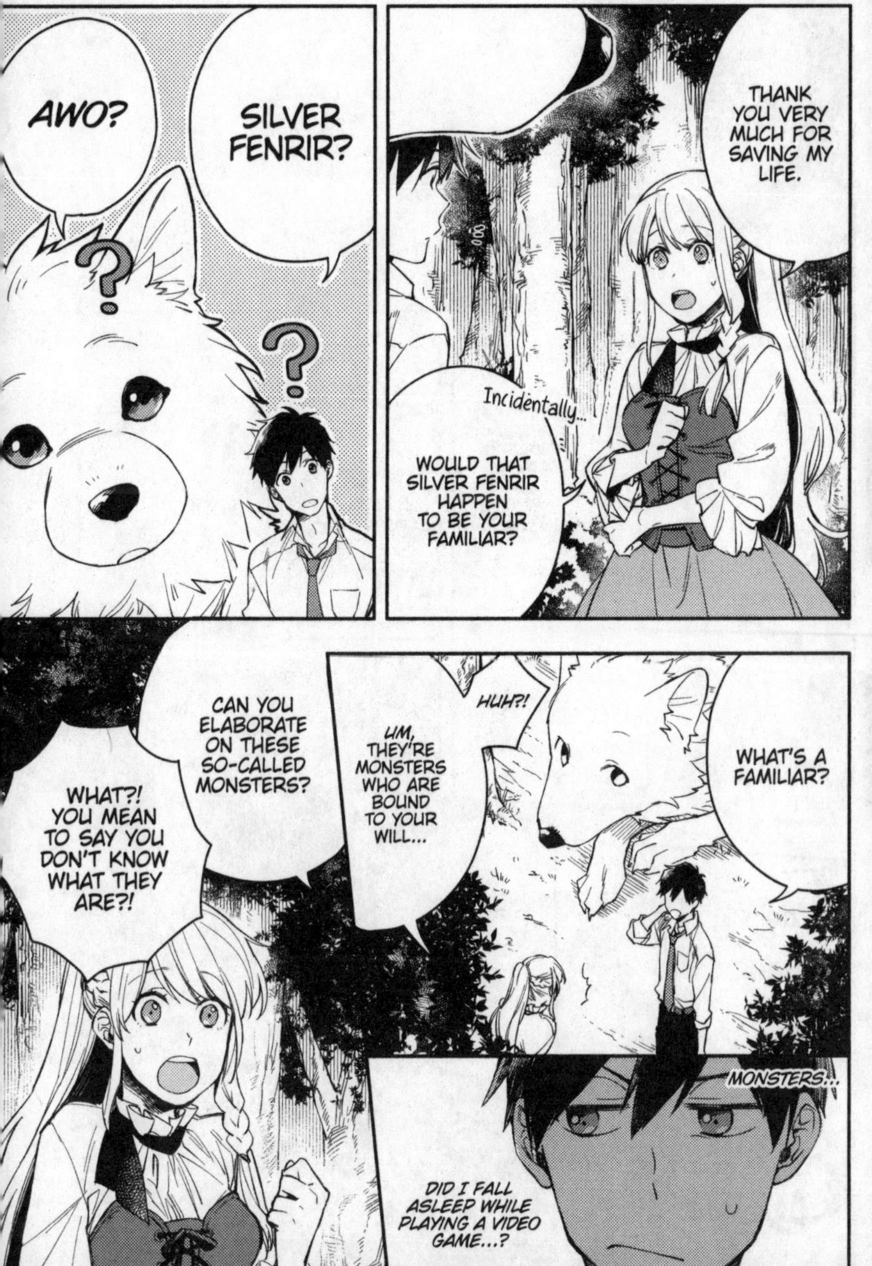

THANK YOU VERY MUCH FOR SAVING MY LIFE.
Incidentally...
WOULD THAT SILVER FENRIR HAPPEN TO BE YOUR FAMILIAR?
SILVER FENRIR?
AWO?
WHAT'S A FAMILIAR?
HUH?!
UM, THEY'RE MONSTERS WHO ARE BOUND TO YOUR WILL...
CAN YOU ELABORATE ON THESE SO-CALLED MONSTERS?
WHAT?! YOU MEAN TO SAY YOU DON'T KNOW WHAT THEY ARE?!
MONSTERS...
DID I FALL ASLEEP WHILE PLAYING A VIDEO GAME...?

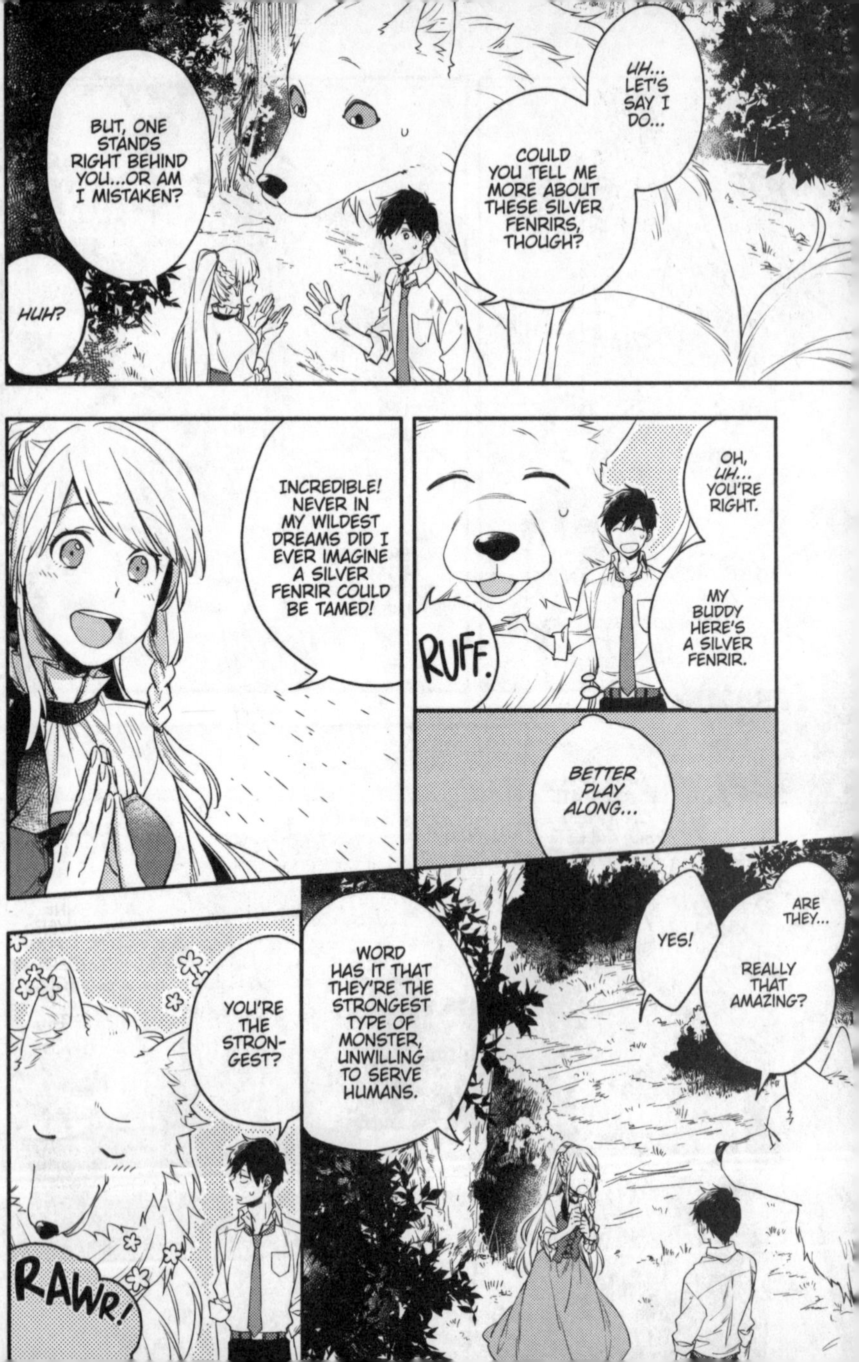
UH... LET'S SAY I DO...
COULD YOU TELL ME MORE ABOUT THESE SILVER FENRIRS, THOUGH?
BUT, ONE STANDS RIGHT BEHIND YOU...OR AM I MISTAKEN?
HUH?
OH, UH... YOU'RE RIGHT.
MY BUDDY HERE'S A SILVER FENRIR.
RUFF.
BETTER PLAY ALONG...
INCREDIBLE! NEVER IN MY WILDEST DREAMS DID I EVER IMAGINE A SILVER FENRIR COULD BE TAMED!
ARE THEY... REALLY THAT AMAZING?
YES!
WORD HAS IT THAT THEY'RE THE STRONGEST TYPE OF MONSTER, UNWILLING TO SERVE HUMANS.
YOU'RE THE STRONG-EST?
RAWR!

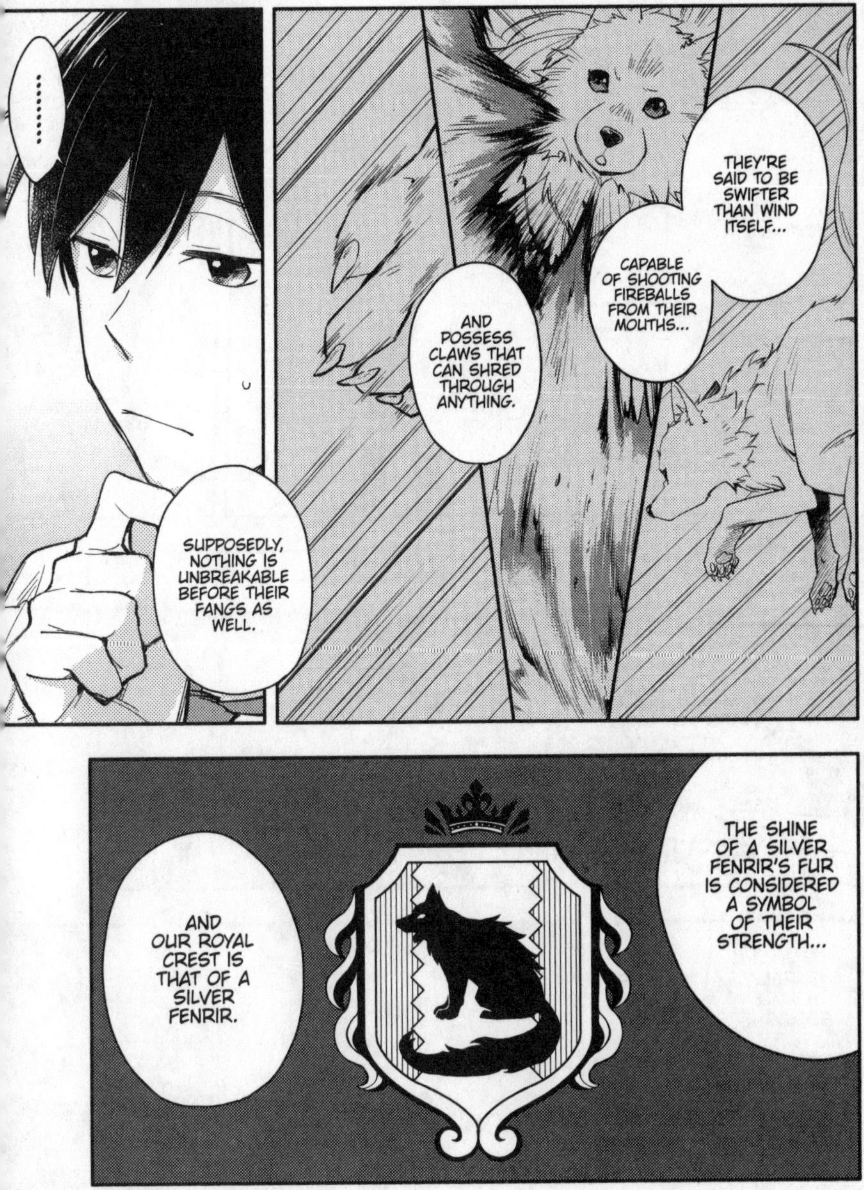
THEY'RE SAID TO BE SWIFTER THAN WIND ITSELF...
CAPABLE OF SHOOTING FIREBALLS FROM THEIR MOUTHS...
AND POSSESS CLAWS THAT CAN SHRED THROUGH ANYTHING.
......
SUPPOSEDLY, NOTHING IS UNBREAKABLE BEFORE THEIR FANGS AS WELL.
THE SHINE OF A SILVER FENRIR'S FUR IS CONSIDERED A SYMBOL OF THEIR STRENGTH...
AND OUR ROYAL CREST IS THAT OF A SILVER FENRIR.

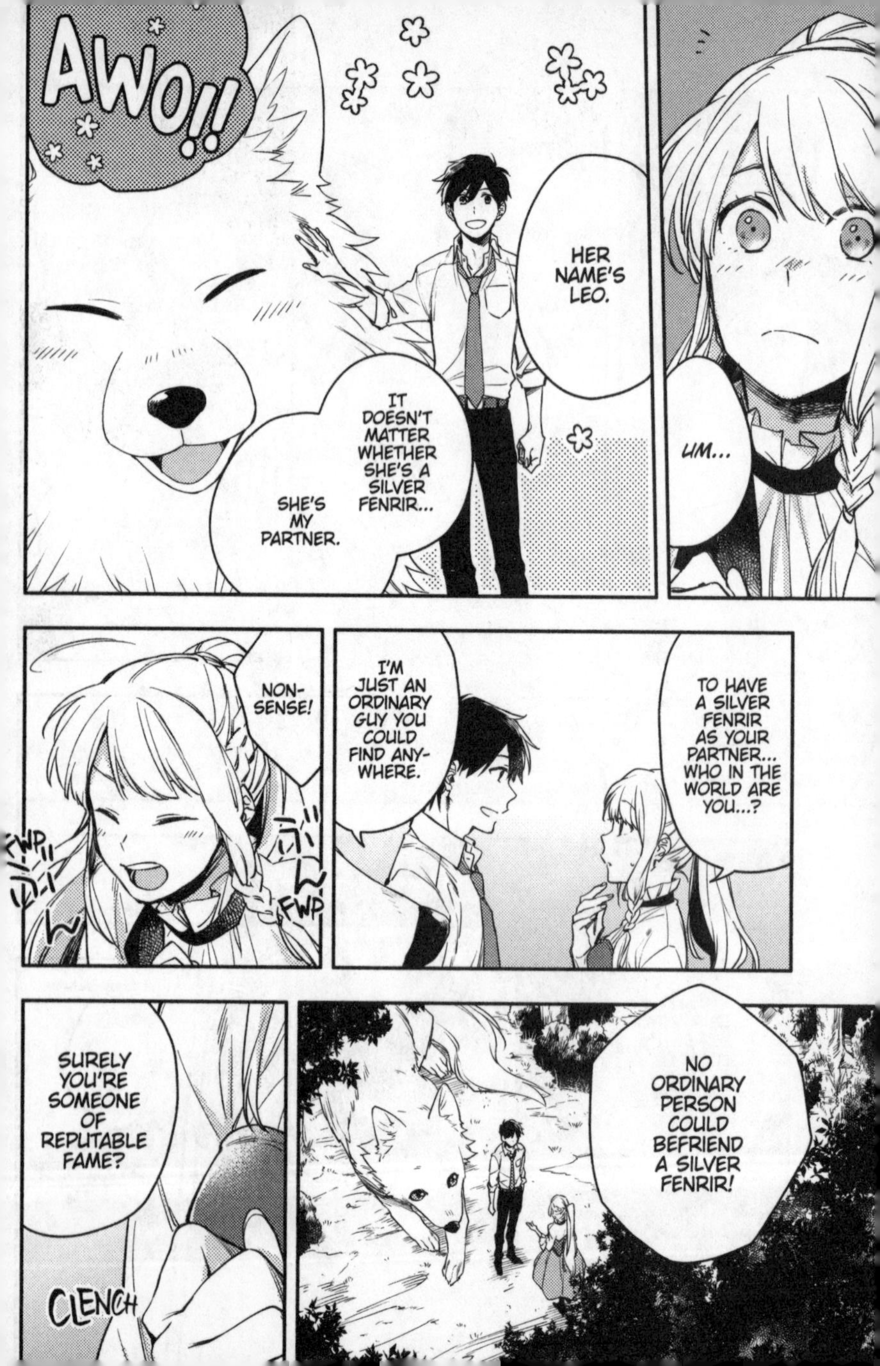
UM...
HER NAME'S LEO.
AWO!!
IT DOESN'T MATTER WHETHER SHE'S A SILVER FENRIR...
SHE'S MY PARTNER.
TO HAVE A SILVER FENRIR AS YOUR PARTNER... WHO IN THE WORLD ARE YOU...?
I'M JUST AN ORDINARY GUY YOU COULD FIND ANY-WHERE.
NON-SENSE!
FWP
FWP
NO ORDINARY PERSON COULD BEFRIEND A SILVER FENRIR!
SURELY YOU'RE SOMEONE OF REPUTABLE FAME?
CLENCH

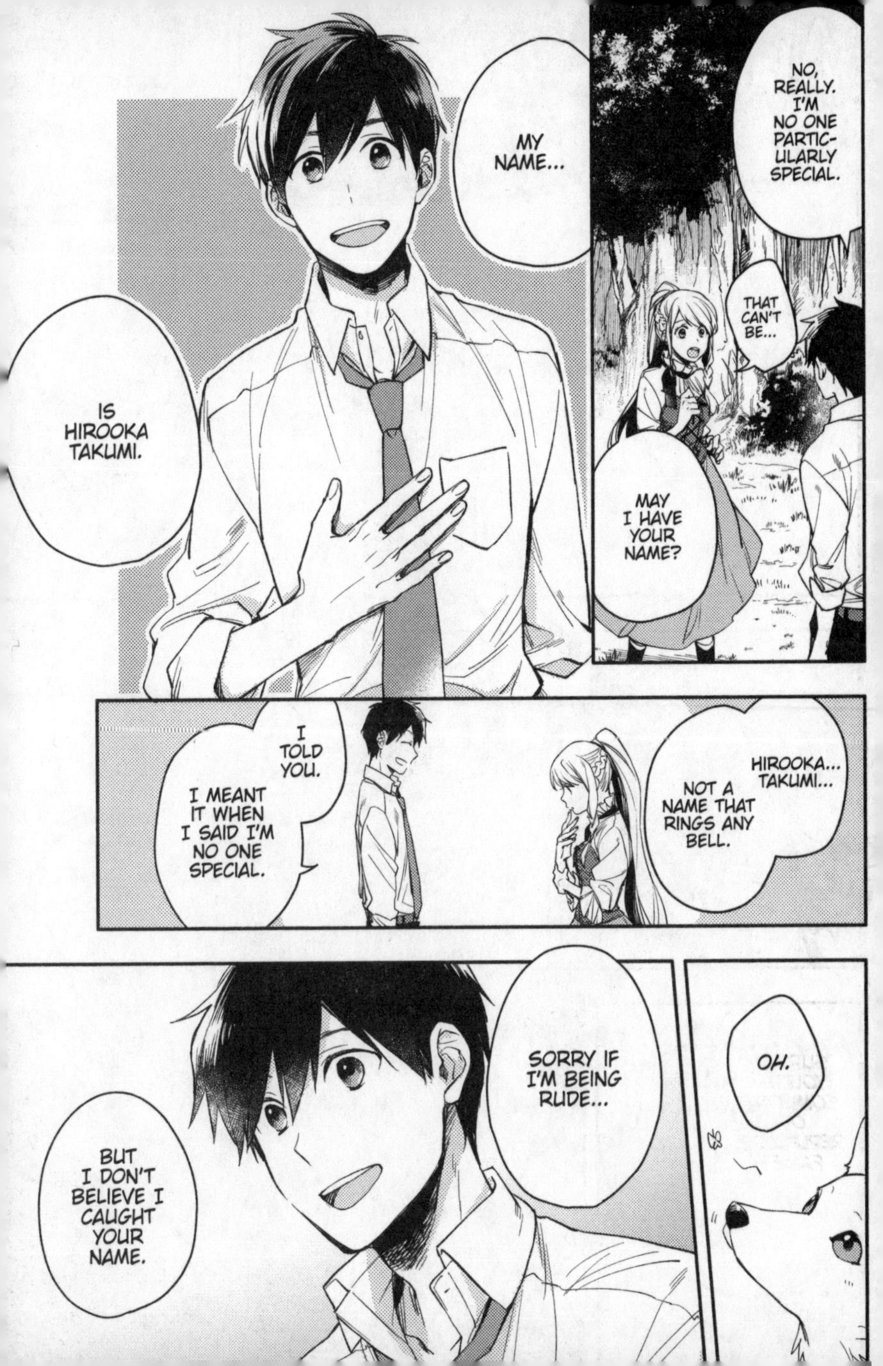
NO, REALLY. I'M NO ONE PARTICULARLY SPECIAL.
THAT CAN'T BE...
MAY I HAVE YOUR NAME?
MY NAME...
IS HIROOKA TAKUMI.
HIROOKA... TAKUMI...
NOT A NAME THAT RINGS ANY BELL.
I TOLD YOU.
I MEANT IT WHEN I SAID I'M NO ONE SPECIAL.
OH.
SORRY IF I'M BEING RUDE...
BUT I DON'T BELIEVE I CAUGHT YOUR NAME.

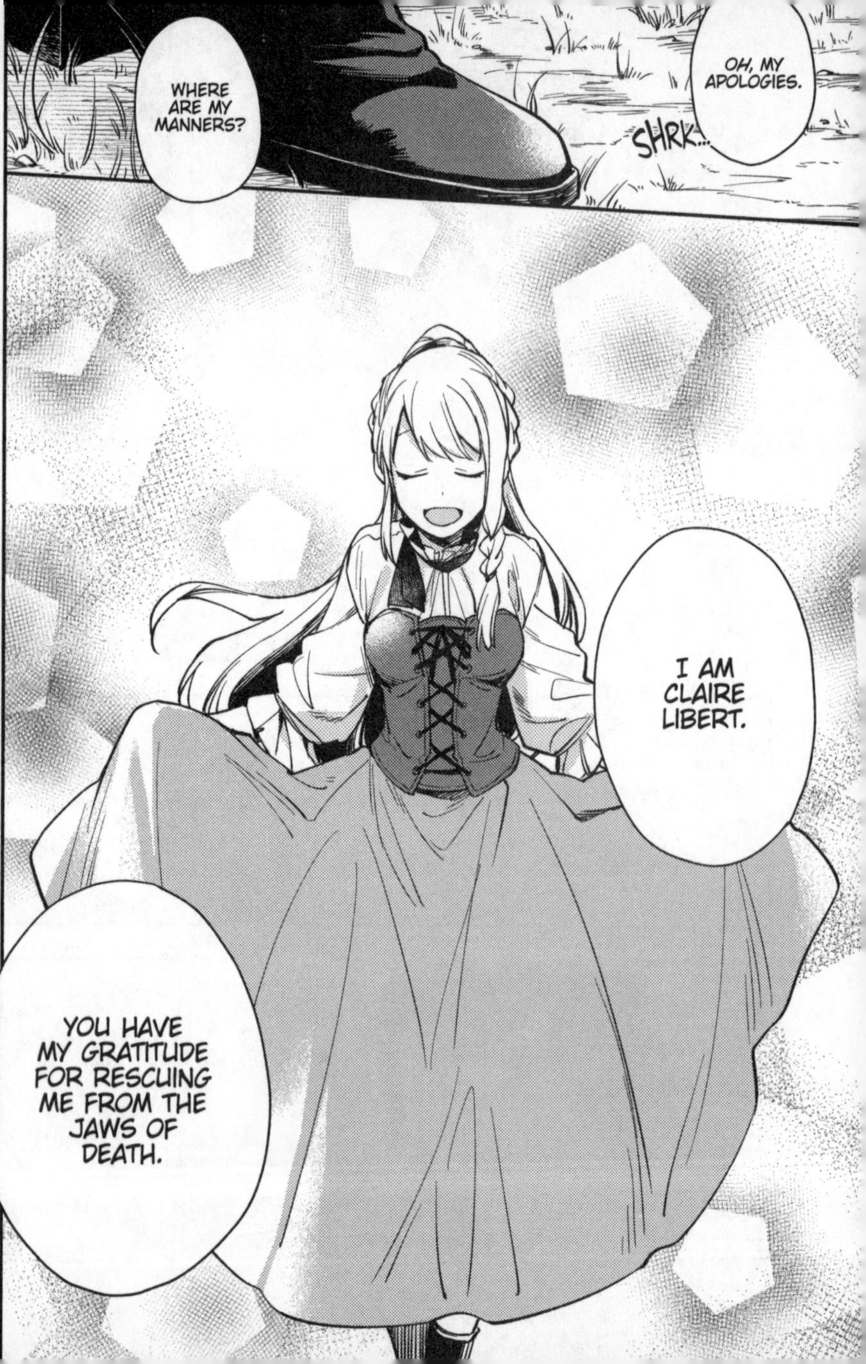
OH, MY APOLOGIES.
SHRK...
WHERE ARE MY MANNERS?
I AM CLAIRE LIBERT.
YOU HAVE MY GRATITUDE FOR RESCUING ME FROM THE JAWS OF DEATH.

EVEN DOGS GO TO OTHER WORLDS

LIFE IN ANOTHER WORLD WITH MY BELOVED HOUND

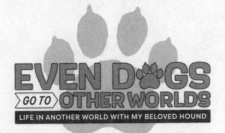

EVEN DOGS GO TO OTHER WORLDS

LIFE IN ANOTHER WORLD WITH MY BELOVED HOUND

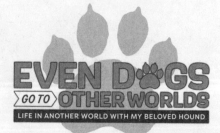

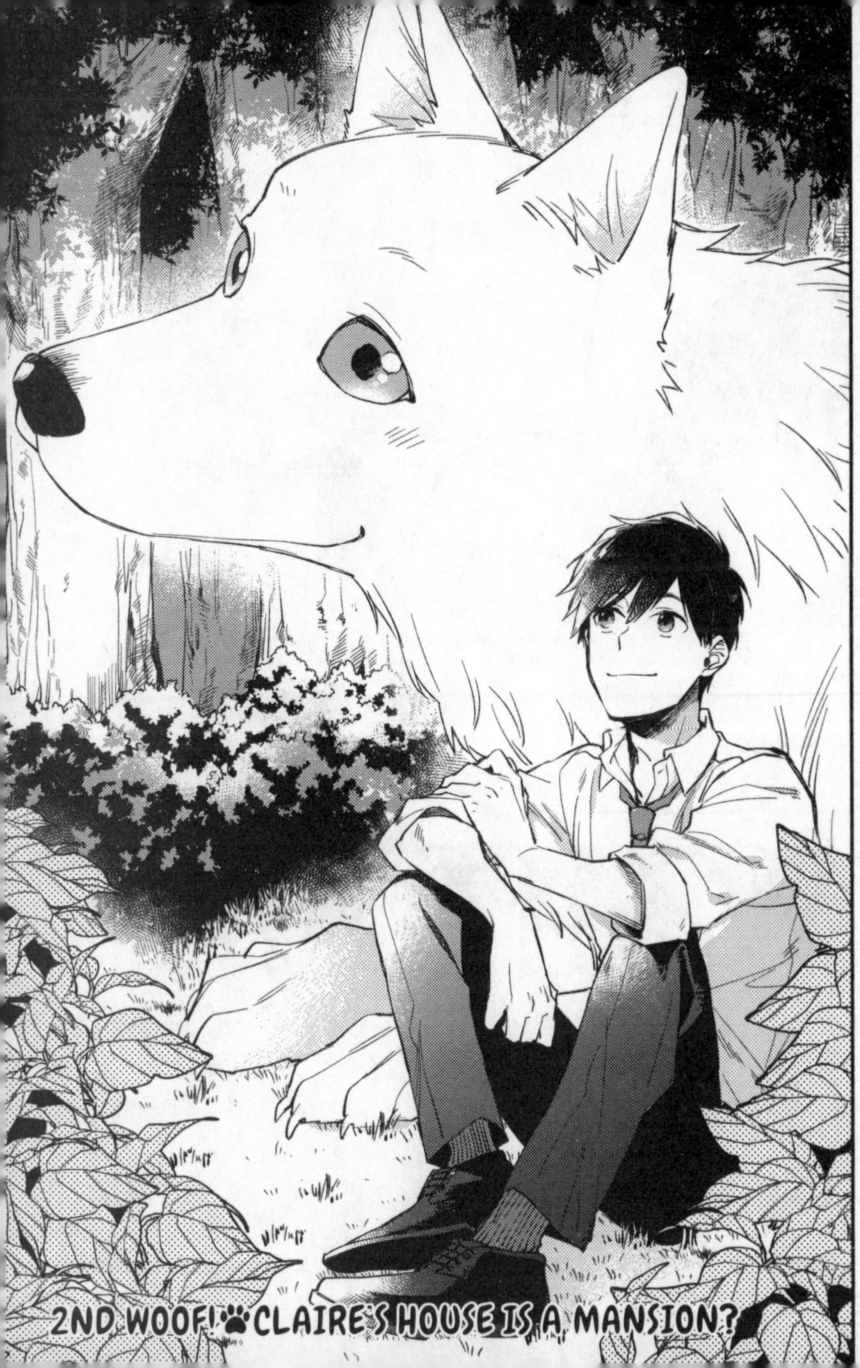
2ND WOOF! CLAIRE'S HOUSE IS A MANSION?

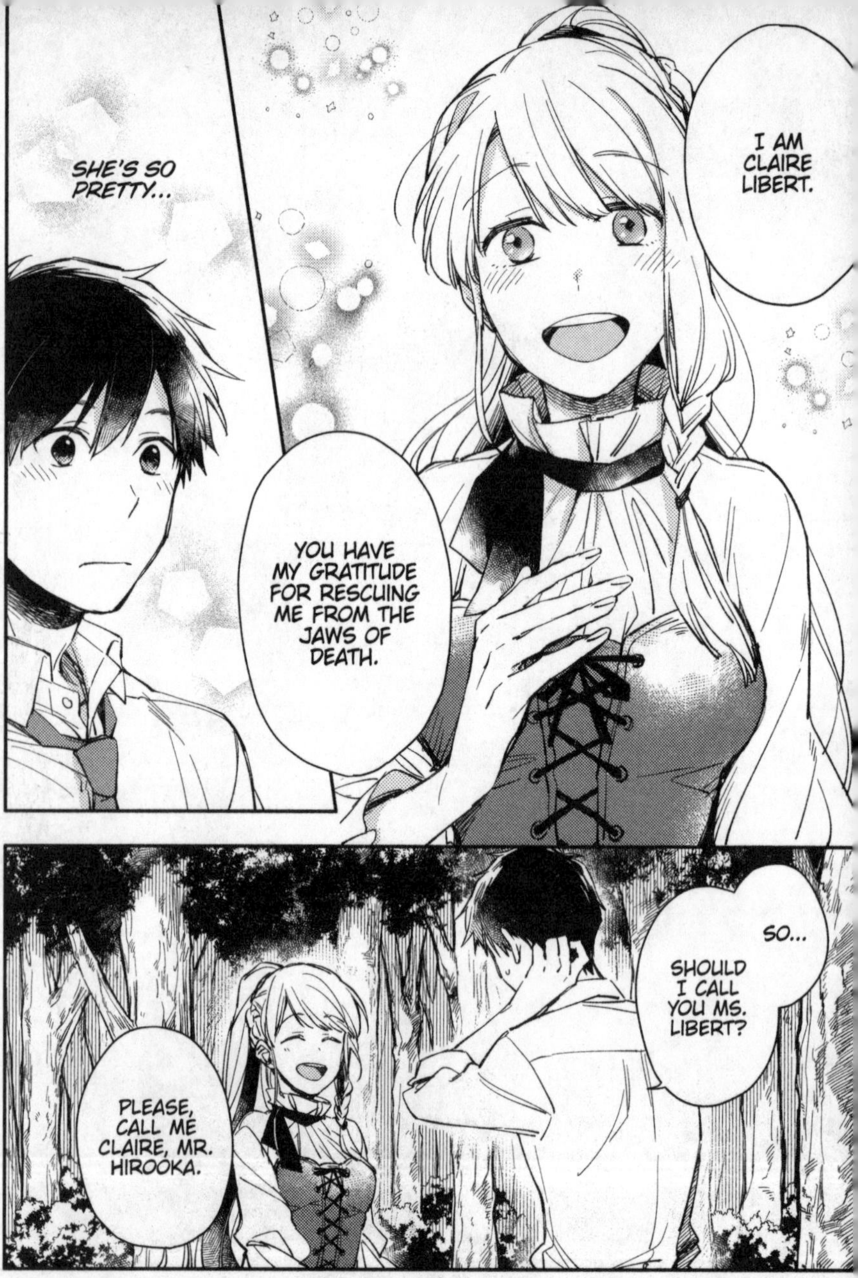
I AM CLAIRE LIBERT.
YOU HAVE MY GRATITUDE FOR RESCUING ME FROM THE JAWS OF DEATH.
SHE'S SO PRETTY...
SO...
SHOULD I CALL YOU MS. LIBERT?
PLEASE, CALL ME CLAIRE, MR. HIROOKA.

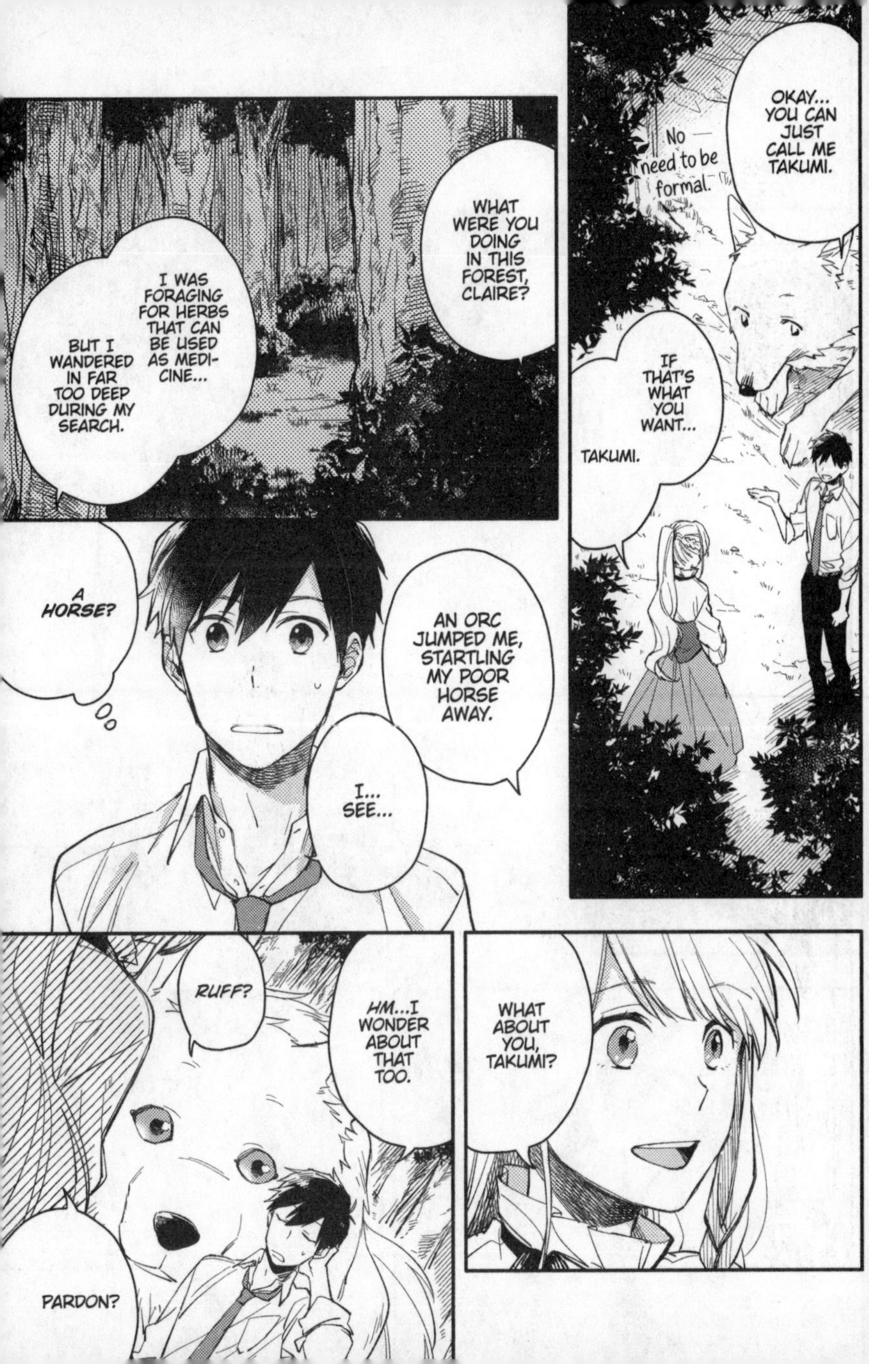
OKAY... YOU CAN JUST CALL ME TAKUMI.
No need to be formal.
IF THAT'S WHAT YOU WANT...
TAKUMI.
WHAT WERE YOU DOING IN THIS FOREST, CLAIRE?
I WAS FORAGING FOR HERBS THAT CAN BE USED AS MEDICINE...
BUT I WANDERED IN FAR TOO DEEP DURING MY SEARCH.
AN ORC JUMPED ME, STARTLING MY POOR HORSE AWAY.
A HORSE?
I... SEE...
WHAT ABOUT YOU, TAKUMI?
HM...I WONDER ABOUT THAT TOO.
RUFF?
PARDON?

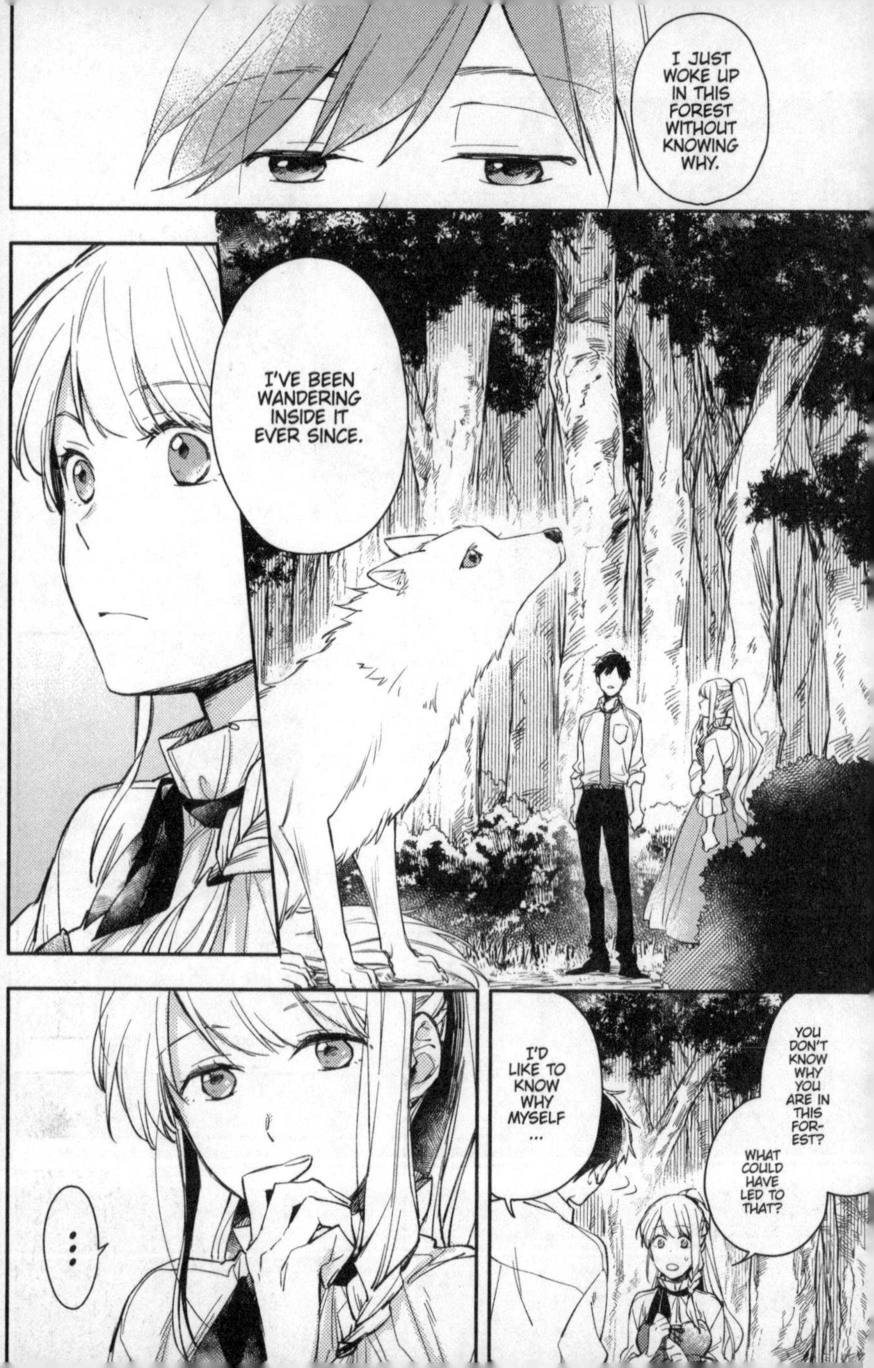
I JUST WOKE UP IN THIS FOREST WITHOUT KNOWING WHY.
I'VE BEEN WANDERING INSIDE IT EVER SINCE.
YOU DON'T KNOW WHY YOU ARE IN THIS FOR-EST?
WHAT COULD HAVE LED TO THAT?
I'D LIKE TO KNOW WHY MYSELF ...
...

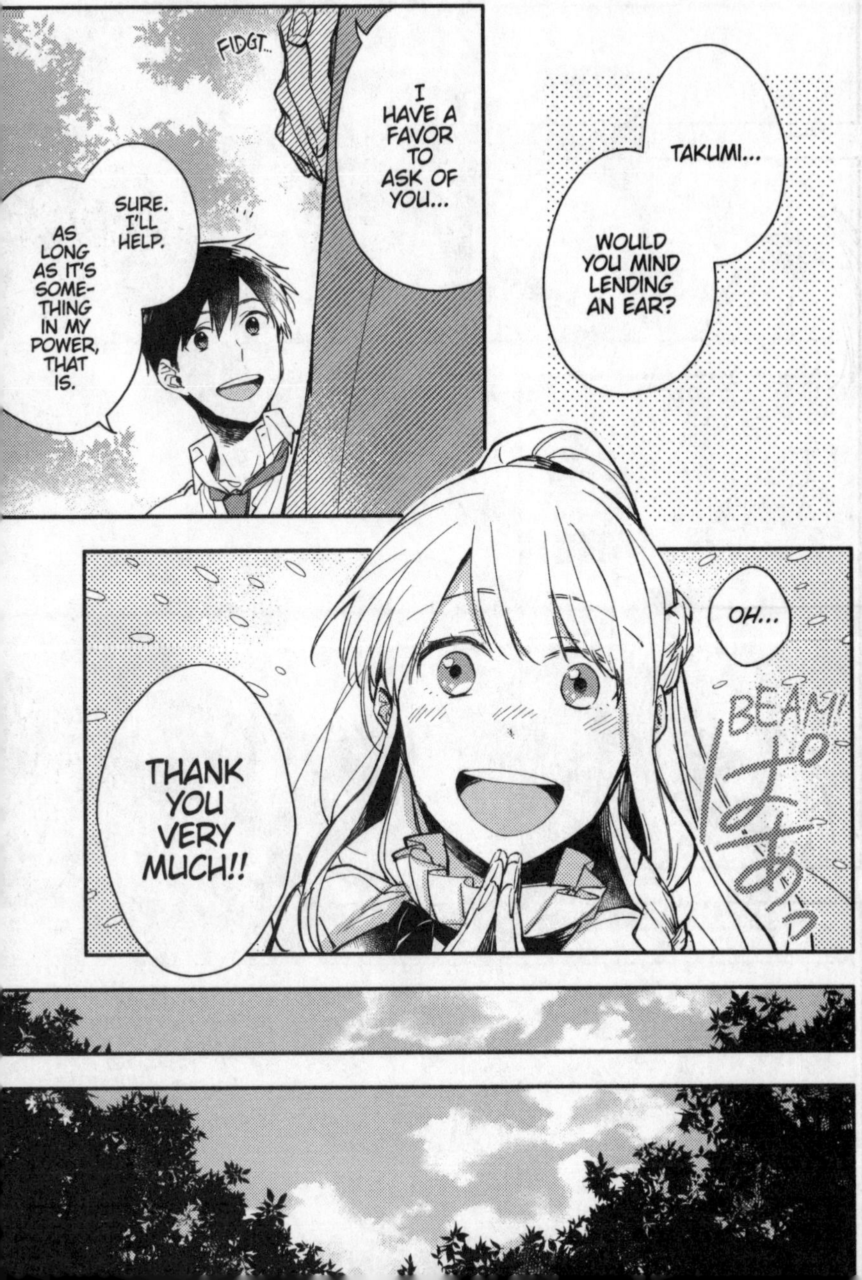
TAKUMI...
WOULD YOU MIND LENDING AN EAR?
FIDGT...
I HAVE A FAVOR TO ASK OF YOU...
SURE. I'LL HELP.
AS LONG AS IT'S SOME-THING IN MY POWER, THAT IS.
OH...
BEAM!
ぱあっ
THANK YOU VERY MUCH!!

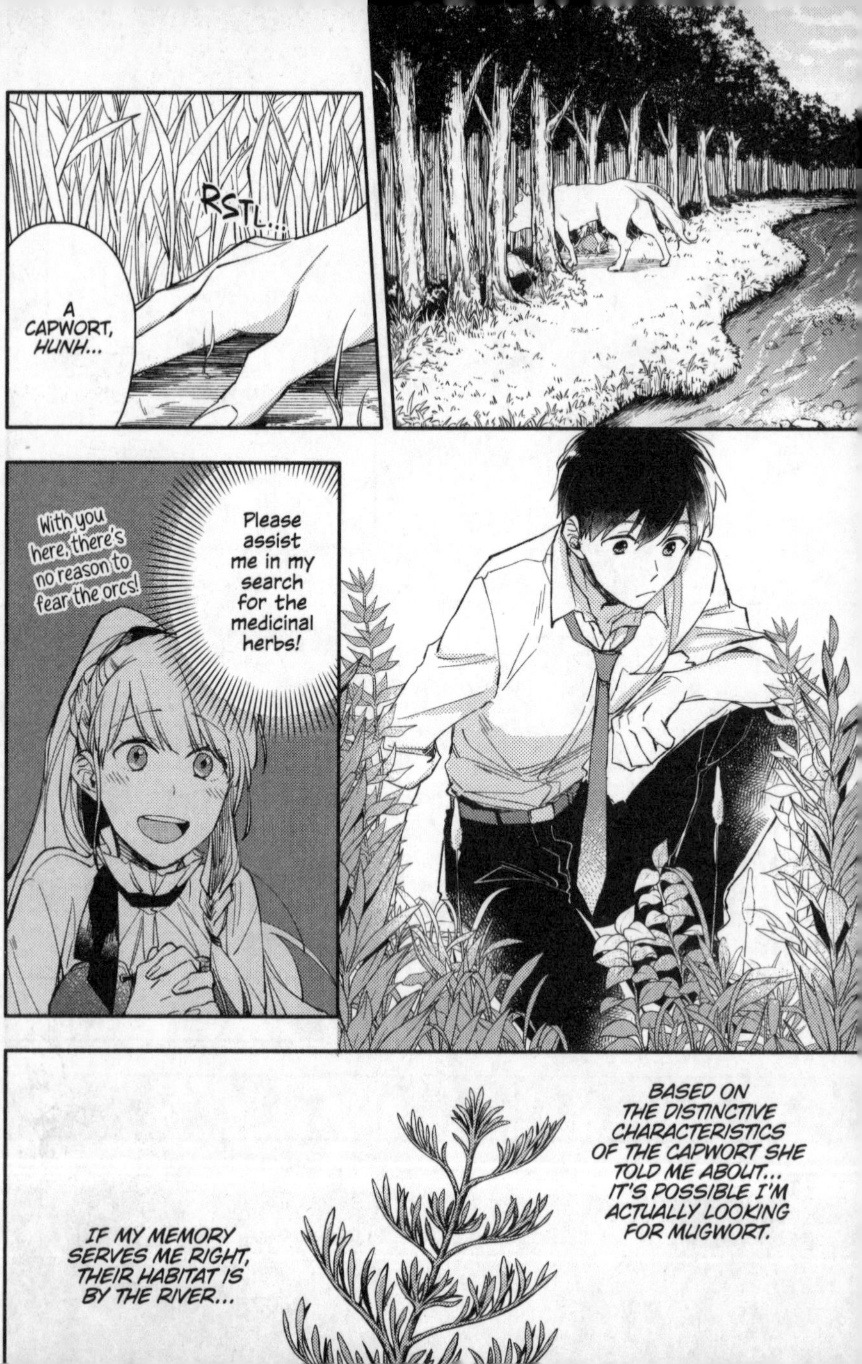
RSTL...
A CAPWORT, HUNH...
Please assist me in my search for the medicinal herbs!
With you here, there's no reason to fear the orcs!
BASED ON THE DISTINCTIVE CHARACTERISTICS OF THE CAPWORT SHE TOLD ME ABOUT... IT'S POSSIBLE I'M ACTUALLY LOOKING FOR MUGWORT.
IF MY MEMORY SERVES ME RIGHT, THEIR HABITAT IS BY THE RIVER...

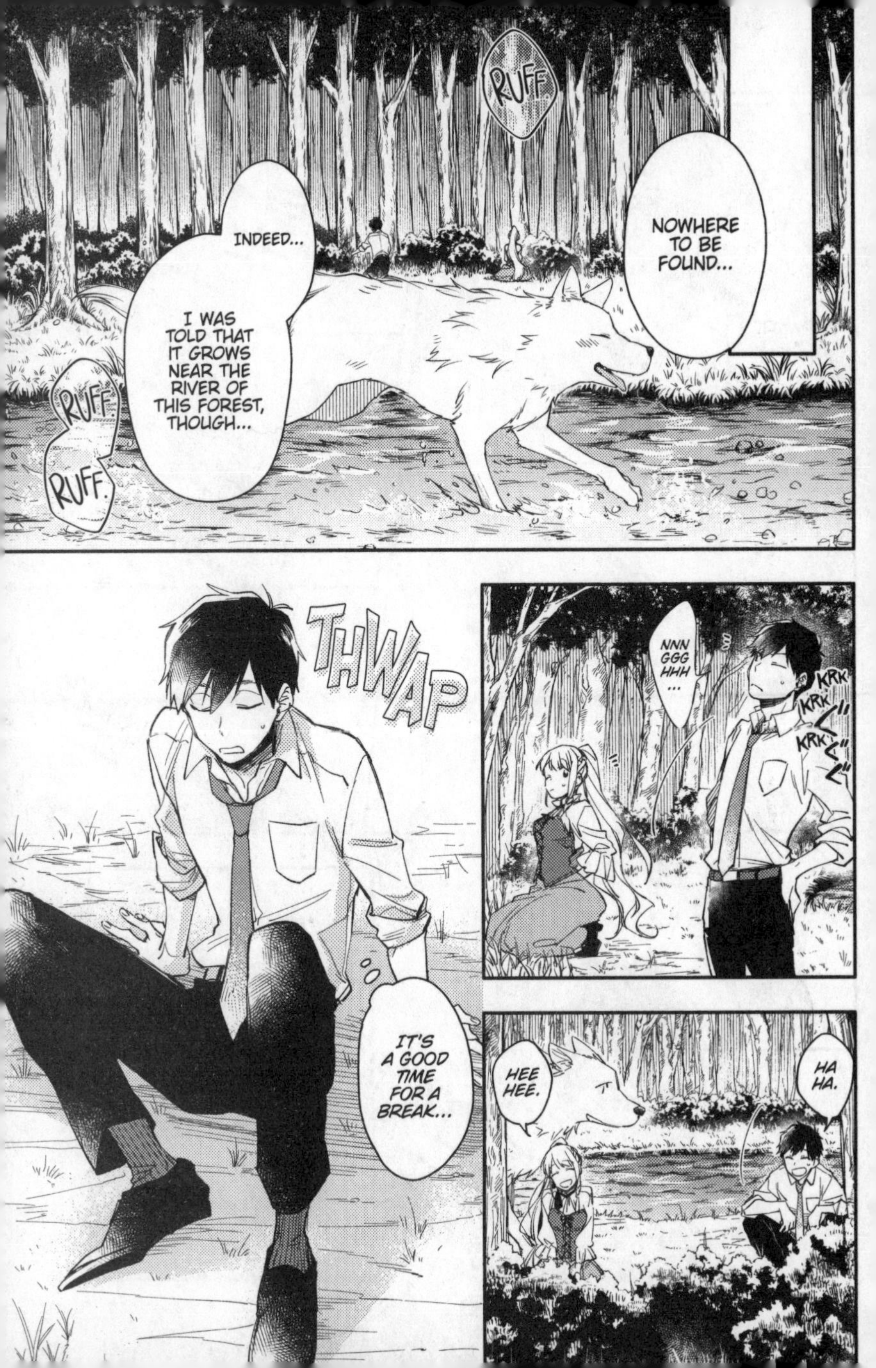
RUFF
NOWHERE TO BE FOUND...
INDEED...
I WAS TOLD THAT IT GROWS NEAR THE RIVER OF THIS FOREST, THOUGH...
RUFF.
RUFF.
NNN GGG HHH...
KRK KRK KRK
HA HA.
HEE HEE.
THWAP
IT'S A GOOD TIME FOR A BREAK...

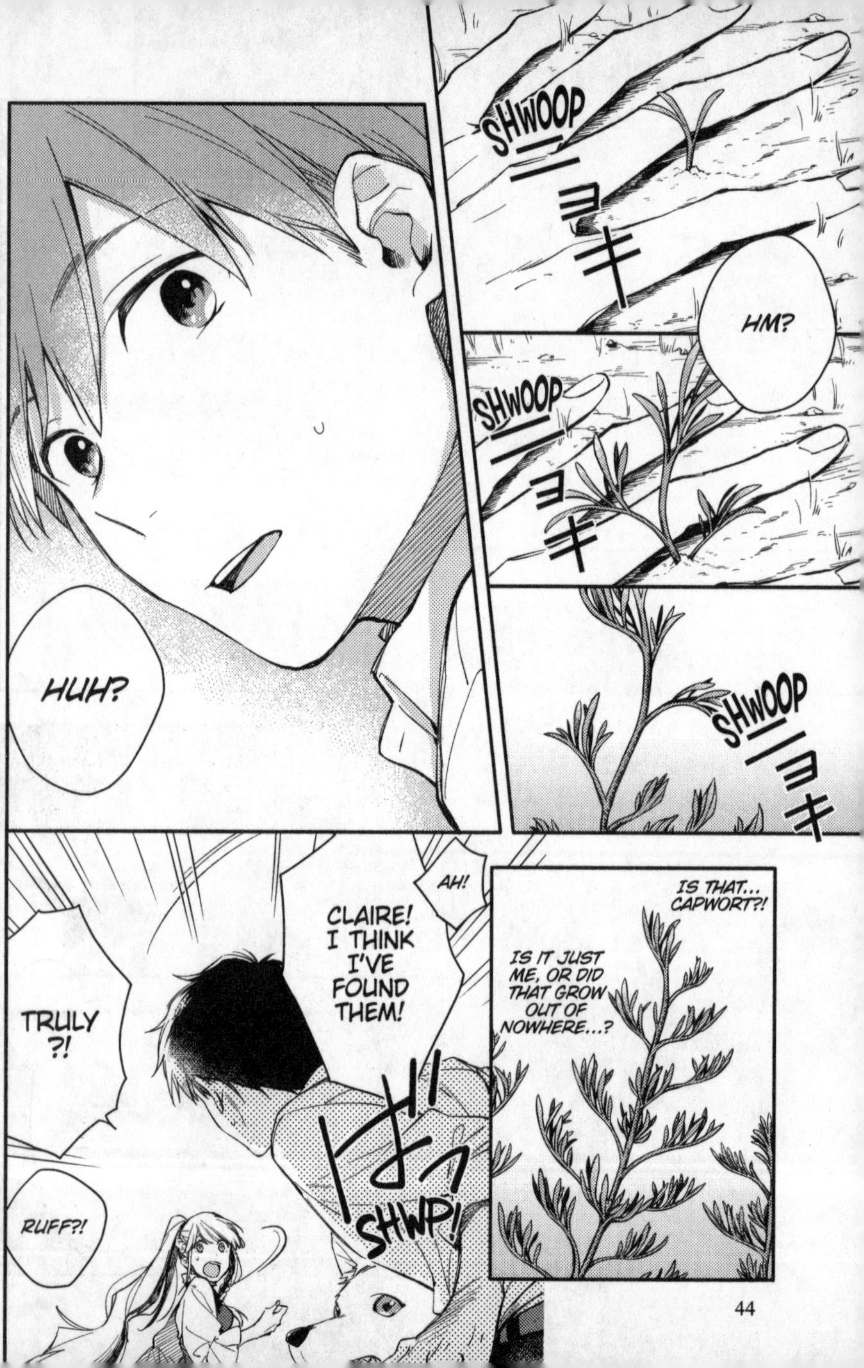
SHWOOP
ニョキ
HM?
SHWOOP
ニョキ
SHWOOP
ニョキ
HUH?
IS THAT... CAPWORT?!
IS IT JUST ME, OR DID THAT GROW OUT OF NOWHERE...?
AH!
CLAIRE! I THINK I'VE FOUND THEM!
TRULY ?!
はっ
SHWP!
RUFF?!

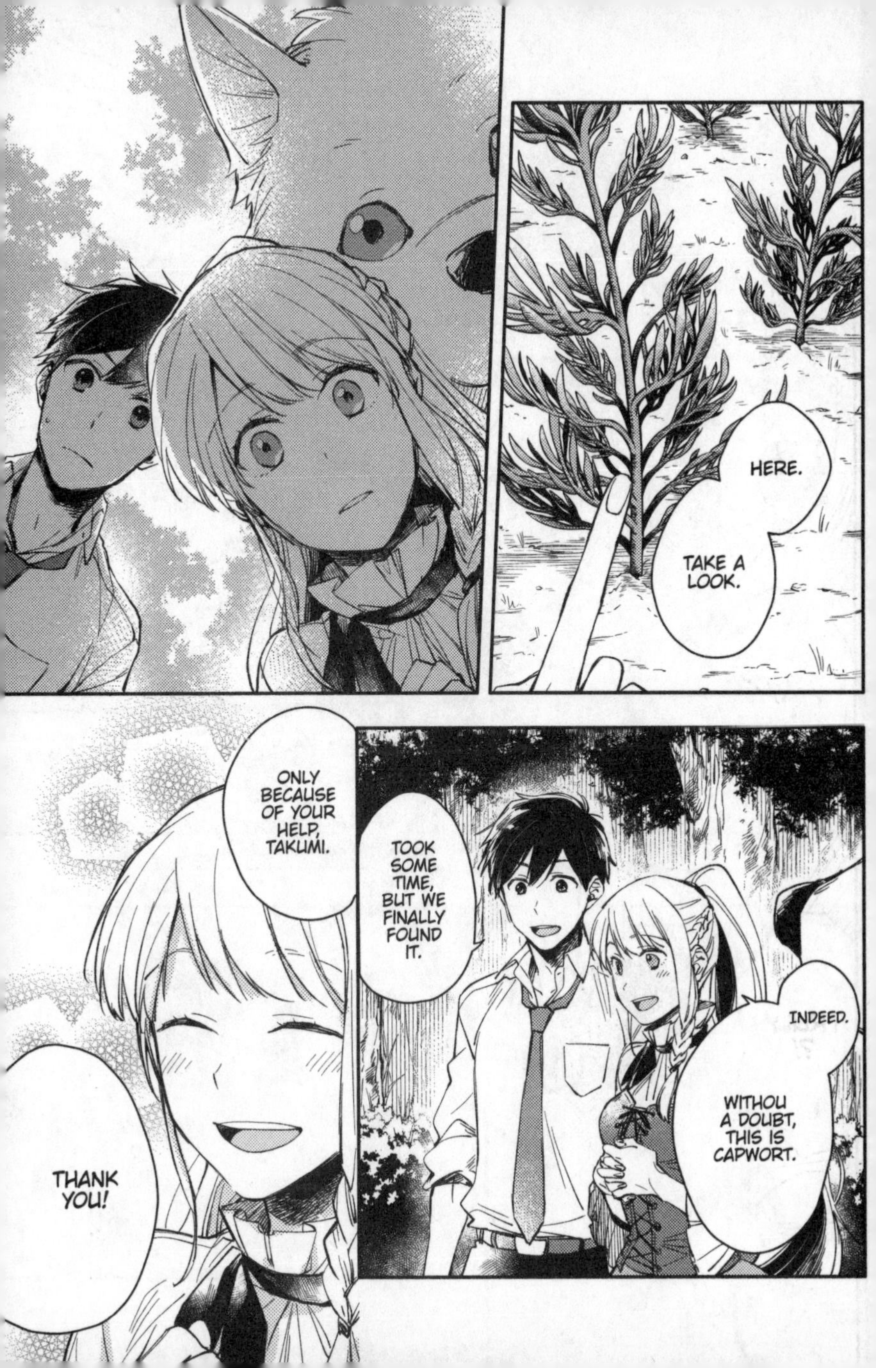
HERE.
TAKE A LOOK.
INDEED.
WITHOU A DOUBT, THIS IS CAPWORT.
TOOK SOME TIME, BUT WE FINALLY FOUND IT.
ONLY BECAUSE OF YOUR HELP, TAKUMI.
THANK YOU!

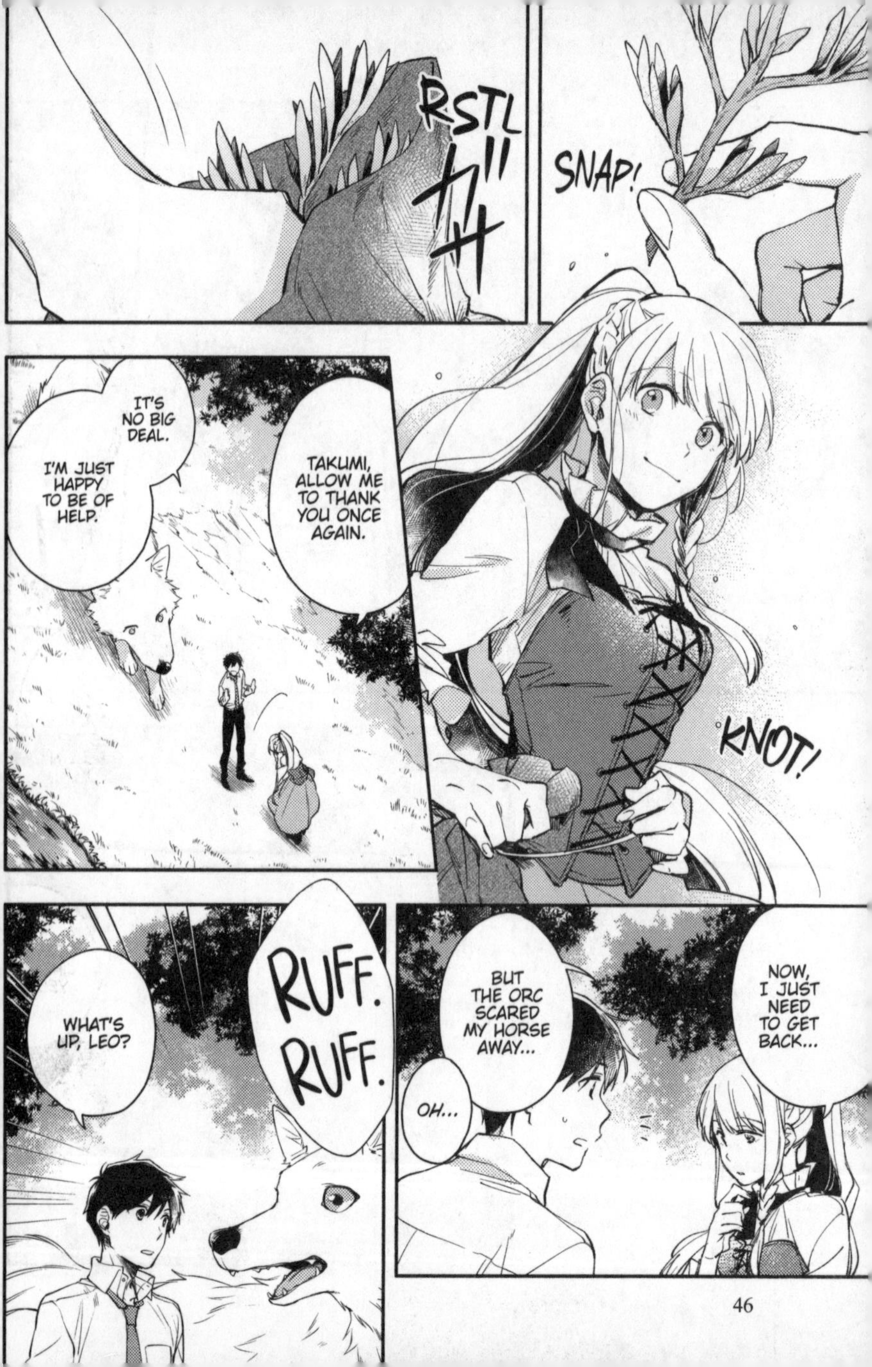
SNAP!
RSTL
KNOT!
TAKUMI, ALLOW ME TO THANK YOU ONCE AGAIN.
IT'S NO BIG DEAL.
I'M JUST HAPPY TO BE OF HELP.
NOW, I JUST NEED TO GET BACK...
BUT THE ORC SCARED MY HORSE AWAY...
OH...
RUFF. RUFF.
WHAT'S UP, LEO?

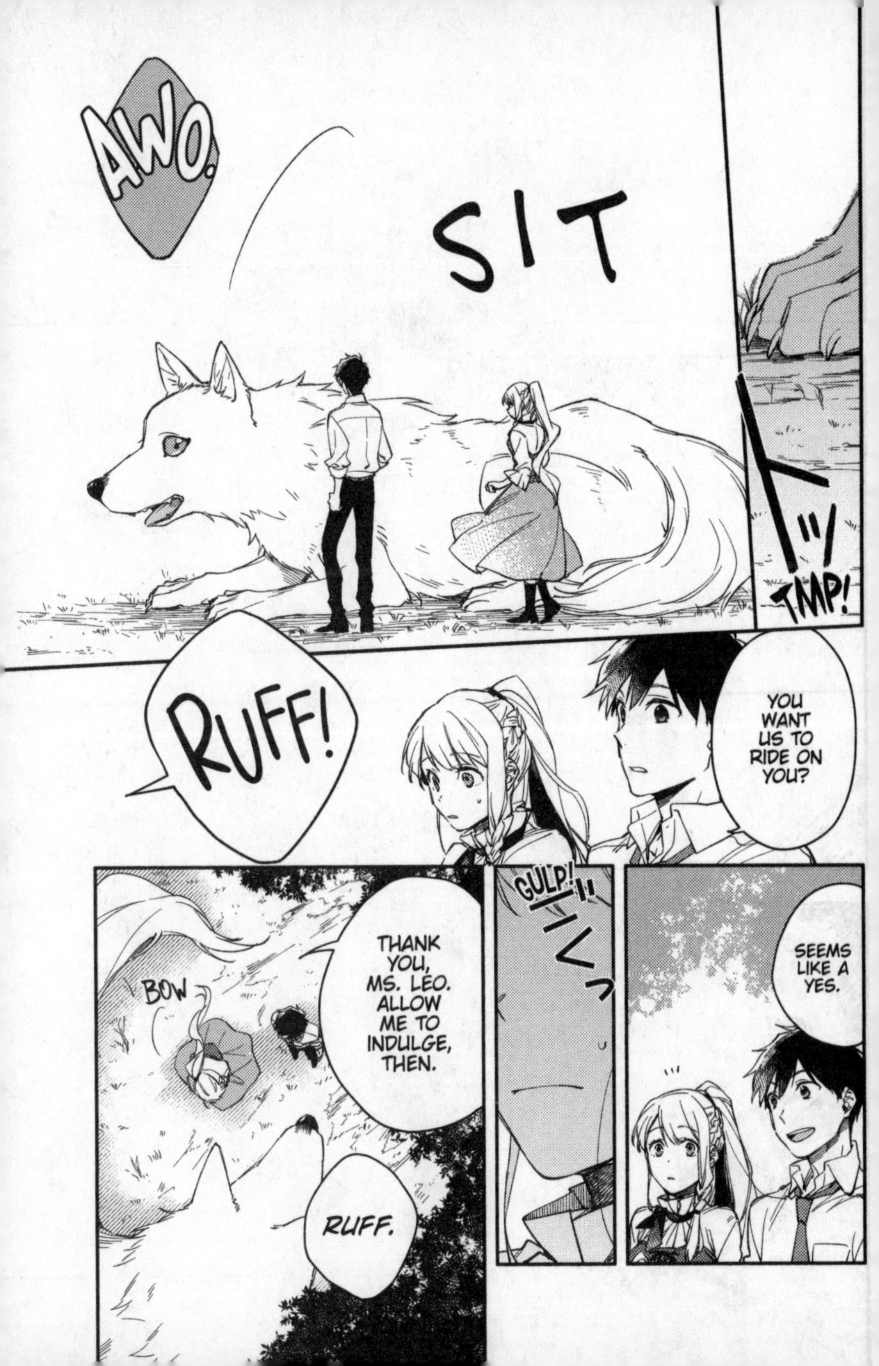
TMP!
SIT
AWO.
YOU WANT US TO RIDE ON YOU?
RUFF!
SEEMS LIKE A YES.
GULP!
THANK YOU, MS. LEO. ALLOW ME TO INDULGE, THEN.
BOW
RUFF.

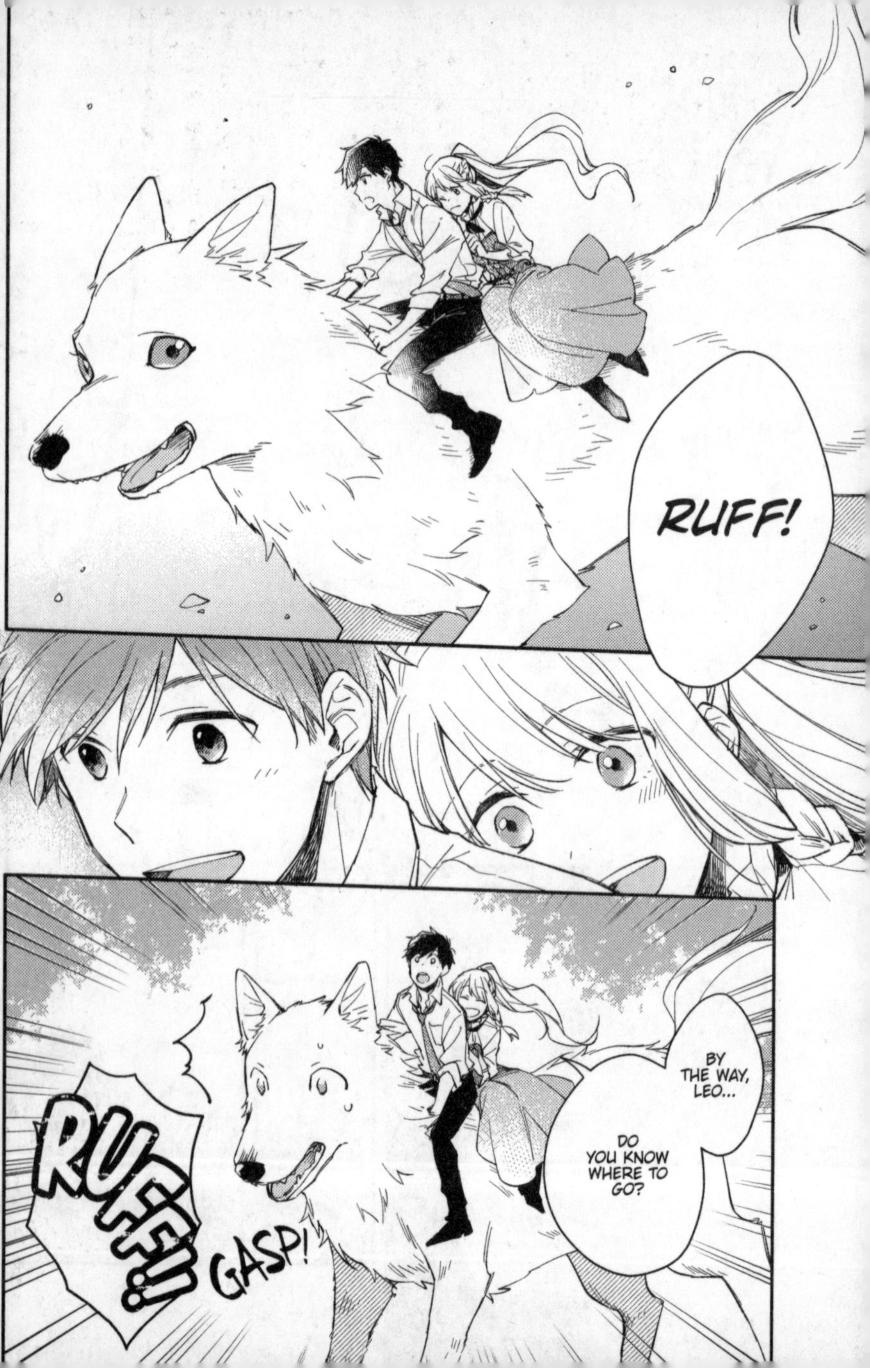
RUFF!
BY THE WAY, LEO...
DO YOU KNOW WHERE TO GO?
GASP!
RUFF!!

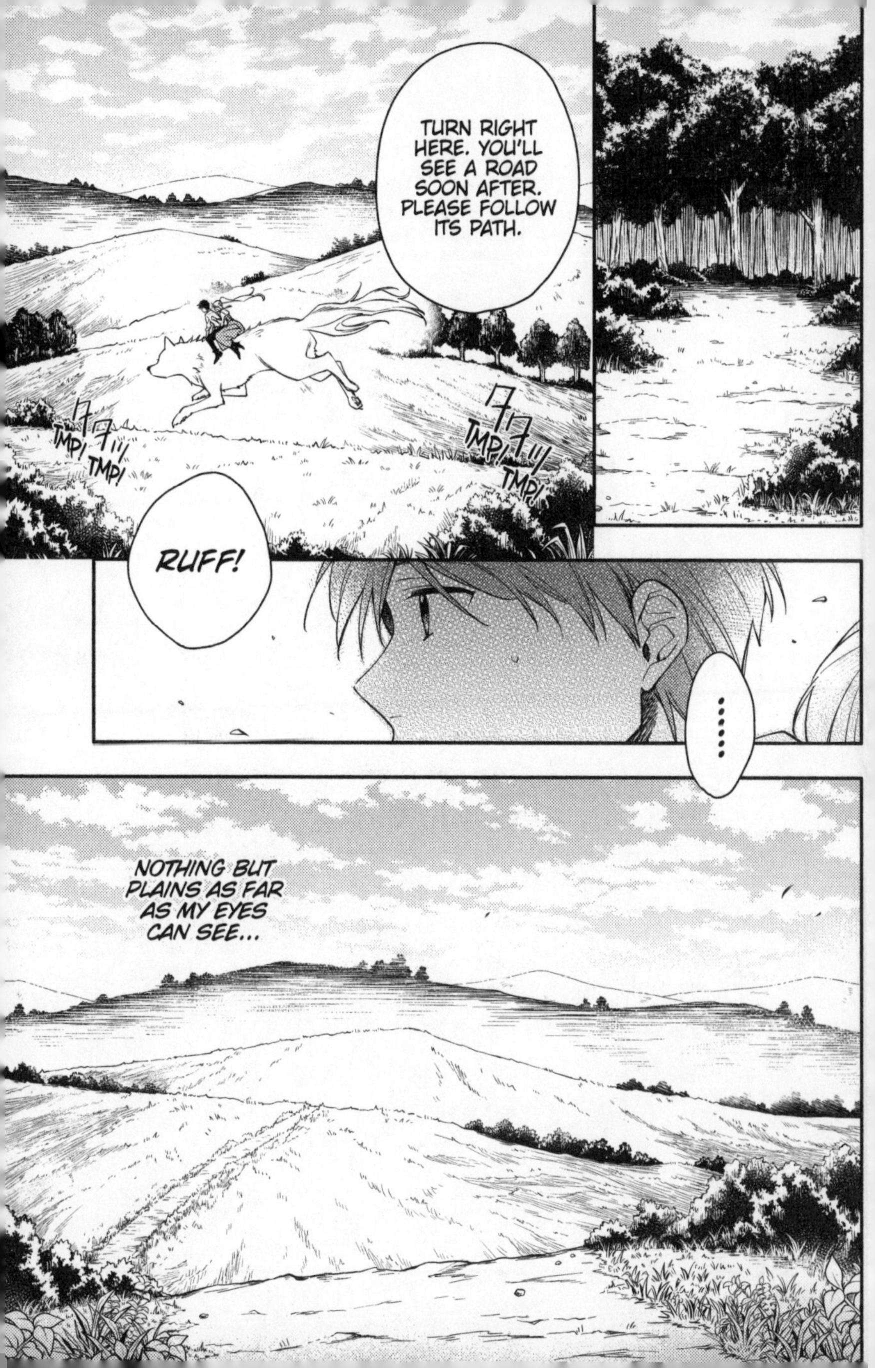
TURN RIGHT HERE. YOU'LL SEE A ROAD SOON AFTER. PLEASE FOLLOW ITS PATH.
TMP! TMP!
TMP! TMP!
RUFF!
......
NOTHING BUT PLAINS AS FAR AS MY EYES CAN SEE...

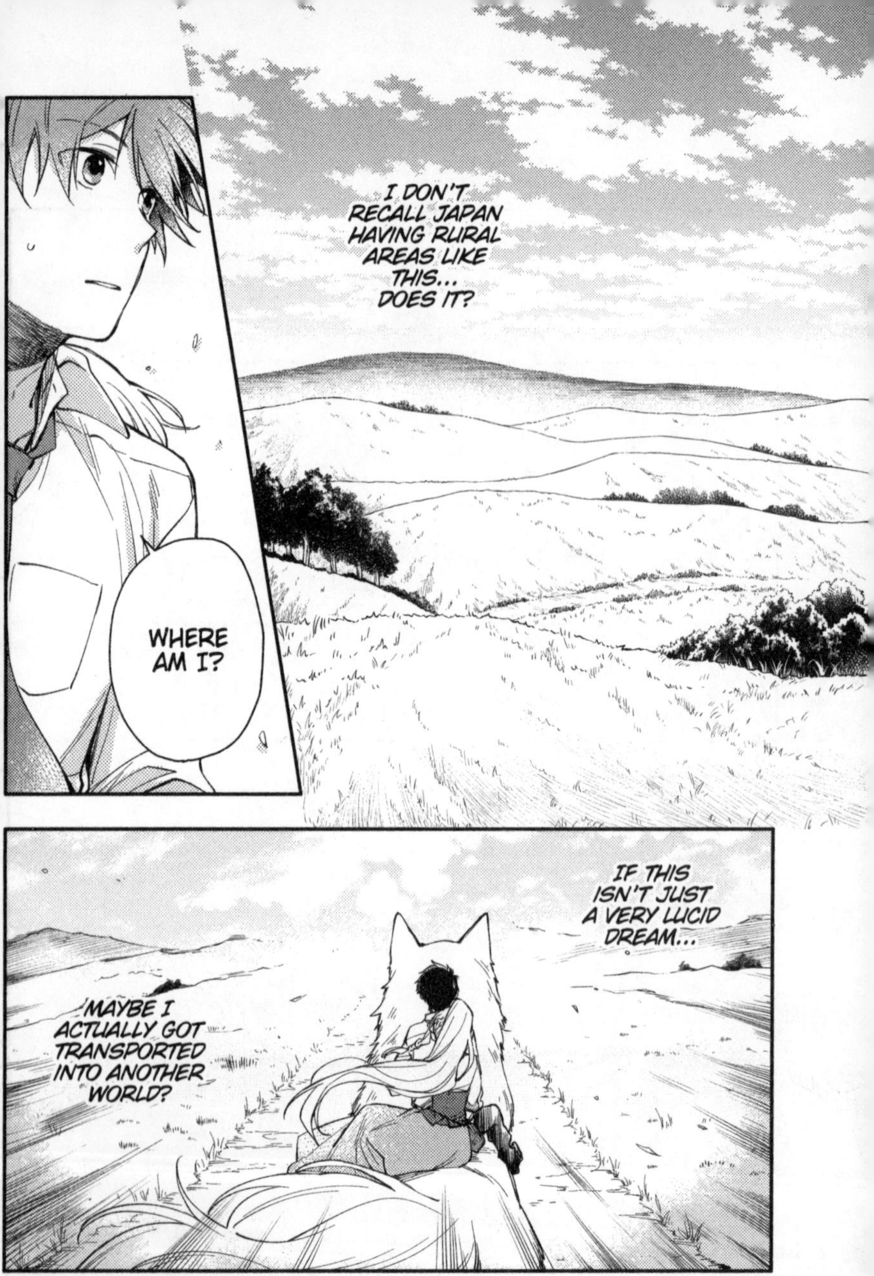
I DON'T RECALL JAPAN HAVING RURAL AREAS LIKE THIS... DOES IT?
WHERE AM I?
IF THIS ISN'T JUST A VERY LUCID DREAM...
MAYBE I ACTUALLY GOT TRANSPORTED INTO ANOTHER WORLD?

NOT SURE IF I SHOULD TRY WRAPPING MY HEAD AROUND IT...

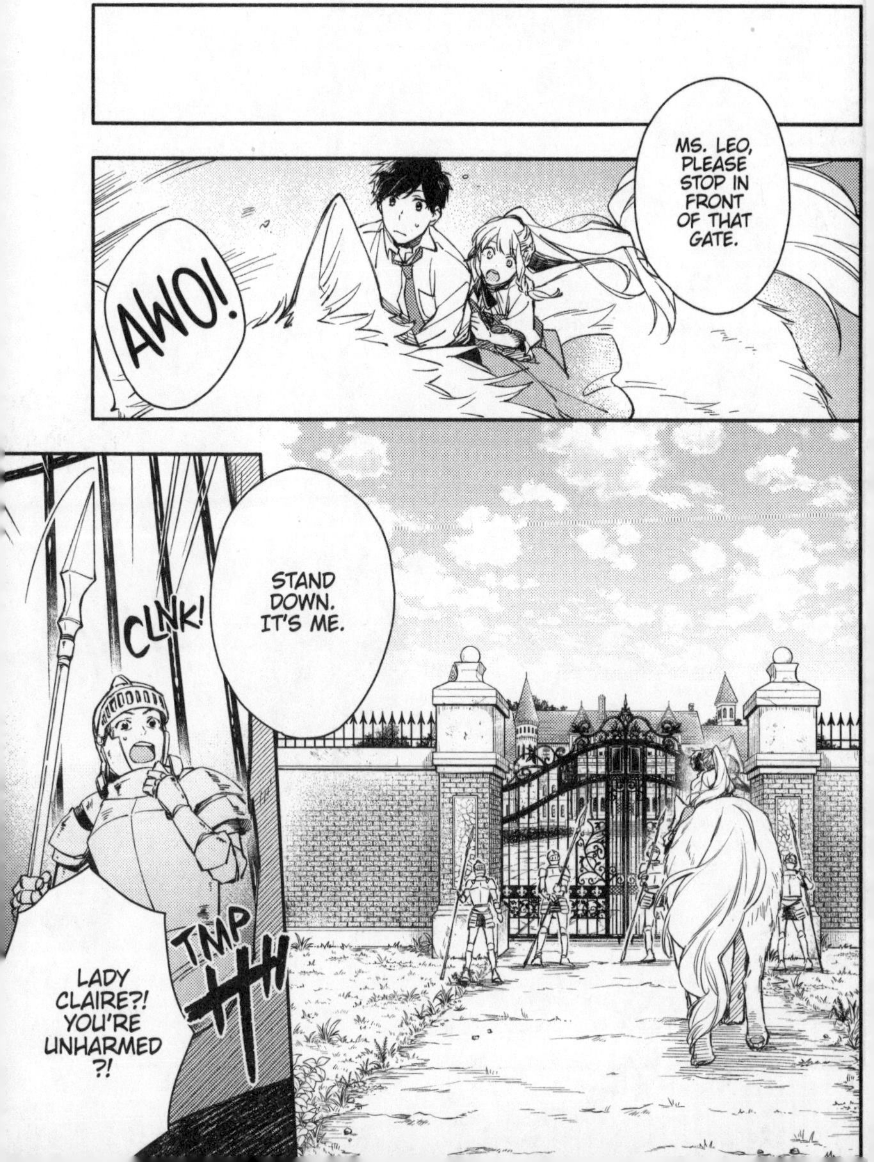
MS. LEO, PLEASE STOP IN FRONT OF THAT GATE.
AWO!
STAND DOWN. IT'S ME.
CLNK!
TMP
LADY CLAIRE?! YOU'RE UNHARMED?!

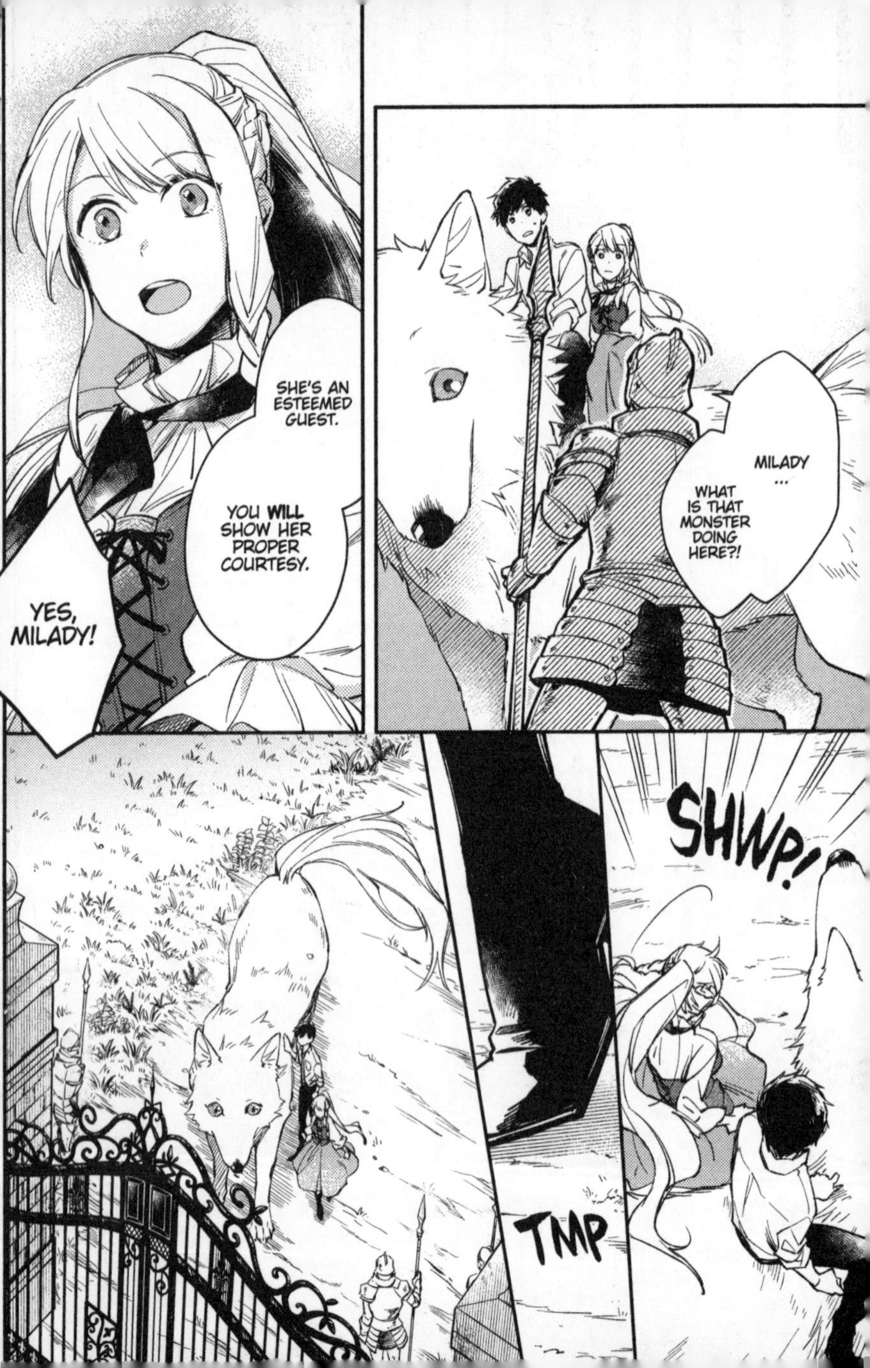
MILADY ... WHAT IS THAT MONSTER DOING HERE?!
SHE'S AN ESTEEMED GUEST.
YOU WILL SHOW HER PROPER COURTESY.
YES, MILADY!
SHWP!
TMP

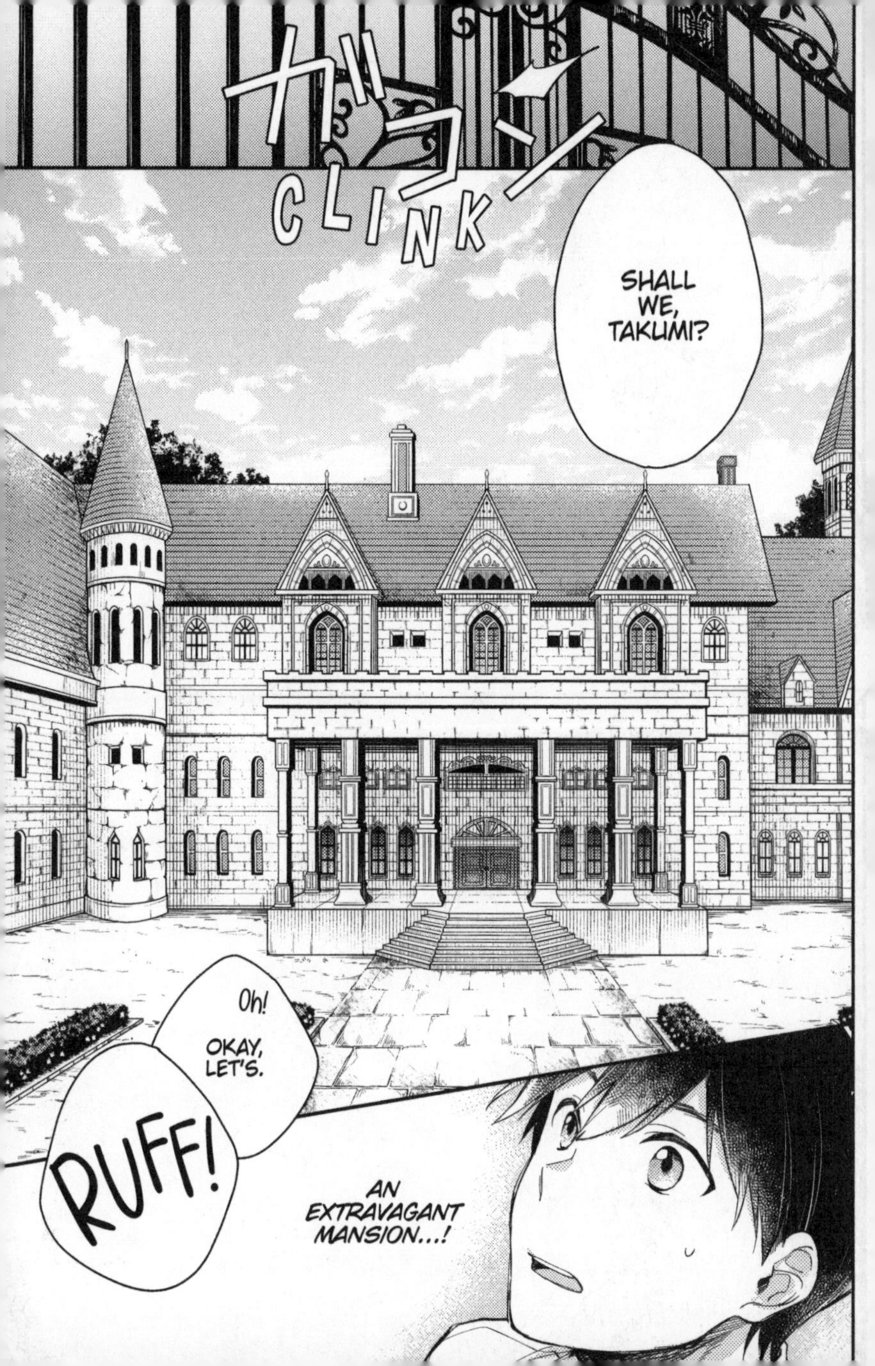
CLINK
SHALL WE, TAKUMI?
Oh!
OKAY, LET'S.
AN EXTRAVAGANT MANSION...!
RUFF!

EVEN DOGS GO TO OTHER WORLDS

LIFE IN ANOTHER WORLD WITH MY BELOVED HOUND

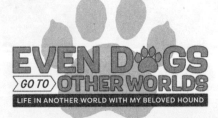

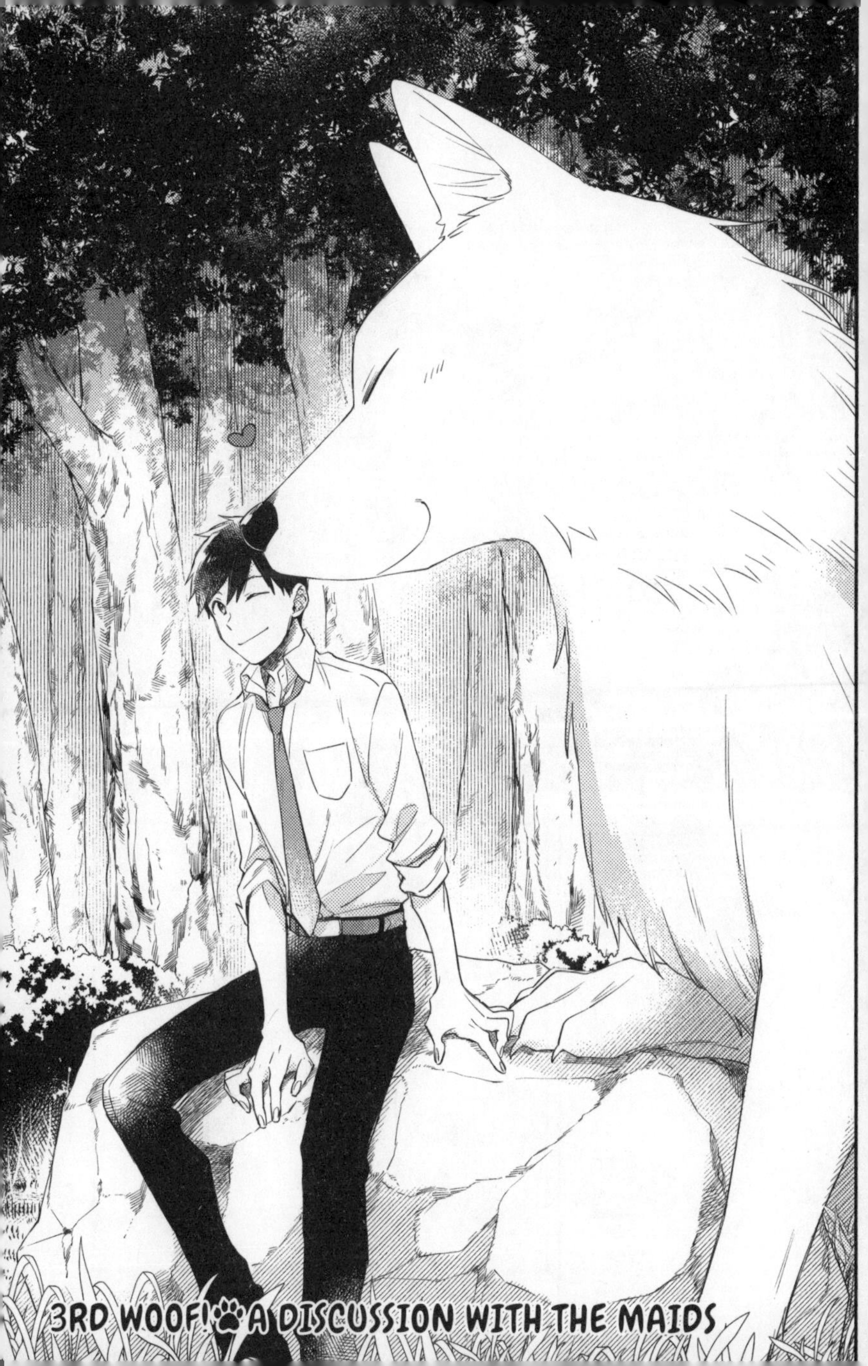
3RD WOOF! A DISCUSSION WITH THE MAIDS

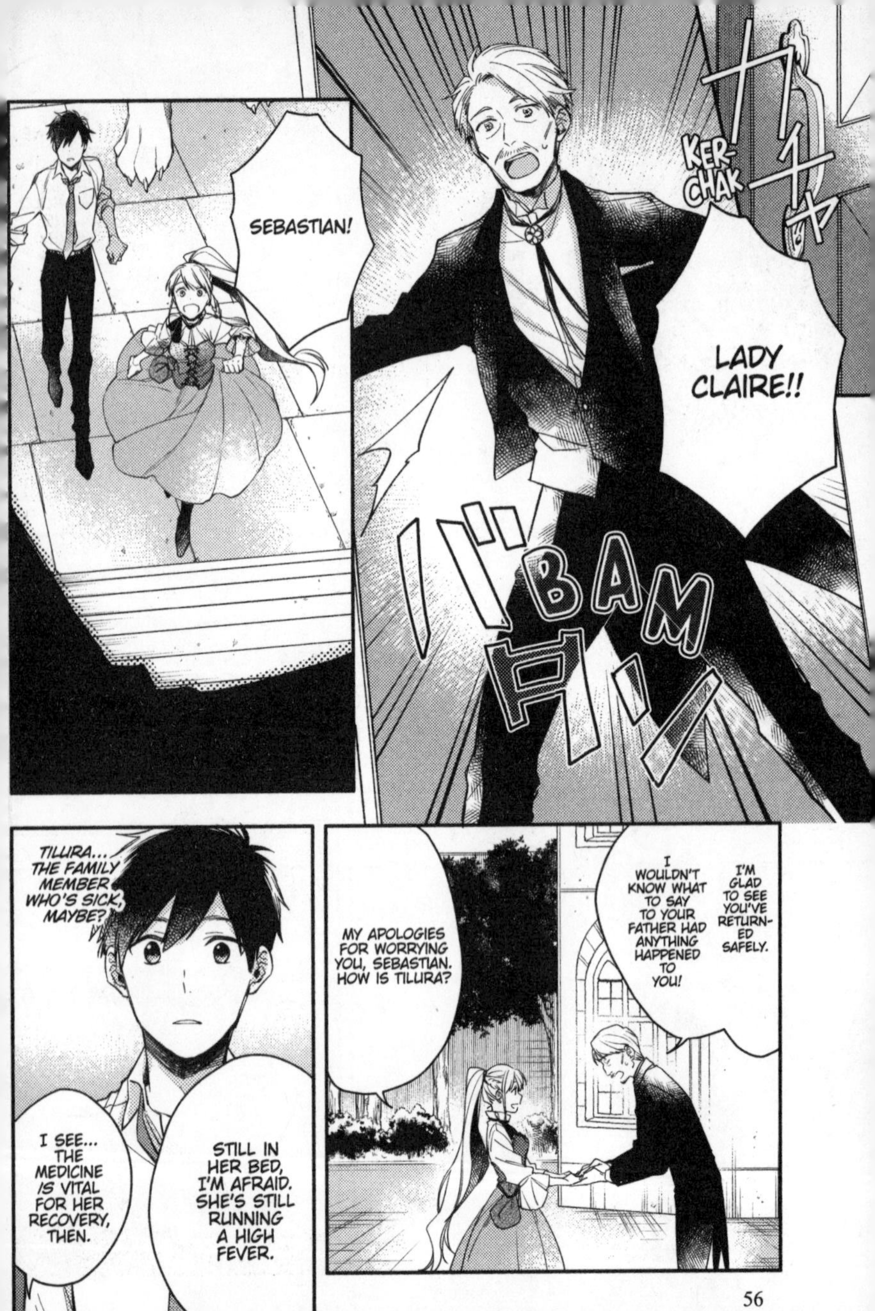
KER-CHAK
LADY CLAIRE!!
BAM
SEBASTIAN!
I'M GLAD TO SEE YOU'VE RETURN-ED SAFELY.
I WOULDN'T KNOW WHAT TO SAY TO YOUR FATHER HAD ANYTHING HAPPENED TO YOU!
MY APOLOGIES FOR WORRYING YOU, SEBASTIAN. HOW IS TILURA?
TILURA... THE FAMILY MEMBER WHO'S SICK, MAYBE?
STILL IN HER BED, I'M AFRAID. SHE'S STILL RUNNING A HIGH FEVER.
I SEE... THE MEDICINE IS VITAL FOR HER RECOVERY, THEN.

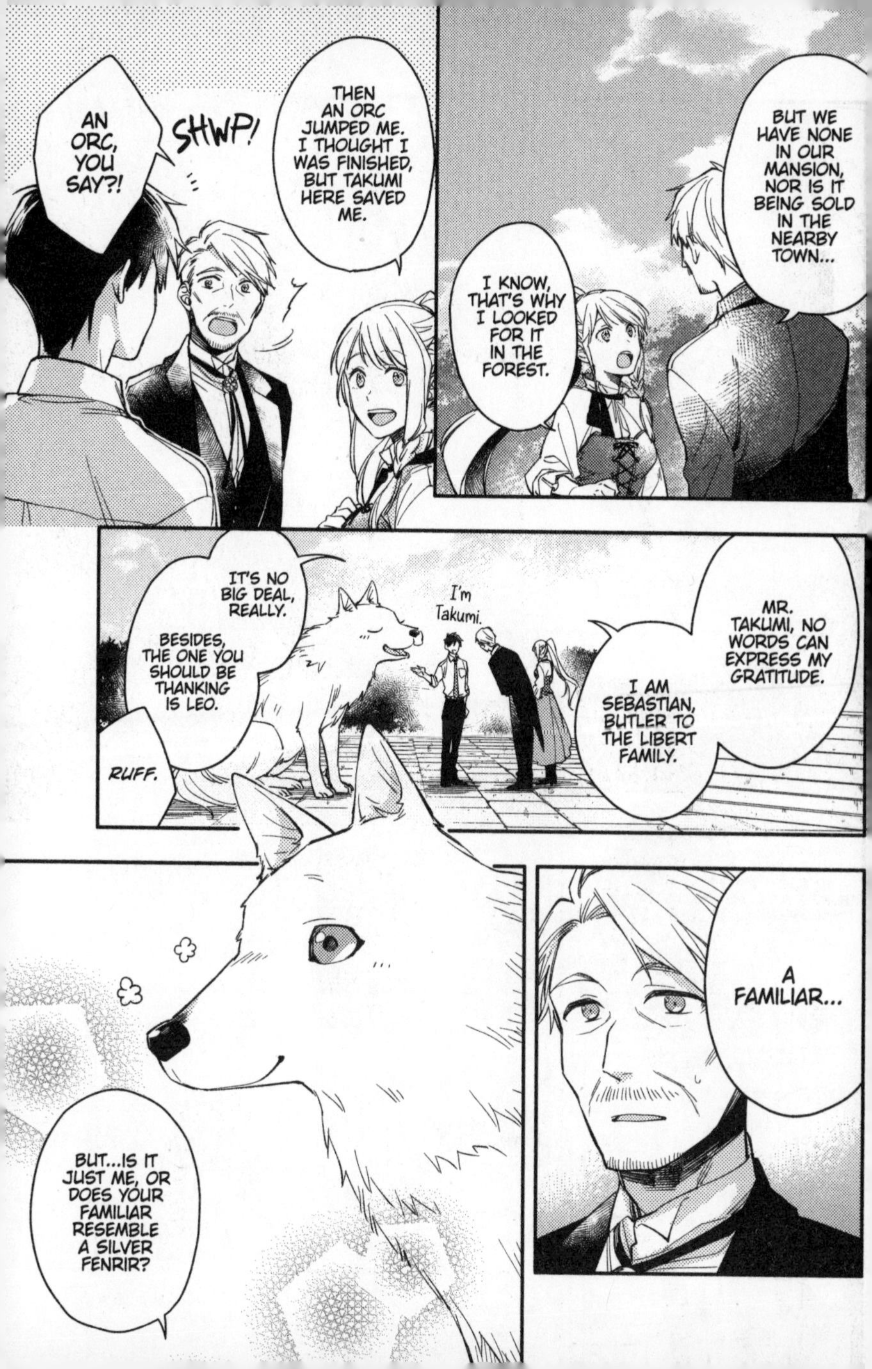
BUT WE HAVE NONE IN OUR MANSION, NOR IS IT BEING SOLD IN THE NEARBY TOWN...
I KNOW, THAT'S WHY I LOOKED FOR IT IN THE FOREST.
THEN AN ORC JUMPED ME. I THOUGHT I WAS FINISHED, BUT TAKUMI HERE SAVED ME.
SHWP!
AN ORC, YOU SAY?!
MR. TAKUMI, NO WORDS CAN EXPRESS MY GRATITUDE.
I AM SEBASTIAN, BUTLER TO THE LIBERT FAMILY.
I'm Takumi.
IT'S NO BIG DEAL, REALLY.
BESIDES, THE ONE YOU SHOULD BE THANKING IS LEO.
RUFF.
A FAMILIAR...
BUT...IS IT JUST ME, OR DOES YOUR FAMILIAR RESEMBLE A SILVER FENRIR?

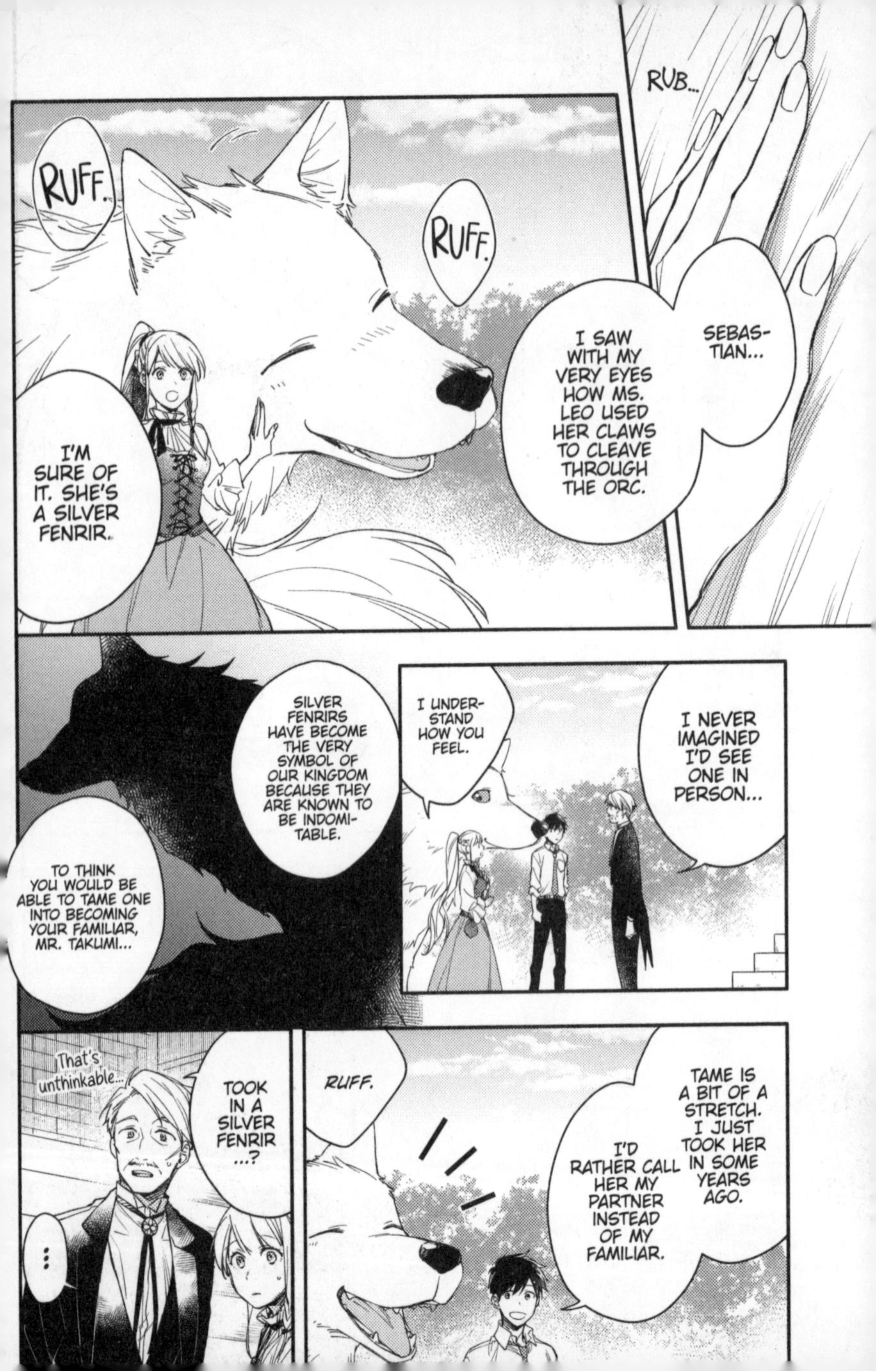
RUB...
SEBASTIAN...
I SAW WITH MY VERY EYES HOW MS. LEO USED HER CLAWS TO CLEAVE THROUGH THE ORC.
RUFF.
RUFF.
I'M SURE OF IT. SHE'S A SILVER FENRIR.
I NEVER IMAGINED I'D SEE ONE IN PERSON...
I UNDERSTAND HOW YOU FEEL.
SILVER FENRIRS HAVE BECOME THE VERY SYMBOL OF OUR KINGDOM BECAUSE THEY ARE KNOWN TO BE INDOMITABLE.
TO THINK YOU WOULD BE ABLE TO TAME ONE INTO BECOMING YOUR FAMILIAR, MR. TAKUMI...
TAME IS A BIT OF A STRETCH. I JUST TOOK HER IN SOME YEARS AGO.
I'D RATHER CALL HER MY PARTNER INSTEAD OF MY FAMILIAR.
RUFF.
TOOK IN A SILVER FENRIR ...?
That's unthinkable...
...

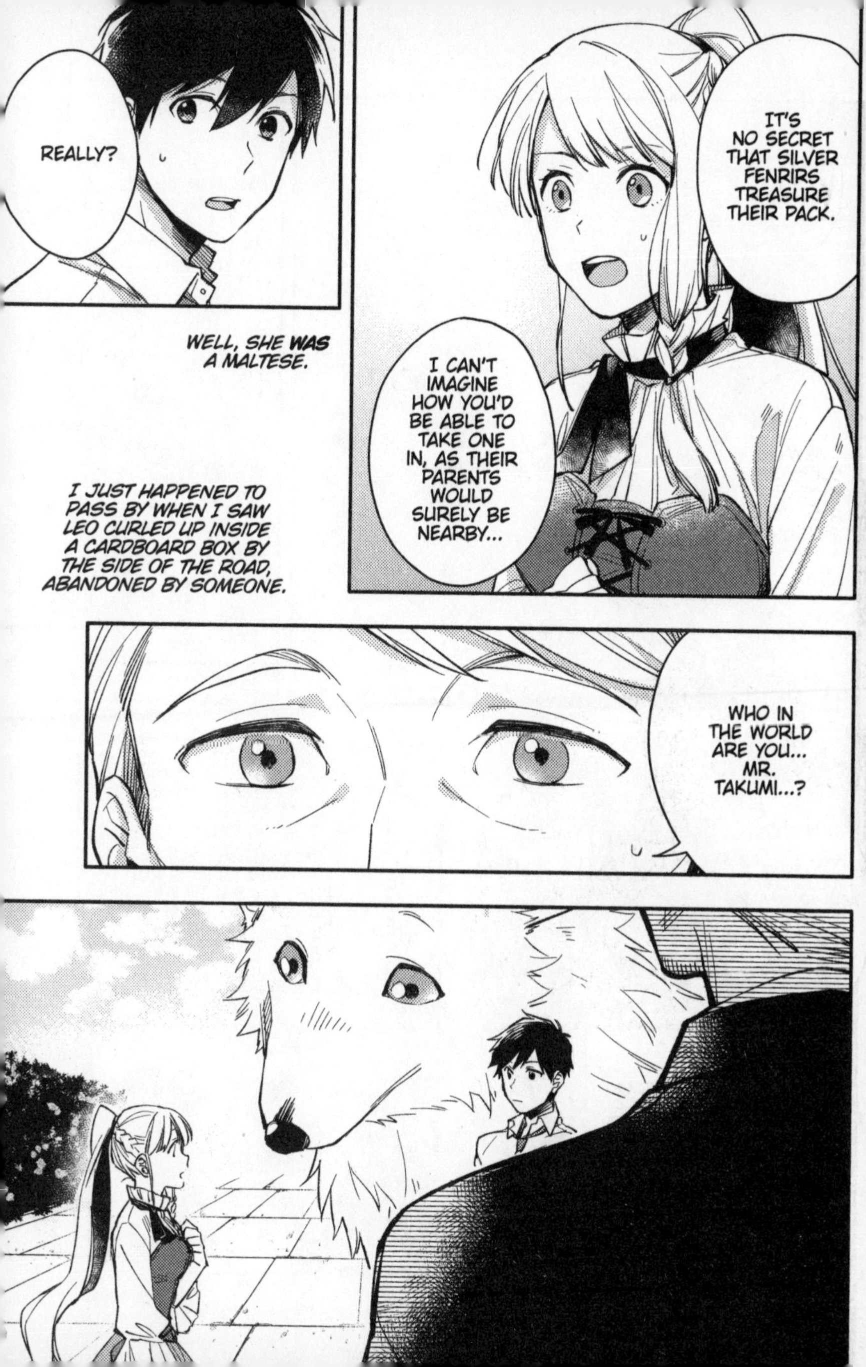
IT'S NO SECRET THAT SILVER FENRIRS TREASURE THEIR PACK.
I CAN'T IMAGINE HOW YOU'D BE ABLE TO TAKE ONE IN, AS THEIR PARENTS WOULD SURELY BE NEARBY...
REALLY?
WELL, SHE WAS A MALTESE.
I JUST HAPPENED TO PASS BY WHEN I SAW LEO CURLED UP INSIDE A CARDBOARD BOX BY THE SIDE OF THE ROAD, ABANDONED BY SOMEONE.
WHO IN THE WORLD ARE YOU... MR. TAKUMI...?

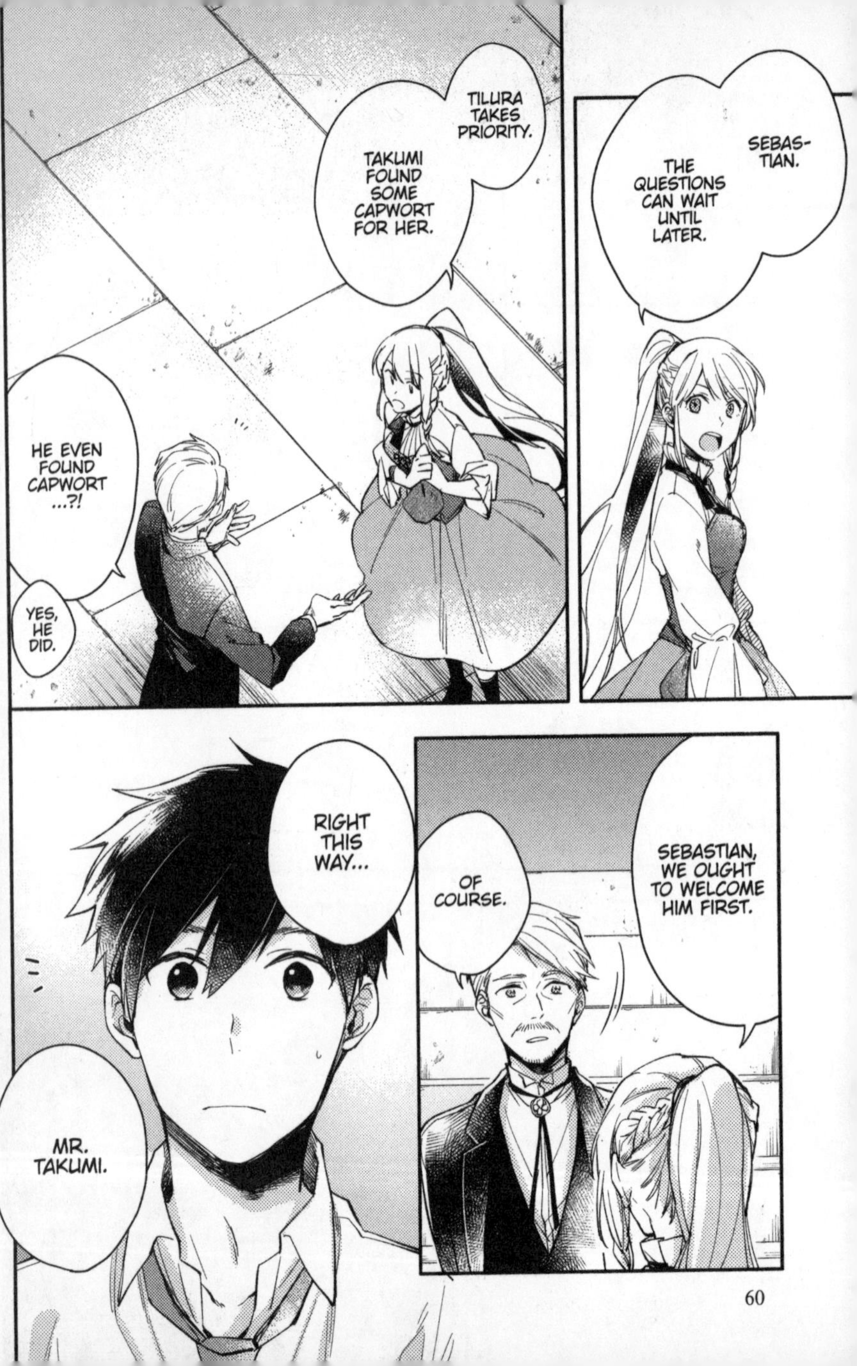
SEBASTIAN.
THE QUESTIONS CAN WAIT UNTIL LATER.
TILURA TAKES PRIORITY.
TAKUMI FOUND SOME CAPWORT FOR HER.
HE EVEN FOUND CAPWORT ...?!
YES, HE DID.
SEBASTIAN, WE OUGHT TO WELCOME HIM FIRST.
OF COURSE.
RIGHT THIS WAY...
MR. TAKUMI.

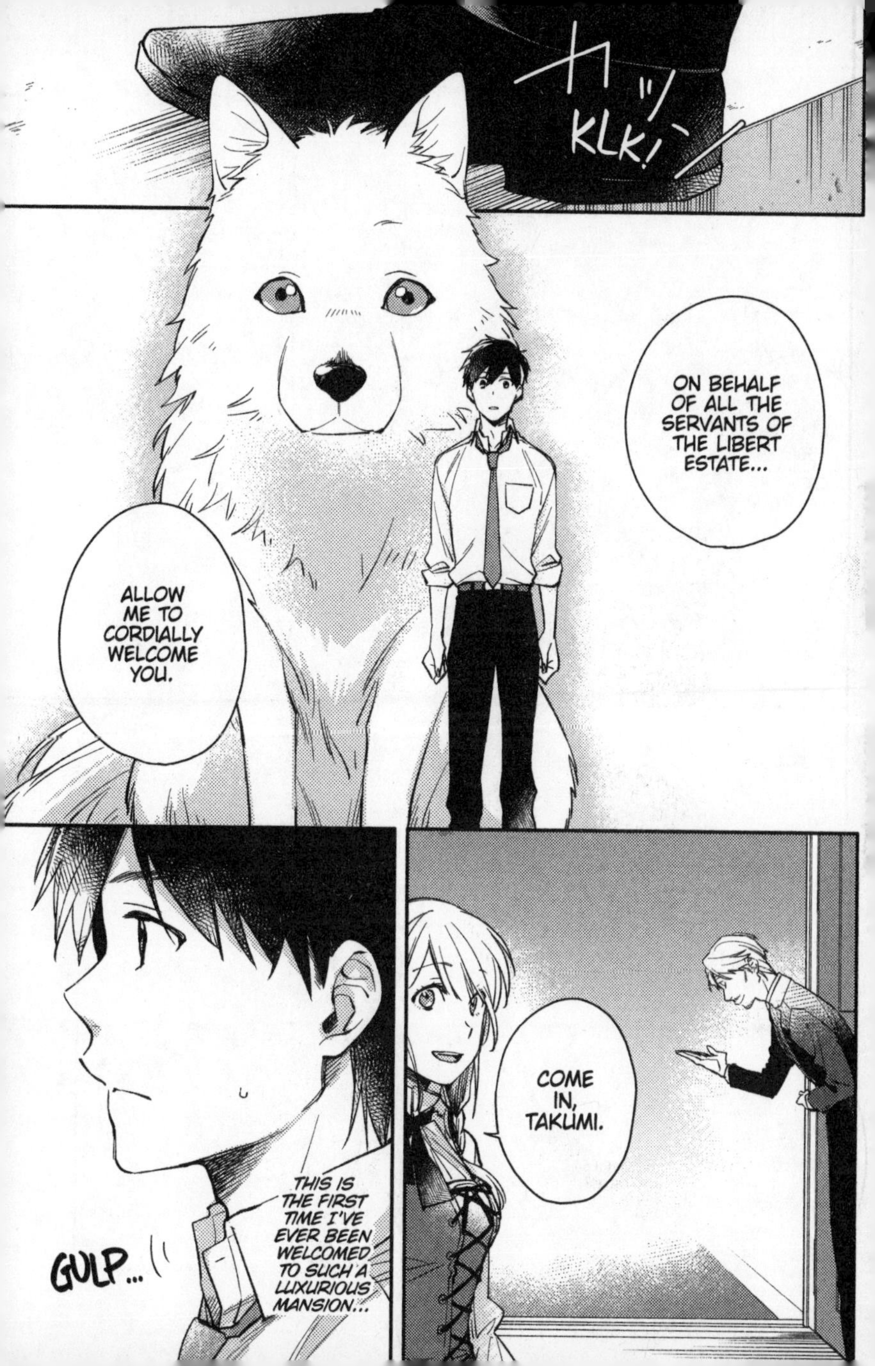
KLK!
ON BEHALF OF ALL THE SERVANTS OF THE LIBERT ESTATE...
ALLOW ME TO CORDIALLY WELCOME YOU.
COME IN, TAKUMI.
THIS IS THE FIRST TIME I'VE EVER BEEN WELCOMED TO SUCH A LUXURIOUS MANSION...
GULP...

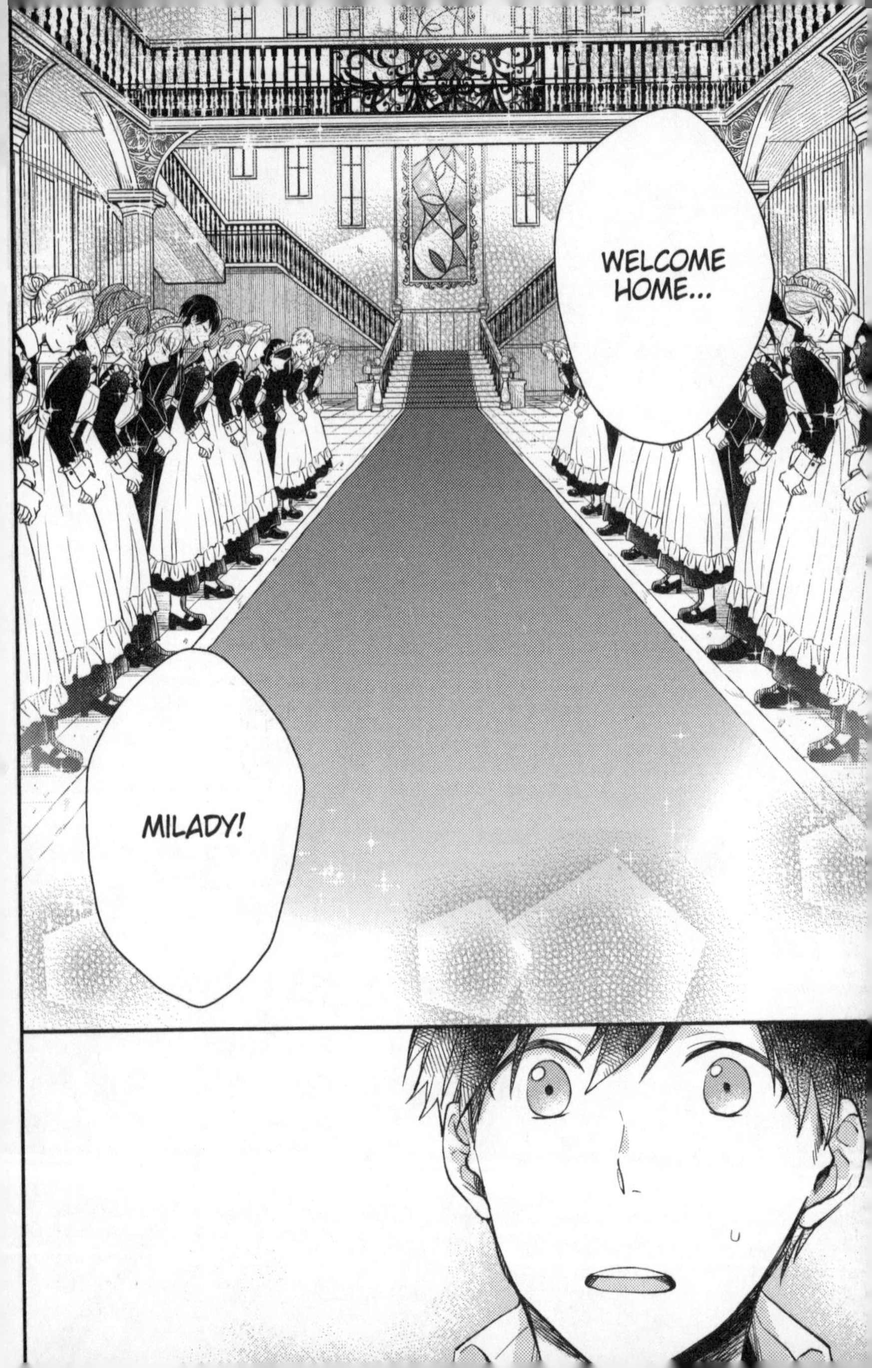
WELCOME HOME...
MILADY!

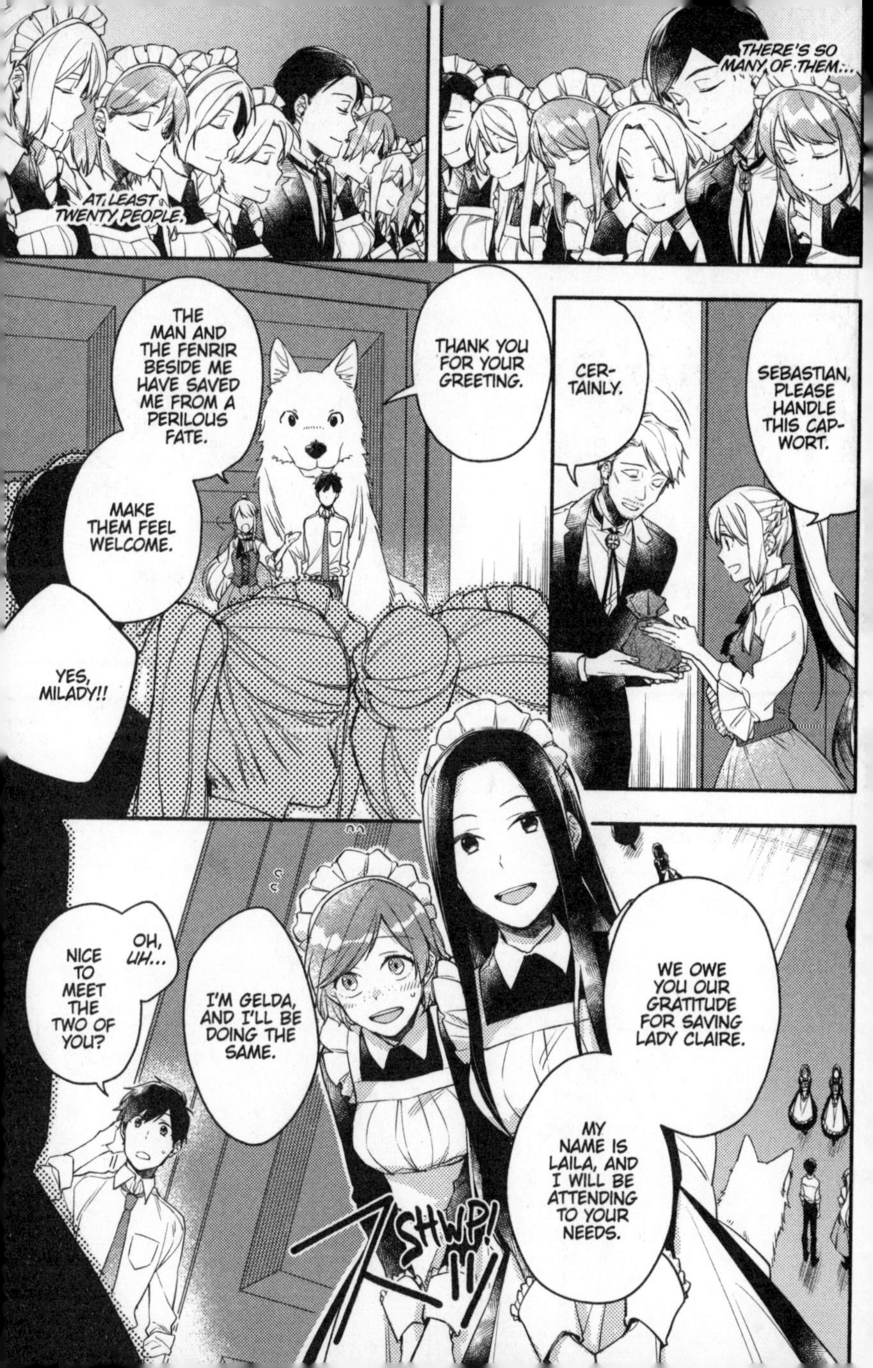
THERE'S SO MANY OF THEM...
AT LEAST TWENTY PEOPLE.
SEBASTIAN, PLEASE HANDLE THIS CAP-WORT.
CER-TAINLY.
THANK YOU FOR YOUR GREETING.
THE MAN AND THE FENRIR BESIDE ME HAVE SAVED ME FROM A PERILOUS FATE.
MAKE THEM FEEL WELCOME.
YES, MILADY!!
WE OWE YOU OUR GRATITUDE FOR SAVING LADY CLAIRE.
MY NAME IS LAILA, AND I WILL BE ATTENDING TO YOUR NEEDS.
SHWP!!
I'M GELDA, AND I'LL BE DOING THE SAME.
OH, UH...
NICE TO MEET THE TWO OF YOU?

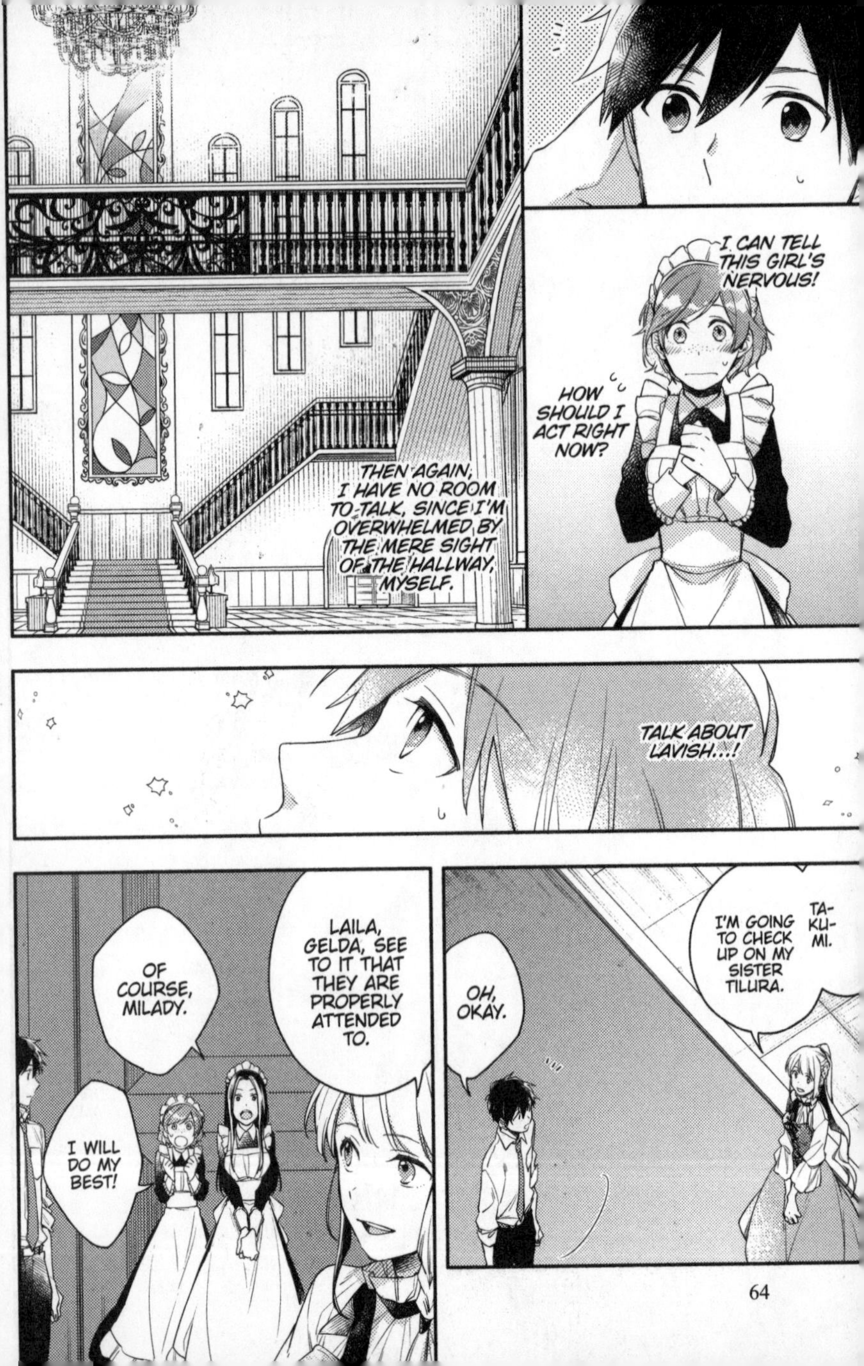
I CAN TELL THIS GIRL'S NERVOUS!
HOW SHOULD I ACT RIGHT NOW?
THEN AGAIN, I HAVE NO ROOM TO TALK, SINCE I'M OVERWHELMED BY THE MERE SIGHT OF THE HALLWAY, MYSELF.
TALK ABOUT LAVISH...!
TAKUMI.
I'M GOING TO CHECK UP ON MY SISTER TILURA.
OH, OKAY.
LAILA, GELDA, SEE TO IT THAT THEY ARE PROPERLY ATTENDED TO.
OF COURSE, MILADY.
I WILL DO MY BEST!

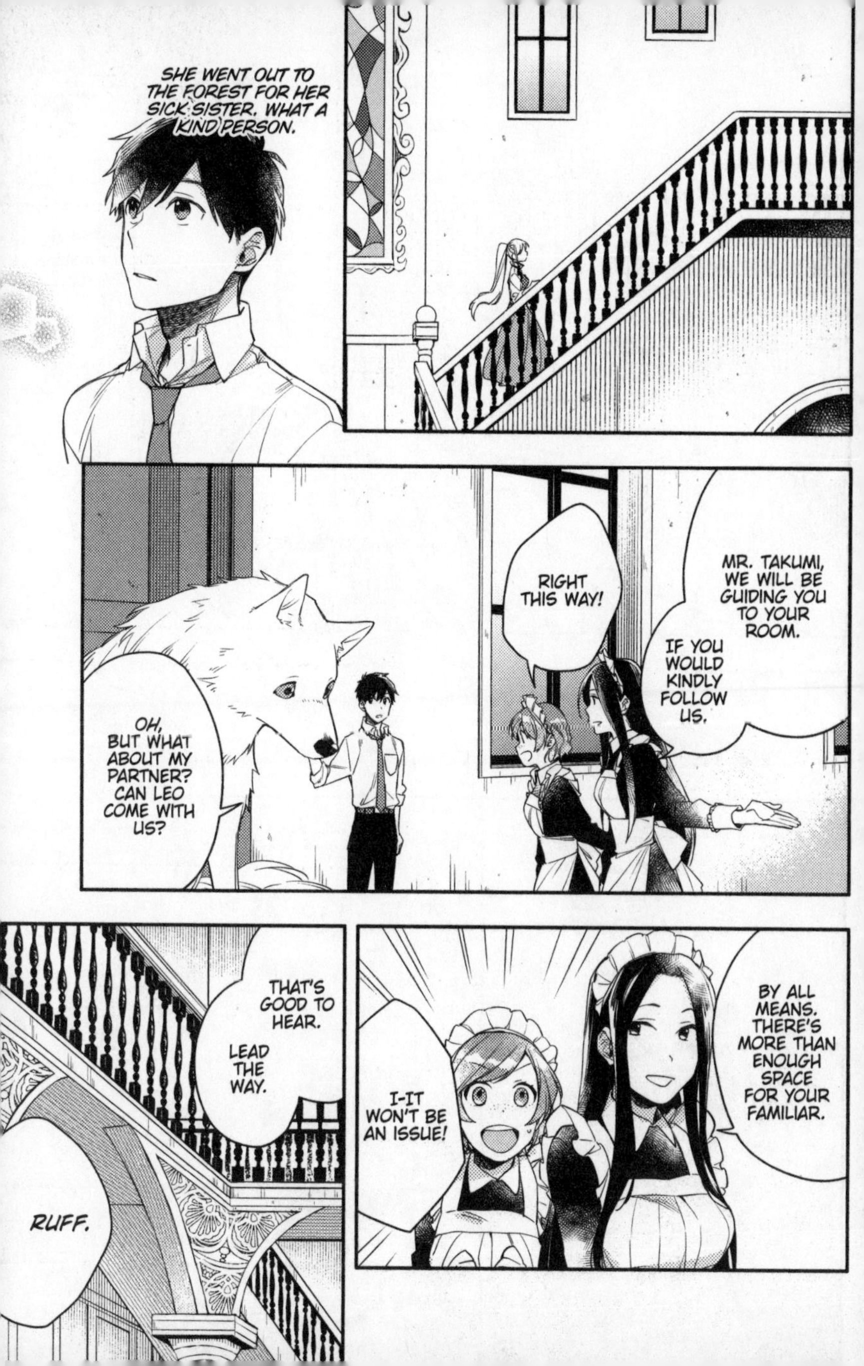
SHE WENT OUT TO THE FOREST FOR HER SICK SISTER. WHAT A KIND PERSON.
MR. TAKUMI, WE WILL BE GUIDING YOU TO YOUR ROOM.
IF YOU WOULD KINDLY FOLLOW US.
RIGHT THIS WAY!
OH, BUT WHAT ABOUT MY PARTNER? CAN LEO COME WITH US?
BY ALL MEANS. THERE'S MORE THAN ENOUGH SPACE FOR YOUR FAMILIAR.
I-IT WON'T BE AN ISSUE!
THAT'S GOOD TO HEAR.
LEAD THE WAY.
RUFF.

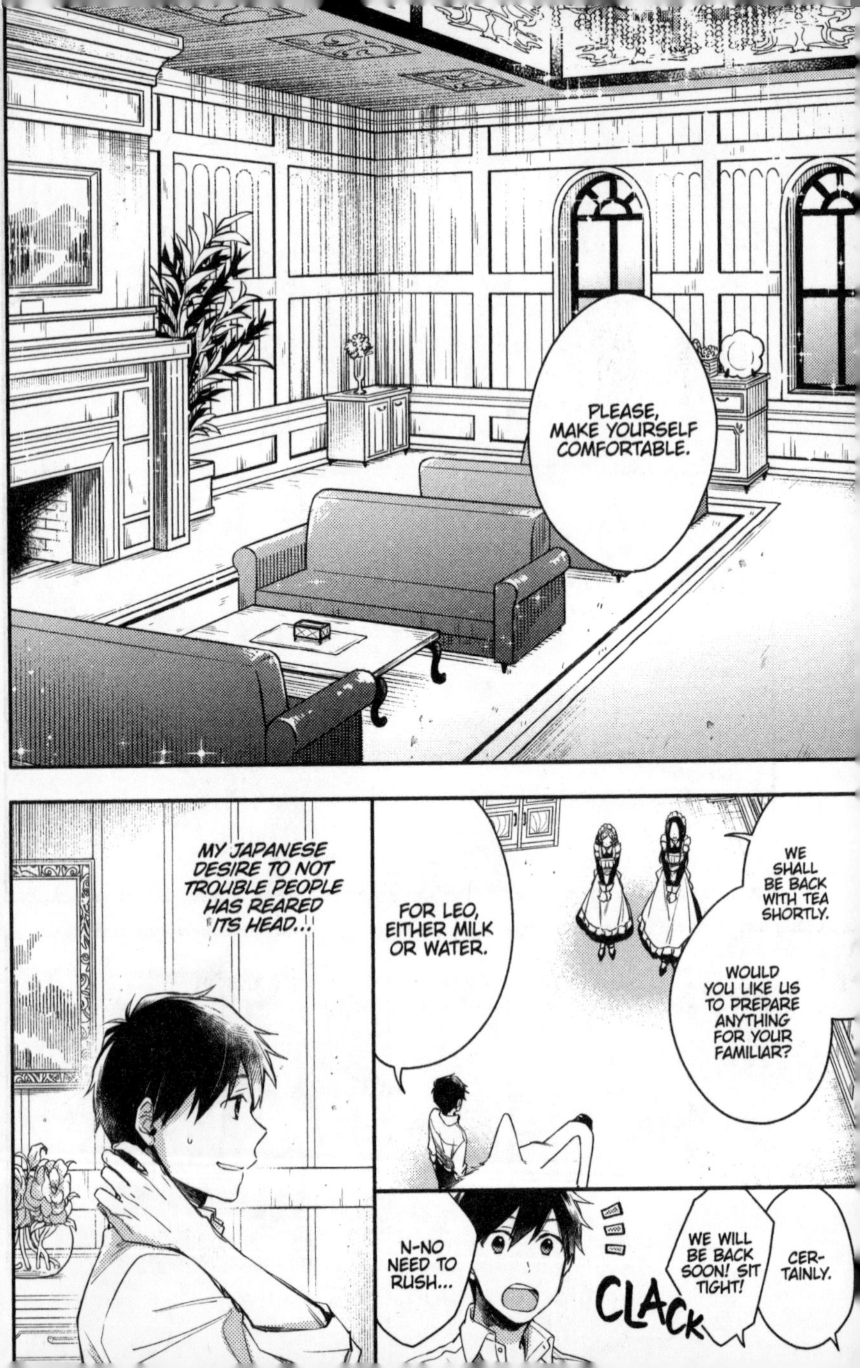
PLEASE, MAKE YOURSELF COMFORTABLE.
WE SHALL BE BACK WITH TEA SHORTLY.
WOULD YOU LIKE US TO PREPARE ANYTHING FOR YOUR FAMILIAR?
FOR LEO, EITHER MILK OR WATER.
CER-TAINLY.
WE WILL BE BACK SOON! SIT TIGHT!
CLACK
N-NO NEED TO RUSH...
MY JAPANESE DESIRE TO NOT TROUBLE PEOPLE HAS REARED ITS HEAD...

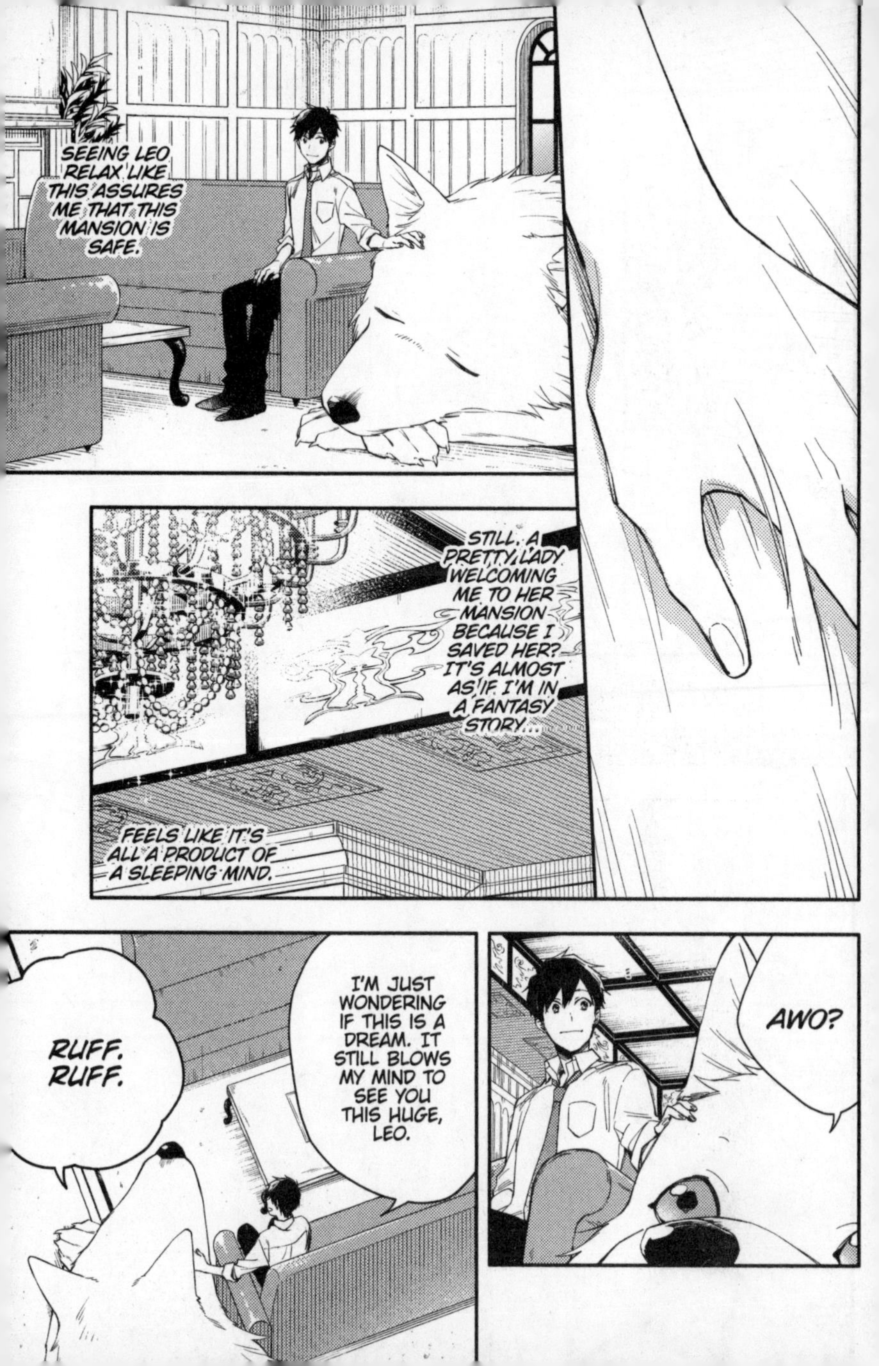
SEEING LEO RELAX LIKE THIS ASSURES ME THAT THIS MANSION IS SAFE.
STILL, A PRETTY LADY WELCOMING ME TO HER MANSION BECAUSE I SAVED HER? IT'S ALMOST AS IF I'M IN A FANTASY STORY...
FEELS LIKE IT'S ALL A PRODUCT OF A SLEEPING MIND.
AWO?
I'M JUST WONDERING IF THIS IS A DREAM. IT STILL BLOWS MY MIND TO SEE YOU THIS HUGE, LEO.
RUFF. RUFF.

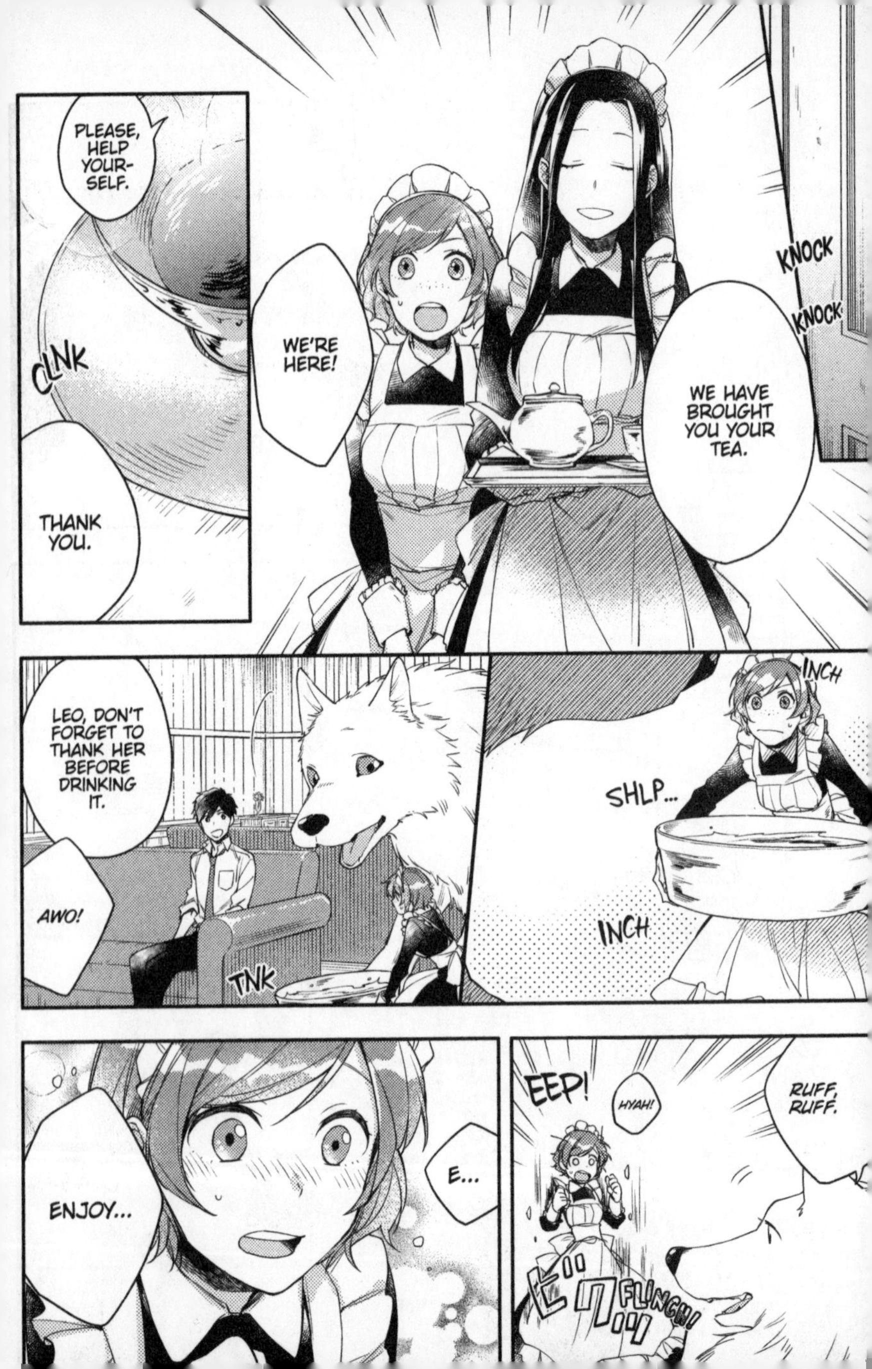
KNOCK
KNOCK
WE HAVE BROUGHT YOU YOUR TEA.
WE'RE HERE!
PLEASE, HELP YOUR-SELF.
CLINK
THANK YOU.
INCH
SHLP...
INCH
LEO, DON'T FORGET TO THANK HER BEFORE DRINKING IT.
AWO!
TNK
RUFF, RUFF.
HYAH!
EEP!
FLINCH!
E...
ENJOY...

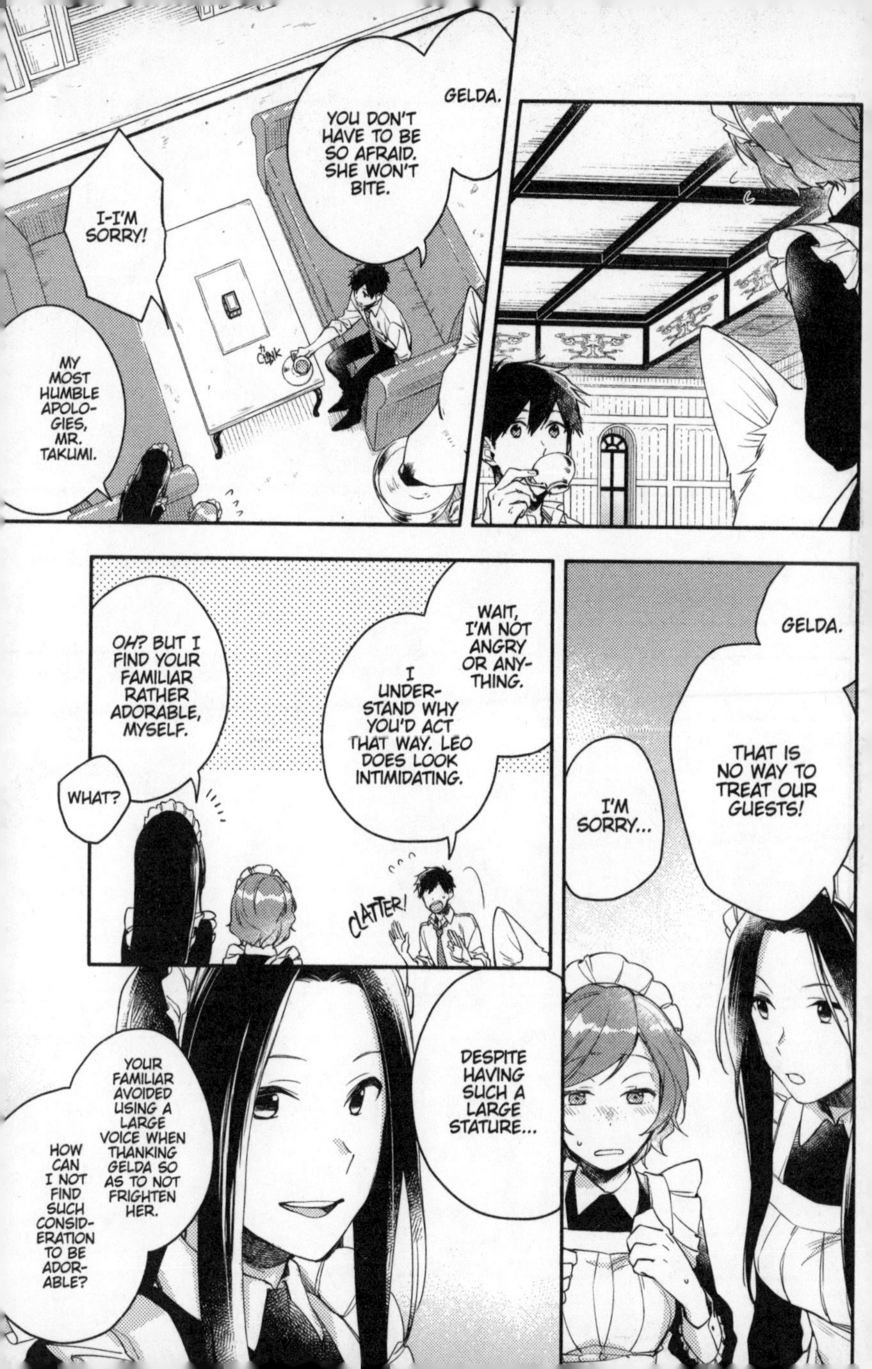
GELDA.
YOU DON'T HAVE TO BE SO AFRAID. SHE WON'T BITE.
I-I'M SORRY!
CLINK
MY MOST HUMBLE APOLOGIES, MR. TAKUMI.
GELDA.
THAT IS NO WAY TO TREAT OUR GUESTS!
I'M SORRY...
WAIT, I'M NOT ANGRY OR ANYTHING.
I UNDERSTAND WHY YOU'D ACT THAT WAY. LEO DOES LOOK INTIMIDATING.
CLATTER!
OH? BUT I FIND YOUR FAMILIAR RATHER ADORABLE, MYSELF.
WHAT?
DESPITE HAVING SUCH A LARGE STATURE...
YOUR FAMILIAR AVOIDED USING A LARGE VOICE WHEN THANKING GELDA SO AS TO NOT FRIGHTEN HER.
HOW CAN I NOT FIND SUCH CONSIDERATION TO BE ADORABLE?

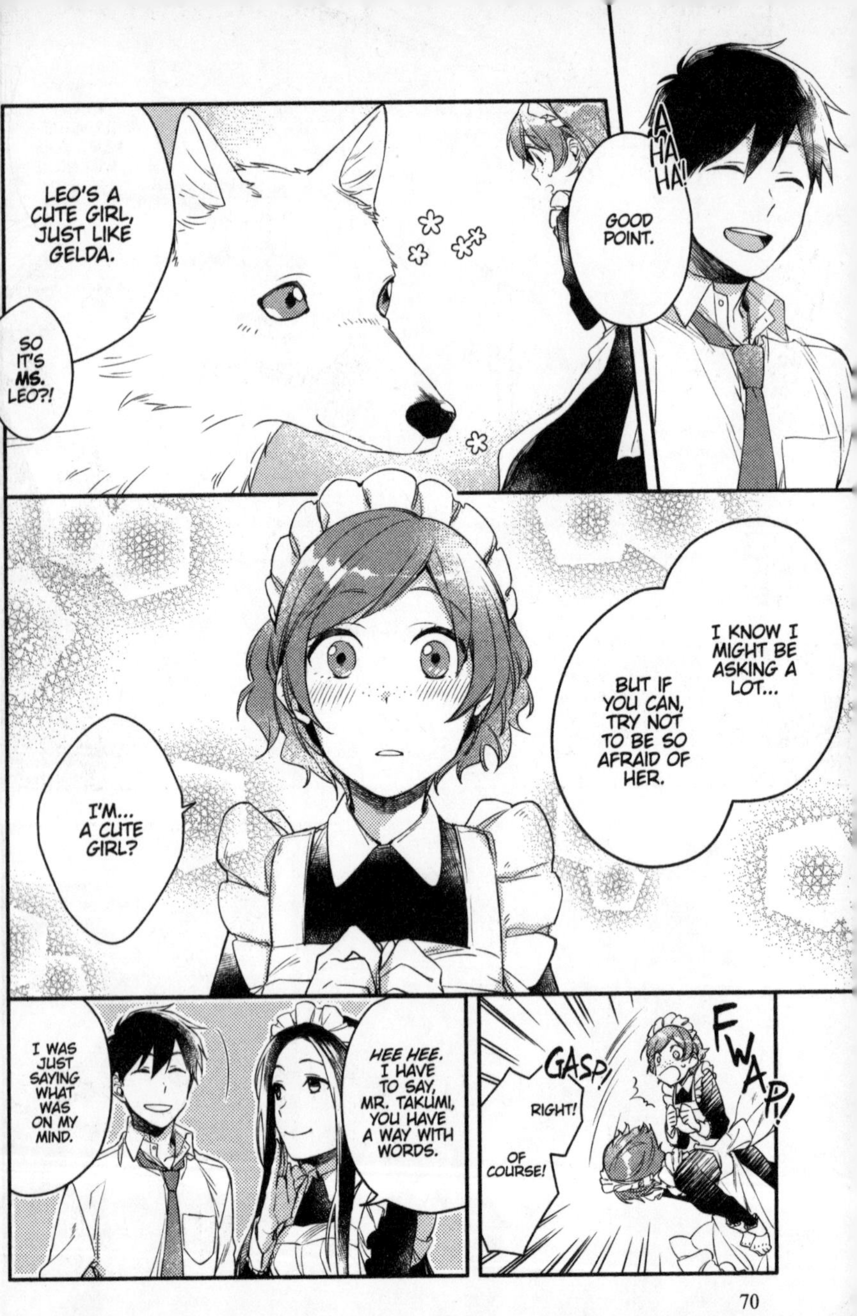
AHAHA!
GOOD POINT.
LEO'S A CUTE GIRL, JUST LIKE GELDA.
SO IT'S MS. LEO?!
I KNOW I MIGHT BE ASKING A LOT...
BUT IF YOU CAN, TRY NOT TO BE SO AFRAID OF HER.
I'M... A CUTE GIRL?
FWAP!
GASP!
RIGHT!
OF COURSE!
HEE HEE. I HAVE TO SAY, MR. TAKUMI, YOU HAVE A WAY WITH WORDS.
I WAS JUST SAYING WHAT WAS ON MY MIND.

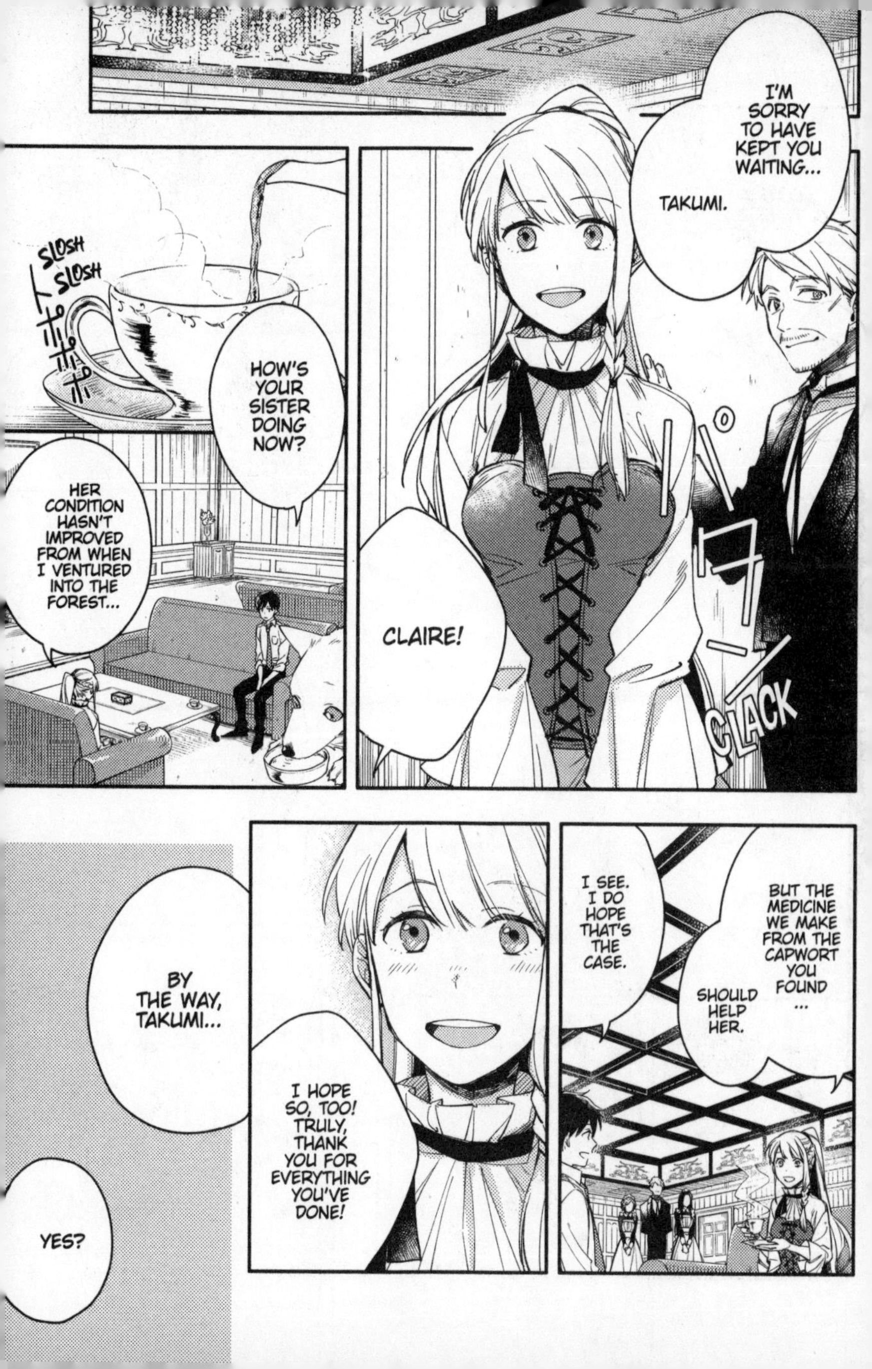
I'M SORRY TO HAVE KEPT YOU WAITING...
TAKUMI.
CLAIRE!
CLACK
SLOSH SLOSH
HOW'S YOUR SISTER DOING NOW?
HER CONDITION HASN'T IMPROVED FROM WHEN I VENTURED INTO THE FOREST...
BUT THE MEDICINE WE MAKE FROM THE CAPWORT YOU FOUND ...
SHOULD HELP HER.
I SEE. I DO HOPE THAT'S THE CASE.
I HOPE SO, TOO! TRULY, THANK YOU FOR EVERYTHING YOU'VE DONE!
BY THE WAY, TAKUMI...
YES?

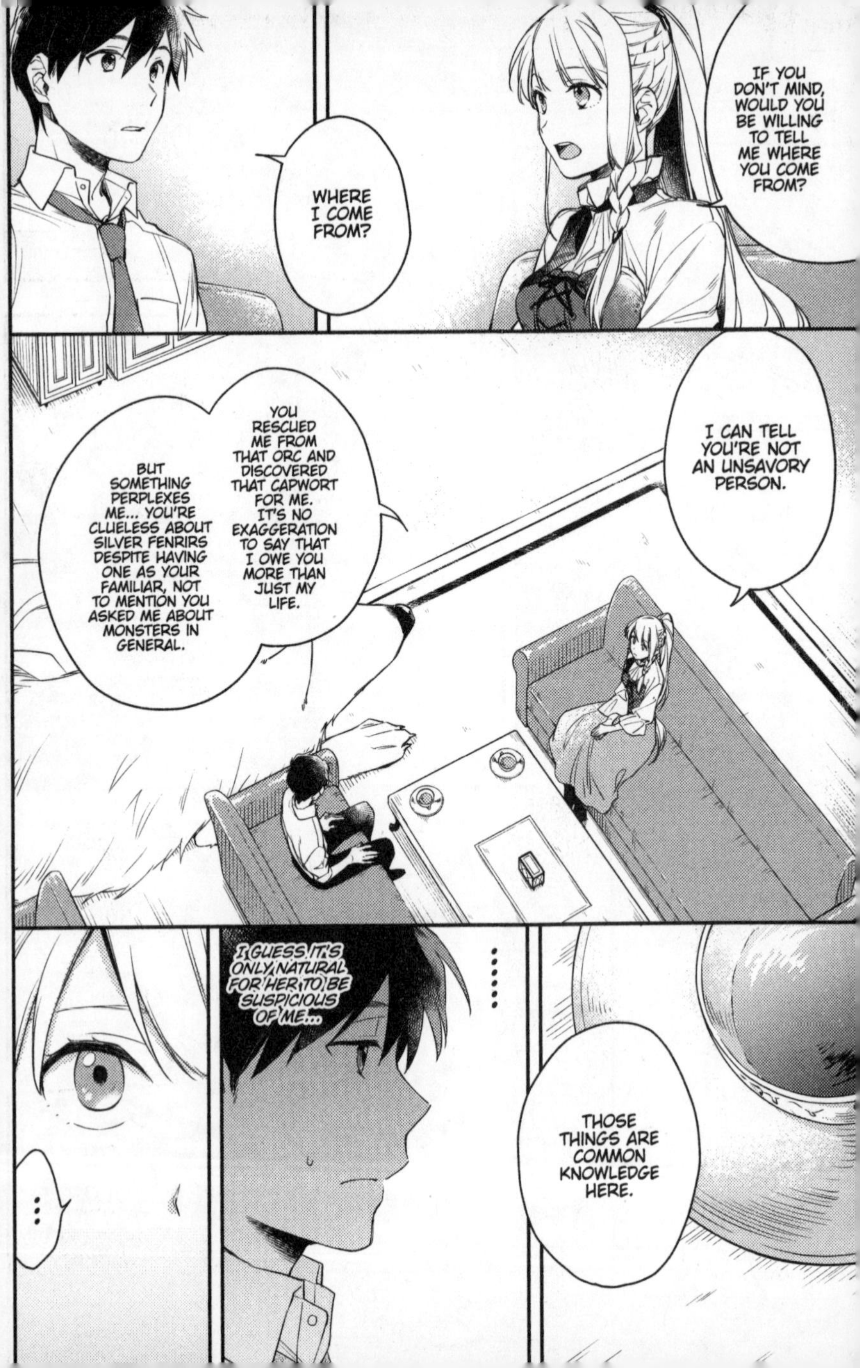
IF YOU DON'T MIND, WOULD YOU BE WILLING TO TELL ME WHERE YOU COME FROM?
WHERE I COME FROM?
I CAN TELL YOU'RE NOT AN UNSAVORY PERSON.
YOU RESCUED ME FROM THAT ORC AND DISCOVERED THAT CAPWORT FOR ME. IT'S NO EXAGGERATION TO SAY THAT I OWE YOU MORE THAN JUST MY LIFE.
BUT SOMETHING PERPLEXES ME... YOU'RE CLUELESS ABOUT SILVER FENRIRS DESPITE HAVING ONE AS YOUR FAMILIAR, NOT TO MENTION YOU ASKED ME ABOUT MONSTERS IN GENERAL.
THOSE THINGS ARE COMMON KNOWLEDGE HERE.
......
I GUESS IT'S ONLY NATURAL FOR HER TO BE SUSPICIOUS OF ME...
...

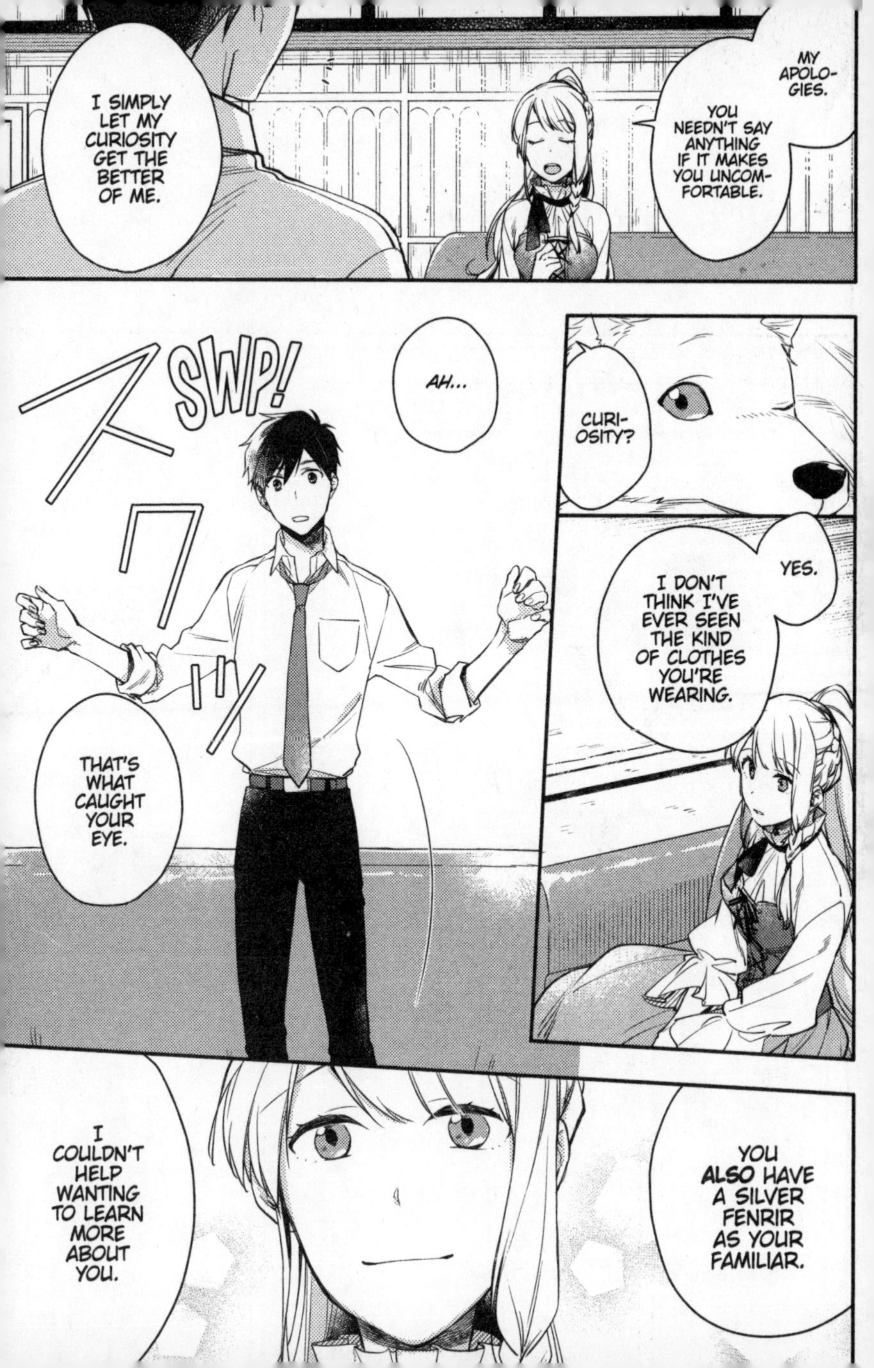
MY APOLOGIES.
YOU NEEDN'T SAY ANYTHING IF IT MAKES YOU UNCOMFORTABLE.
I SIMPLY LET MY CURIOSITY GET THE BETTER OF ME.
CURIOSITY?
YES.
I DON'T THINK I'VE EVER SEEN THE KIND OF CLOTHES YOU'RE WEARING.
AH...
SWP!
THAT'S WHAT CAUGHT YOUR EYE.
YOU ALSO HAVE A SILVER FENRIR AS YOUR FAMILIAR.
I COULDN'T HELP WANTING TO LEARN MORE ABOUT YOU.

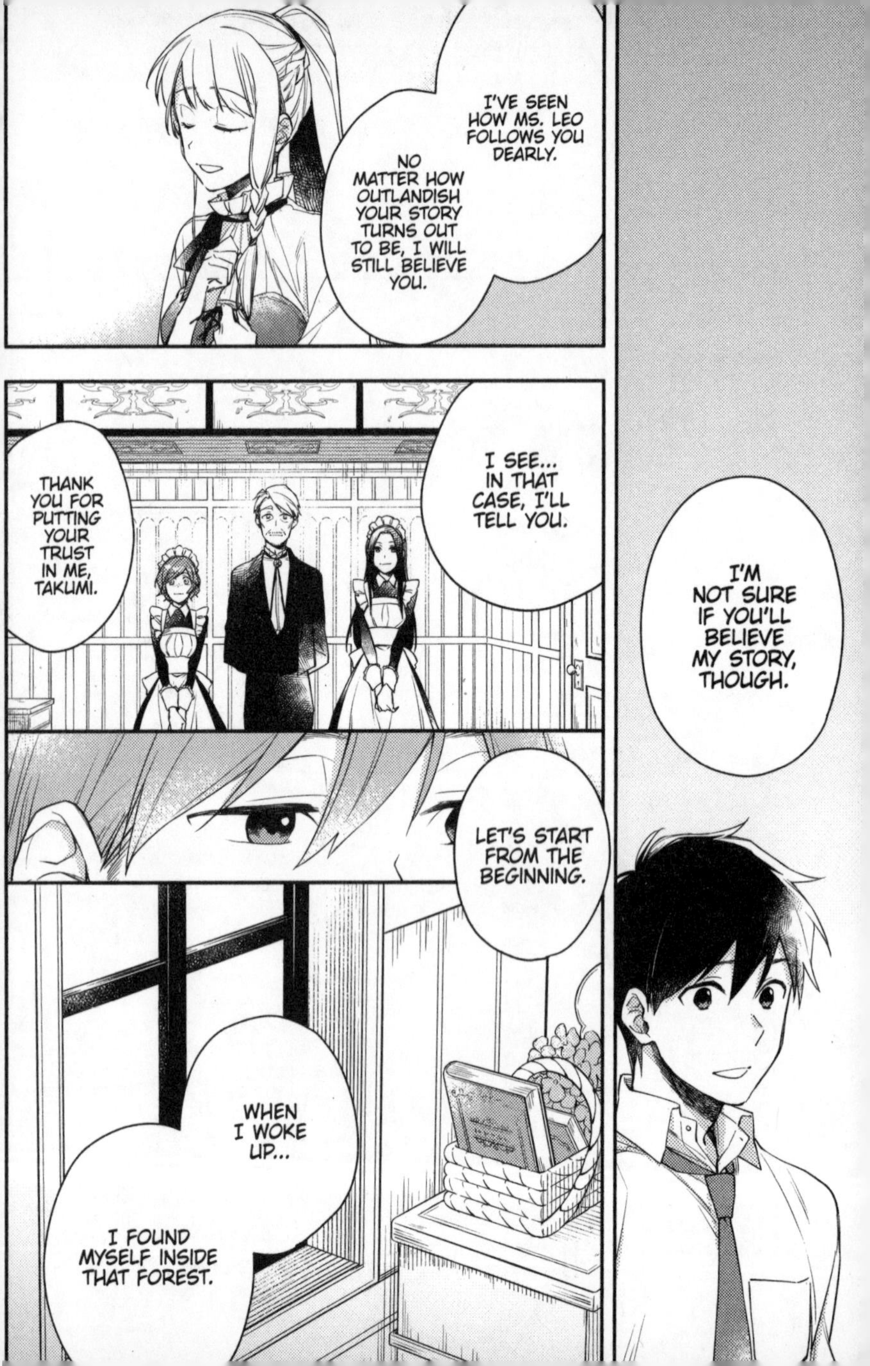

I'VE SEEN HOW MS. LEO FOLLOWS YOU DEARLY.
NO MATTER HOW OUTLANDISH YOUR STORY TURNS OUT TO BE, I WILL STILL BELIEVE YOU.
I SEE... IN THAT CASE, I'LL TELL YOU.
THANK YOU FOR PUTTING YOUR TRUST IN ME, TAKUMI.
I'M NOT SURE IF YOU'LL BELIEVE MY STORY, THOUGH.
LET'S START FROM THE BEGINNING.
WHEN I WOKE UP...
I FOUND MYSELF INSIDE THAT FOREST.

EVEN DOGS GO TO OTHER WORLDS

LIFE IN ANOTHER WORLD WITH MY BELOVED HOUND

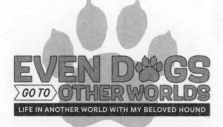

EVEN DOGS GO TO OTHER WORLDS

LIFE IN ANOTHER WORLD WITH MY BELOVED HOUND

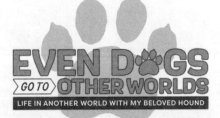

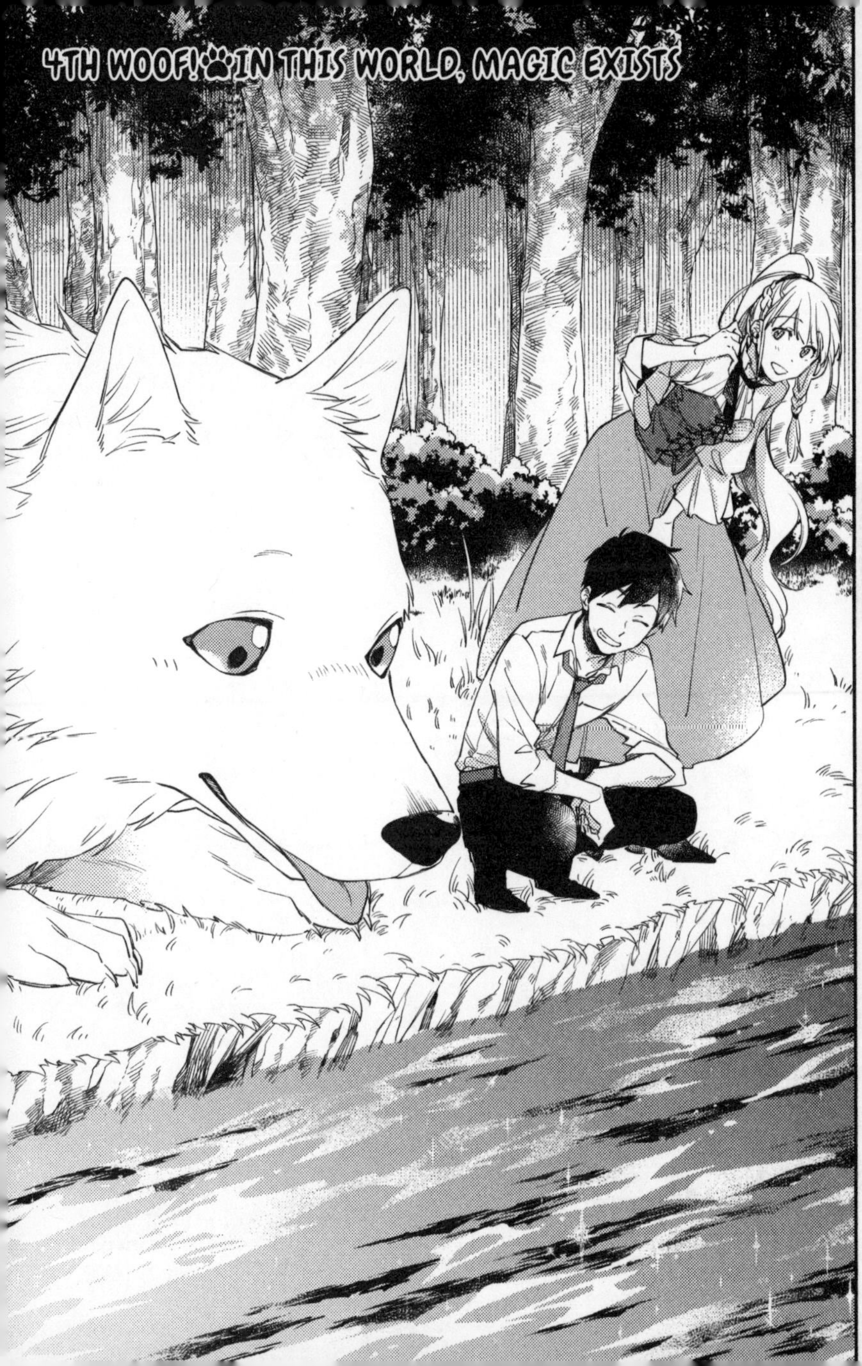
4TH WOOF! IN THIS WORLD, MAGIC EXISTS

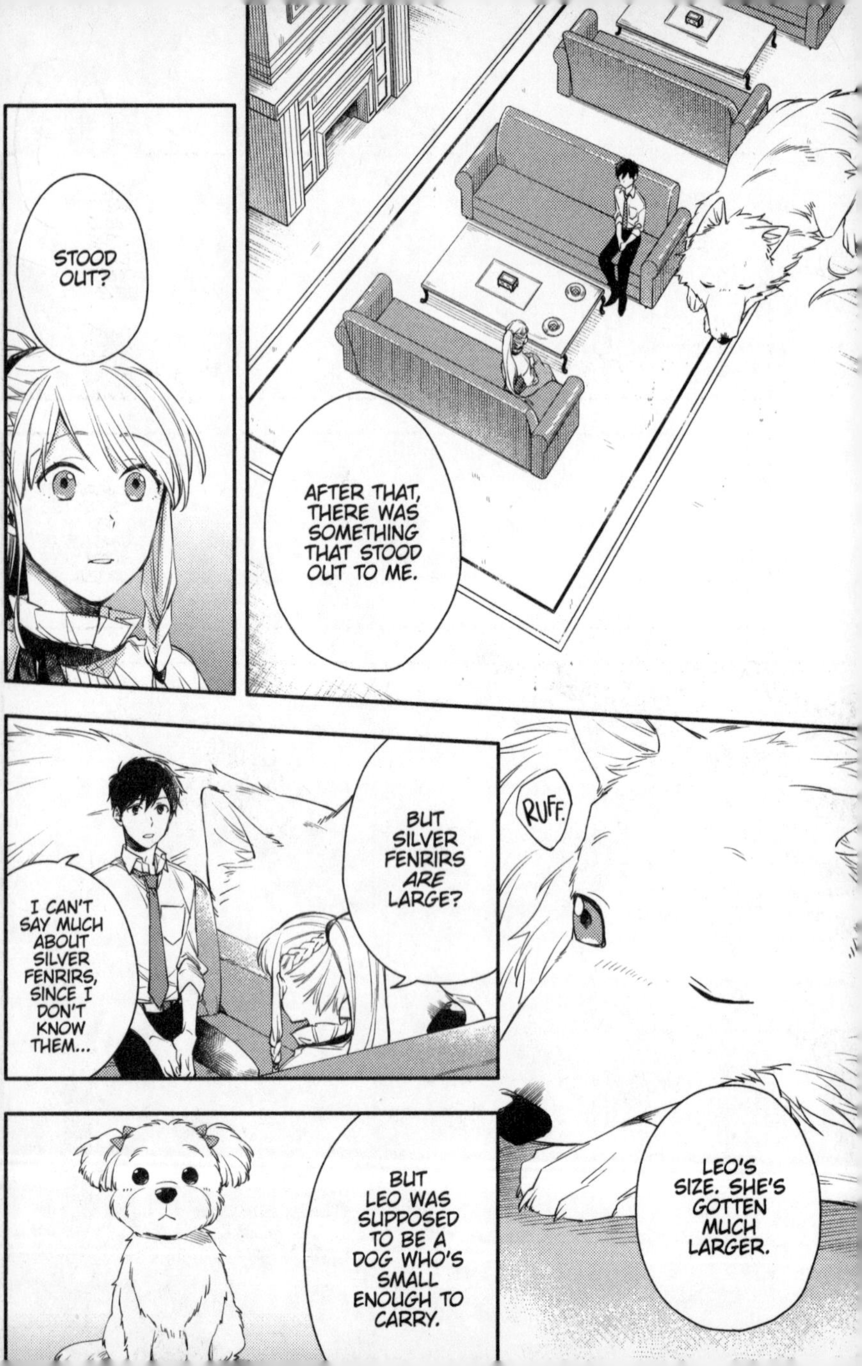
AFTER THAT, THERE WAS SOMETHING THAT STOOD OUT TO ME.
STOOD OUT?
RUFF.
LEO'S SIZE. SHE'S GOTTEN MUCH LARGER.
BUT SILVER FENRIRS *ARE* LARGE?
I CAN'T SAY MUCH ABOUT SILVER FENRIRS, SINCE I DON'T KNOW THEM...
BUT LEO WAS SUPPOSED TO BE A DOG WHO'S SMALL ENOUGH TO CARRY.

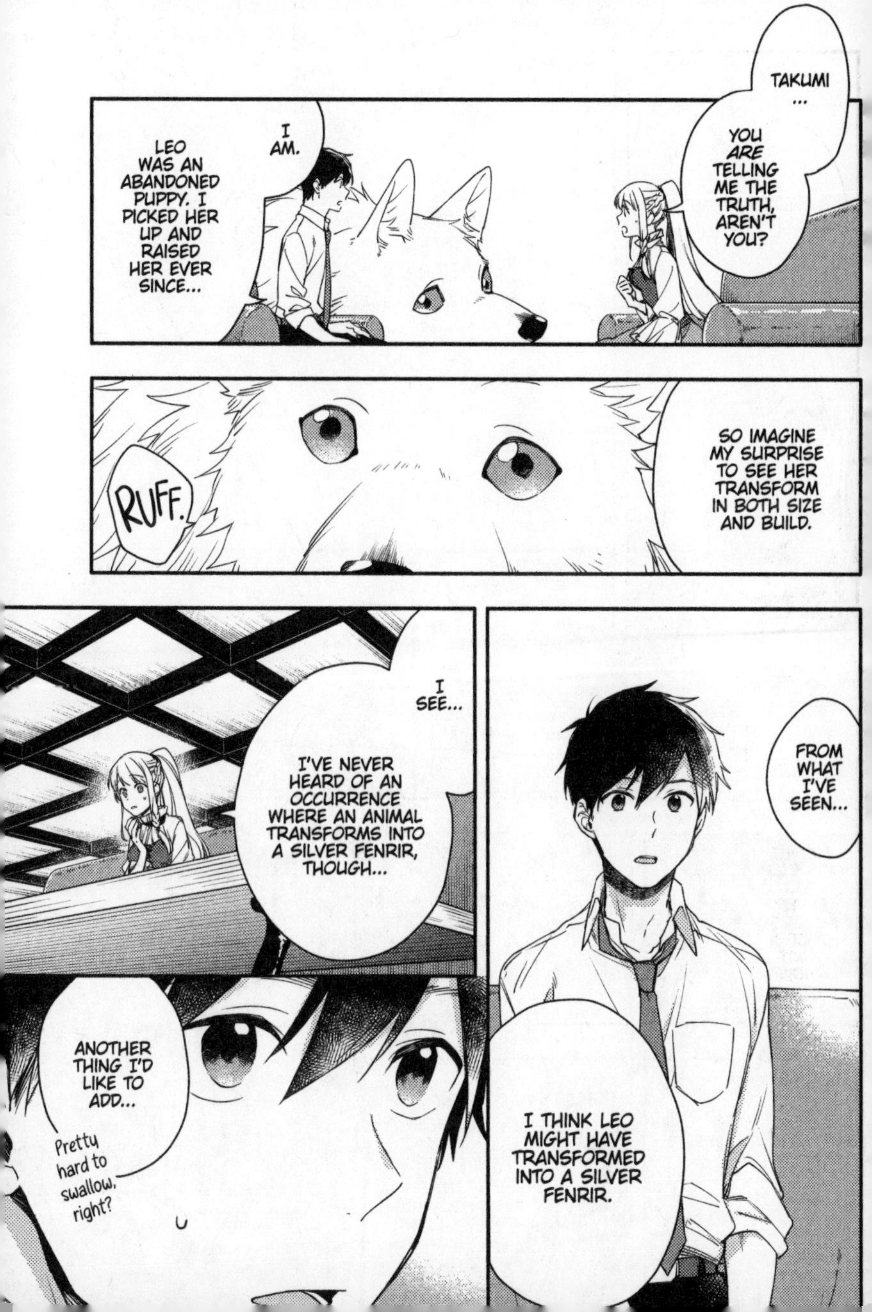
TAKUMI ...
YOU ARE TELLING ME THE TRUTH, AREN'T YOU?
I AM.
LEO WAS AN ABANDONED PUPPY. I PICKED HER UP AND RAISED HER EVER SINCE...
SO IMAGINE MY SURPRISE TO SEE HER TRANSFORM IN BOTH SIZE AND BUILD.
RUFF.
FROM WHAT I'VE SEEN...
I THINK LEO MIGHT HAVE TRANSFORMED INTO A SILVER FENRIR.
I SEE...
I'VE NEVER HEARD OF AN OCCURRENCE WHERE AN ANIMAL TRANSFORMS INTO A SILVER FENRIR, THOUGH...
ANOTHER THING I'D LIKE TO ADD...
Pretty hard to swallow, right?

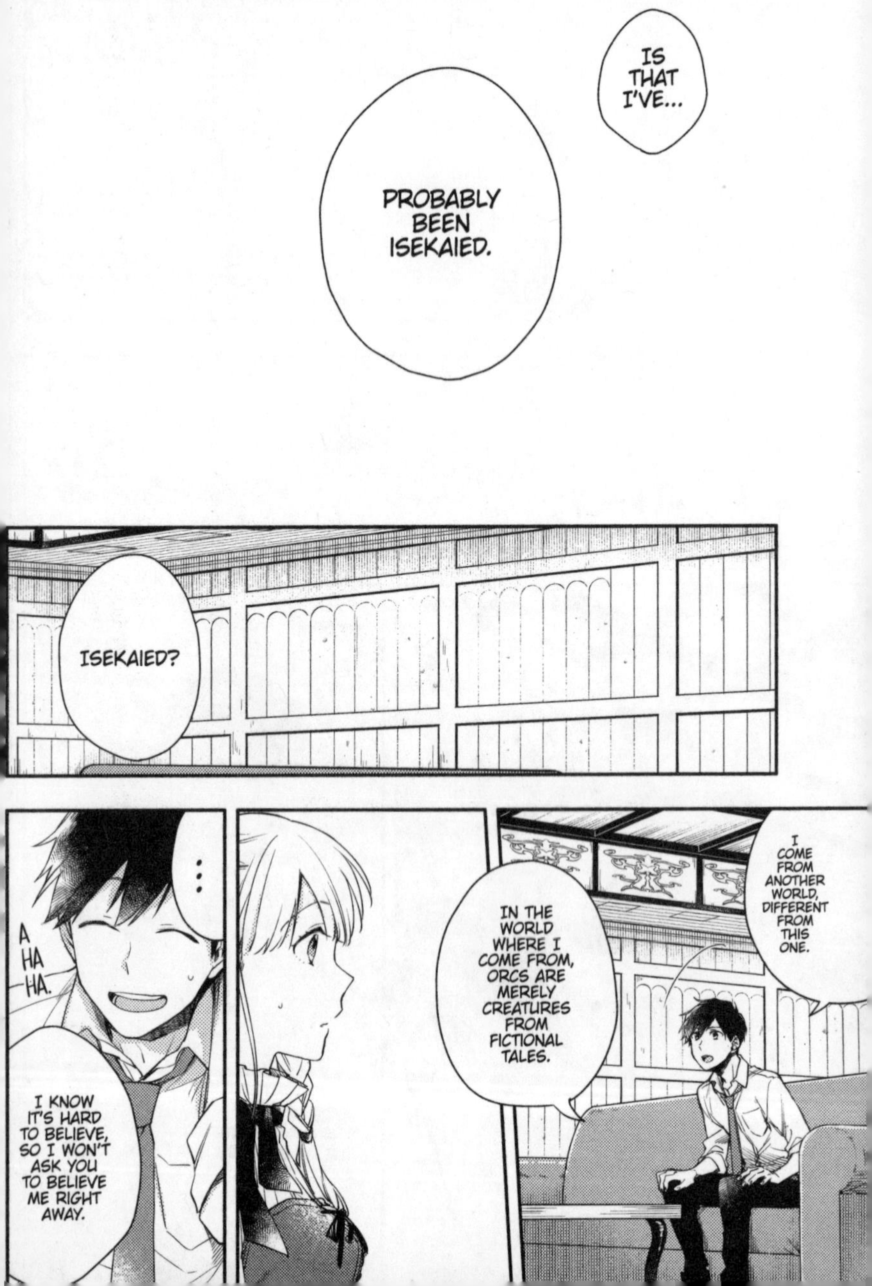
IS THAT I'VE...
PROBABLY BEEN ISEKAIED.
ISEKAIED?
I COME FROM ANOTHER WORLD, DIFFERENT FROM THIS ONE.
IN THE WORLD WHERE I COME FROM, ORCS ARE MERELY CREATURES FROM FICTIONAL TALES.
...
A HA HA.
I KNOW IT'S HARD TO BELIEVE, SO I WON'T ASK YOU TO BELIEVE ME RIGHT AWAY.

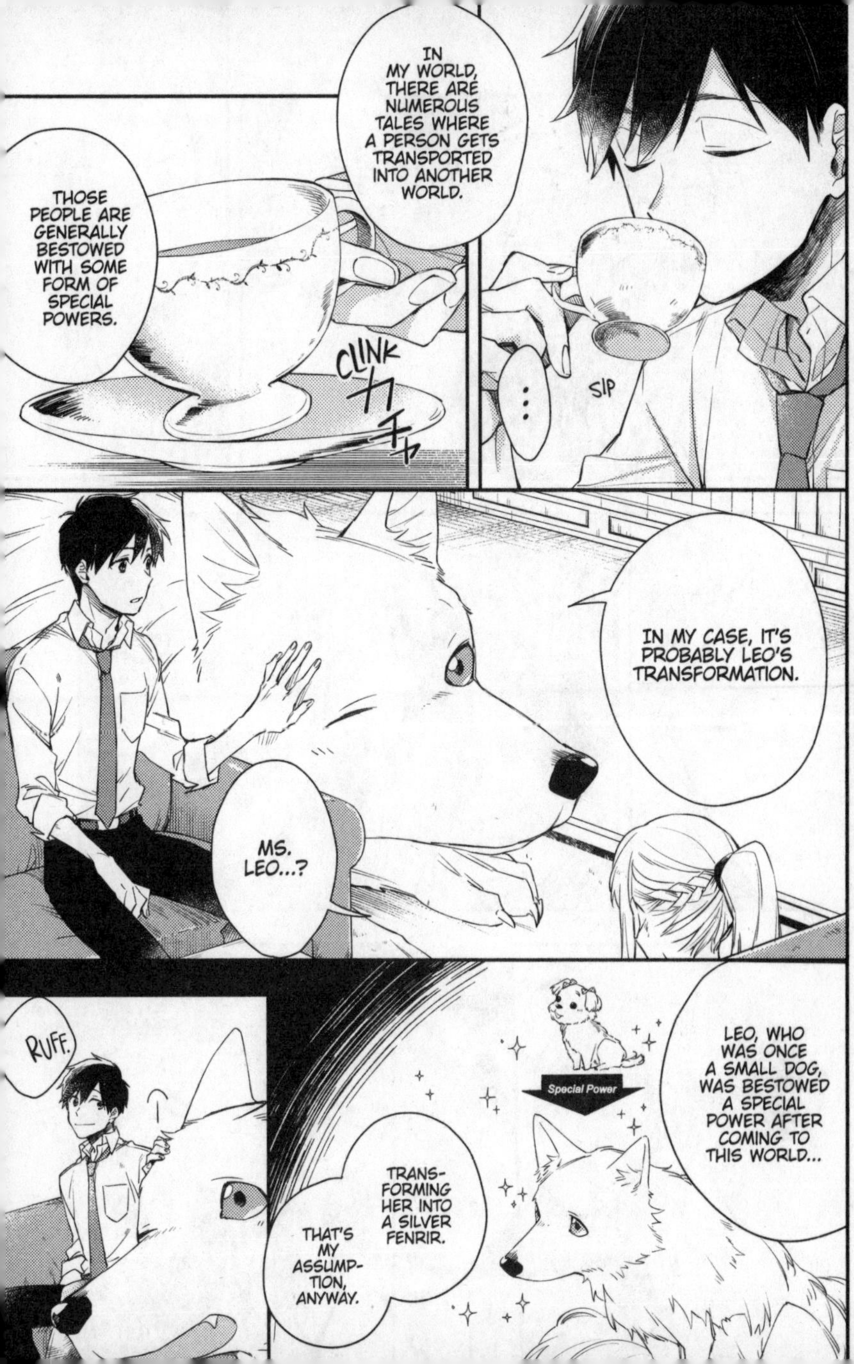
IN MY WORLD, THERE ARE NUMEROUS TALES WHERE A PERSON GETS TRANSPORTED INTO ANOTHER WORLD.
...
SIP
THOSE PEOPLE ARE GENERALLY BESTOWED WITH SOME FORM OF SPECIAL POWERS.
CLINK
カチャ
IN MY CASE, IT'S PROBABLY LEO'S TRANSFORMATION.
MS. LEO...?
LEO, WHO WAS ONCE A SMALL DOG, WAS BESTOWED A SPECIAL POWER AFTER COMING TO THIS WORLD...
Special Power
TRANS-FORMING HER INTO A SILVER FENRIR.
THAT'S MY ASSUMP-TION, ANYWAY.
RUFF.

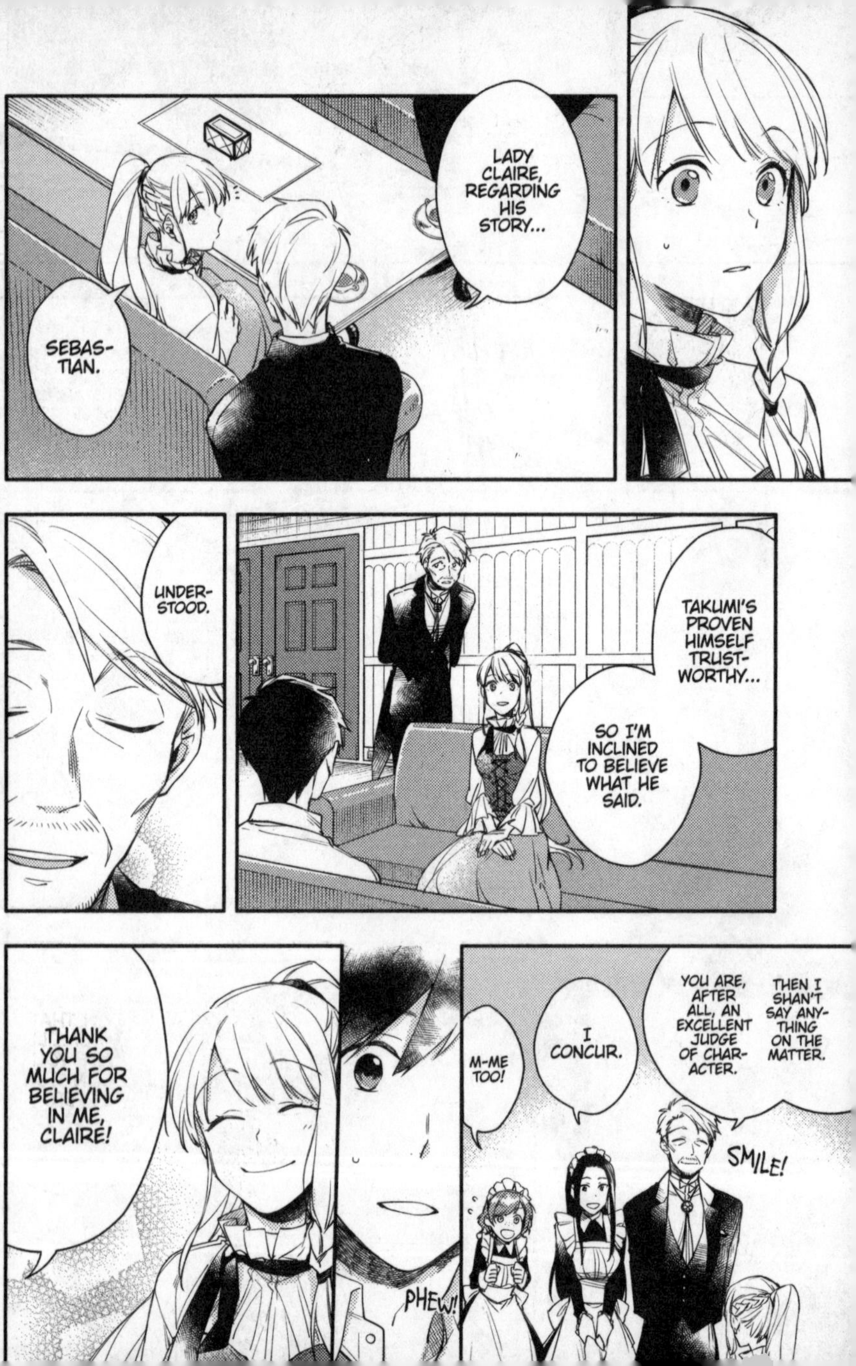
LADY CLAIRE, REGARDING HIS STORY...
SEBAS-TIAN.
TAKUMI'S PROVEN HIMSELF TRUST-WORTHY...
SO I'M INCLINED TO BELIEVE WHAT HE SAID.
UNDER-STOOD.
THEN I SHAN'T SAY ANY-THING ON THE MATTER.
YOU ARE, AFTER ALL, AN EXCELLENT JUDGE OF CHAR-ACTER.
I CONCUR.
M-ME TOO!
SMILE!
THANK YOU SO MUCH FOR BELIEVING IN ME, CLAIRE!
PHEW!

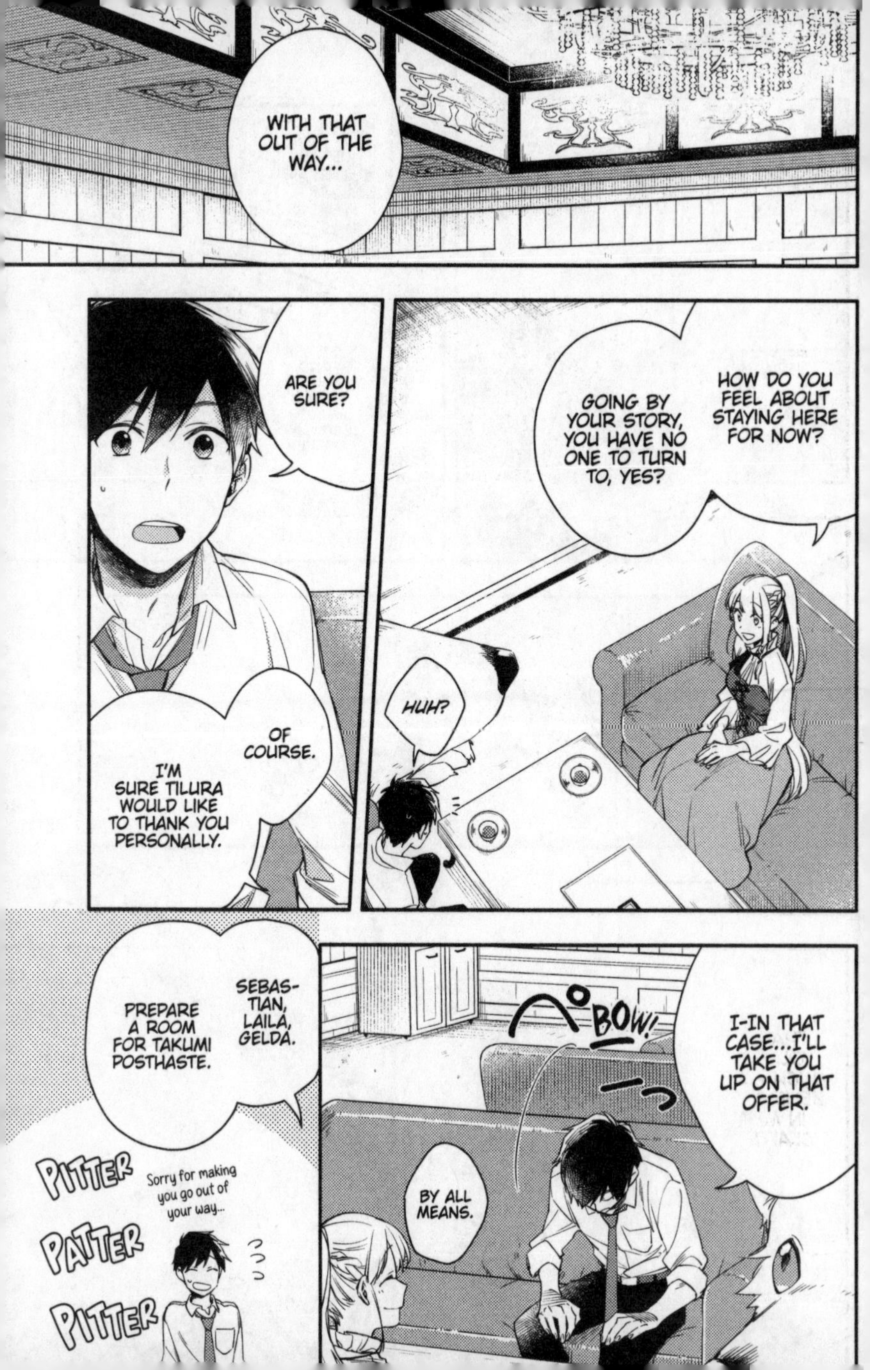
WITH THAT OUT OF THE WAY...
HOW DO YOU FEEL ABOUT STAYING HERE FOR NOW?
GOING BY YOUR STORY, YOU HAVE NO ONE TO TURN TO, YES?
HUH?
ARE YOU SURE?
OF COURSE.
I'M SURE TILURA WOULD LIKE TO THANK YOU PERSONALLY.
I-IN THAT CASE...I'LL TAKE YOU UP ON THAT OFFER.
BOW!
BY ALL MEANS.
SEBAS-TIAN, LAILA, GELDA.
PREPARE A ROOM FOR TAKUMI POSTHASTE.
PITTER
PATTER
PITTER
Sorry for making you go out of your way...

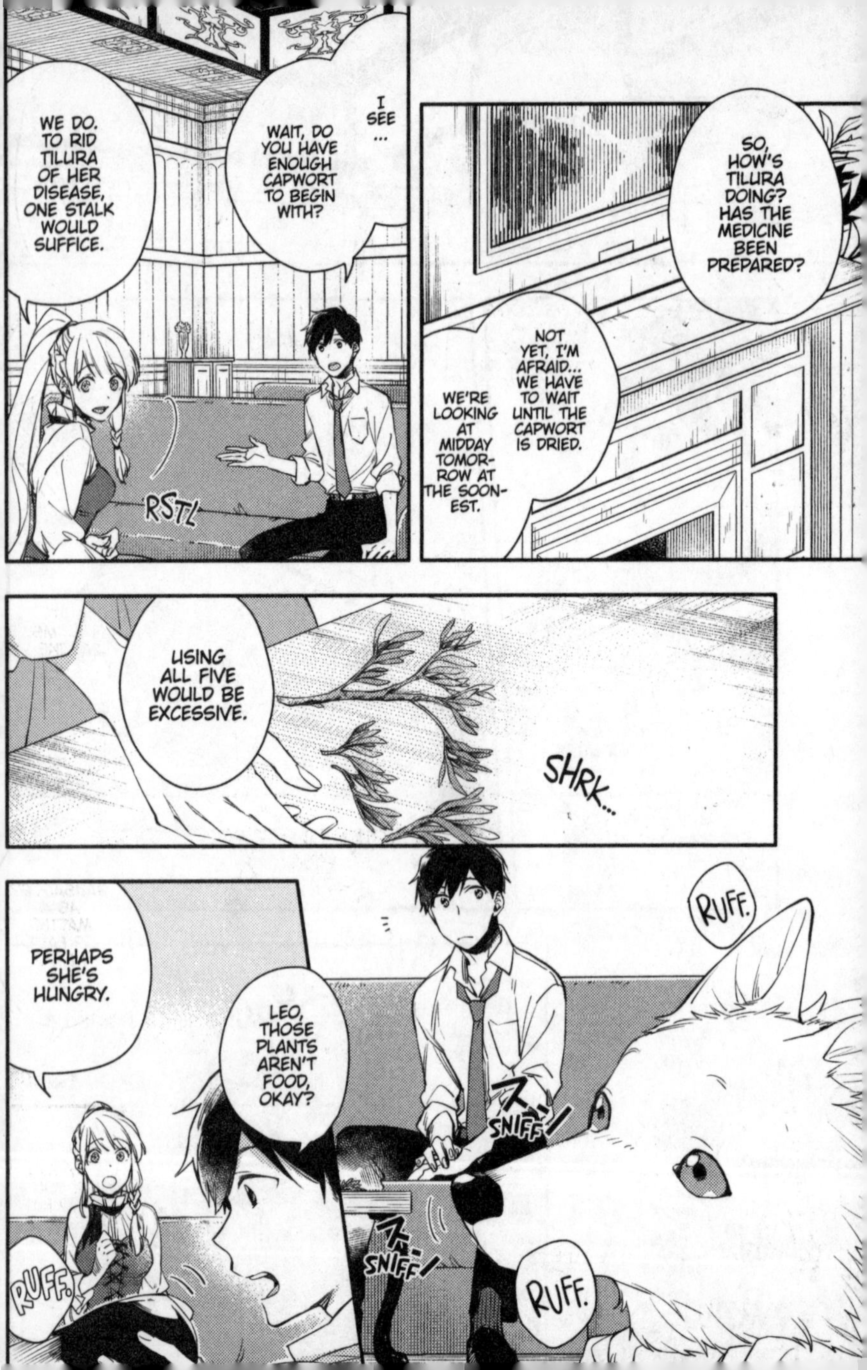
SO, HOW'S TILURA DOING? HAS THE MEDICINE BEEN PREPARED?
NOT YET, I'M AFRAID... WE HAVE TO WAIT UNTIL THE CAPWORT IS DRIED.
WE'RE LOOKING AT MIDDAY TOMORROW AT THE SOONEST.
I SEE ...
WAIT, DO YOU HAVE ENOUGH CAPWORT TO BEGIN WITH?
WE DO. TO RID TILURA OF HER DISEASE, ONE STALK WOULD SUFFICE.
RSTL
USING ALL FIVE WOULD BE EXCESSIVE.
SHRK...
RUFF.
LEO, THOSE PLANTS AREN'T FOOD, OKAY?
SNIFF!
PERHAPS SHE'S HUNGRY.
SNIFF!
RUFF.
RUFF.

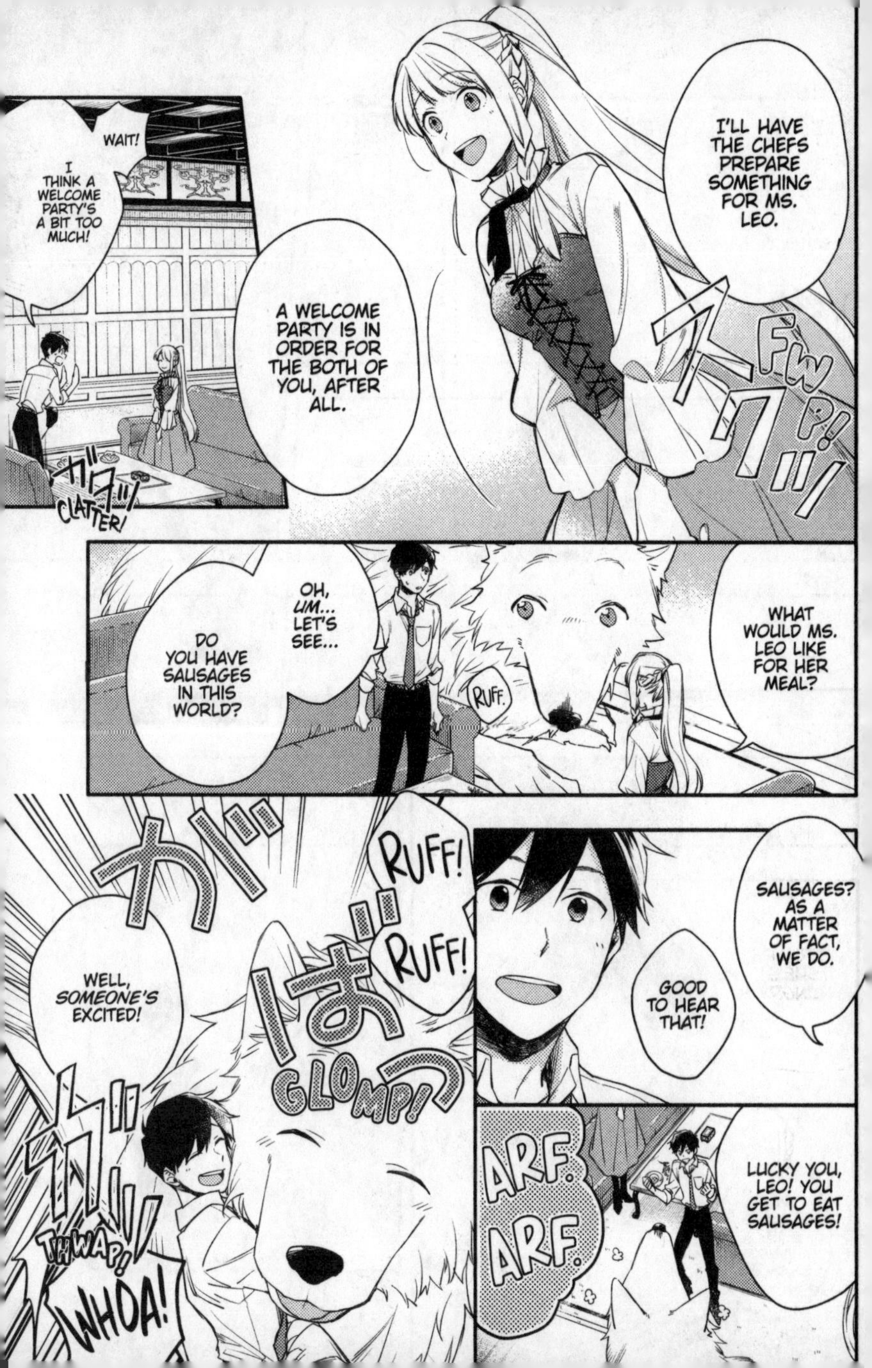
I'LL HAVE THE CHEFS PREPARE SOMETHING FOR MS. LEO.
FWP!
A WELCOME PARTY IS IN ORDER FOR THE BOTH OF YOU, AFTER ALL.
WAIT!
I THINK A WELCOME PARTY'S A BIT TOO MUCH!
CLATTER!
WHAT WOULD MS. LEO LIKE FOR HER MEAL?
OH, UM... LET'S SEE...
DO YOU HAVE SAUSAGES IN THIS WORLD?
RUFF.
SAUSAGES? AS A MATTER OF FACT, WE DO.
GOOD TO HEAR THAT!
LUCKY YOU, LEO! YOU GET TO EAT SAUSAGES!
ARF.
ARF.
RUFF!
RUFF!
GLOMP!
WELL, SOMEONE'S EXCITED!
THWAP!
WHOA!

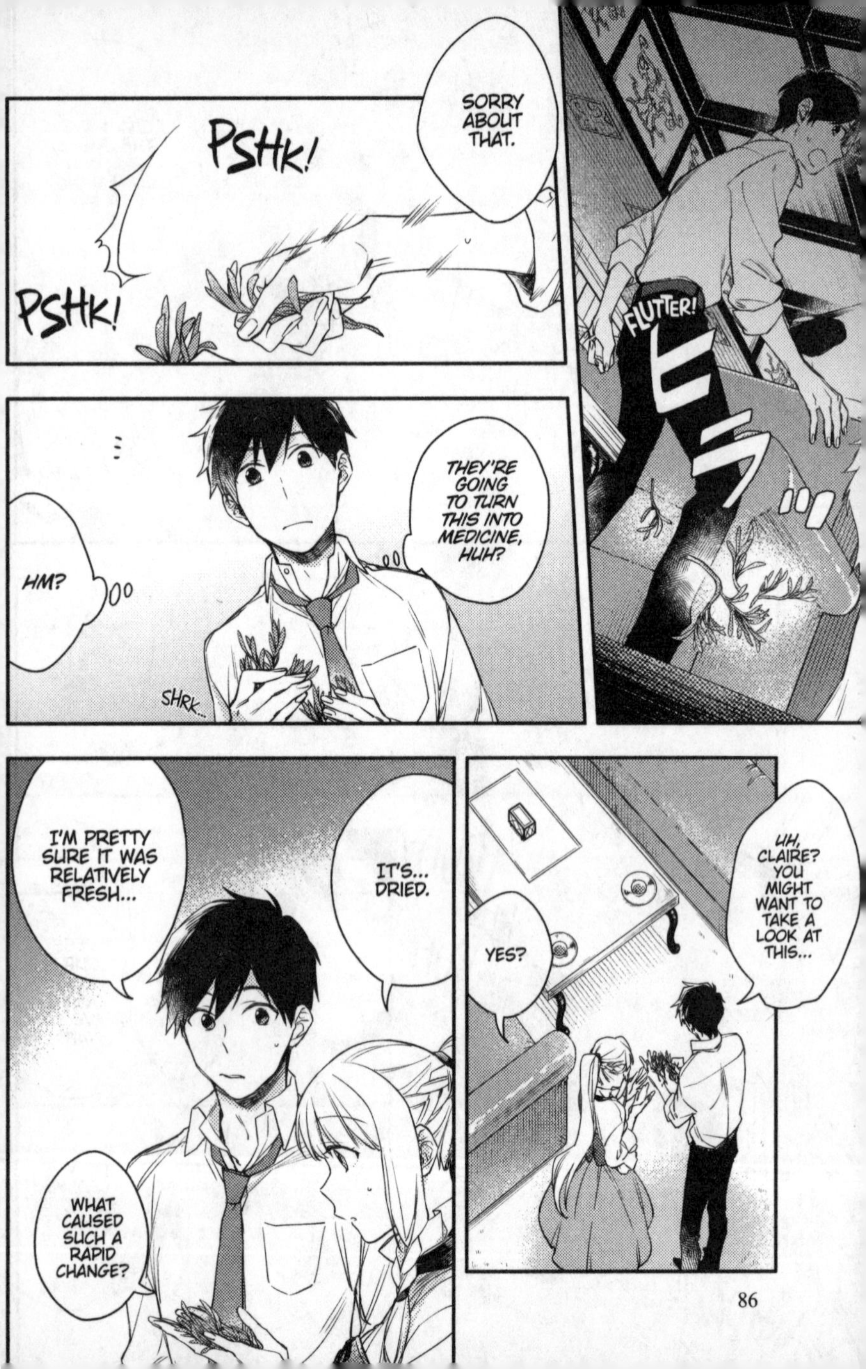
FLUTTER!
ヒラ
SORRY ABOUT THAT.
PSHK!
PSHK!
THEY'RE GOING TO TURN THIS INTO MEDICINE, HUH?
HM?
SHRK...
UH, CLAIRE? YOU MIGHT WANT TO TAKE A LOOK AT THIS...
YES?
IT'S... DRIED.
I'M PRETTY SURE IT WAS RELATIVELY FRESH...
WHAT CAUSED SUCH A RAPID CHANGE?

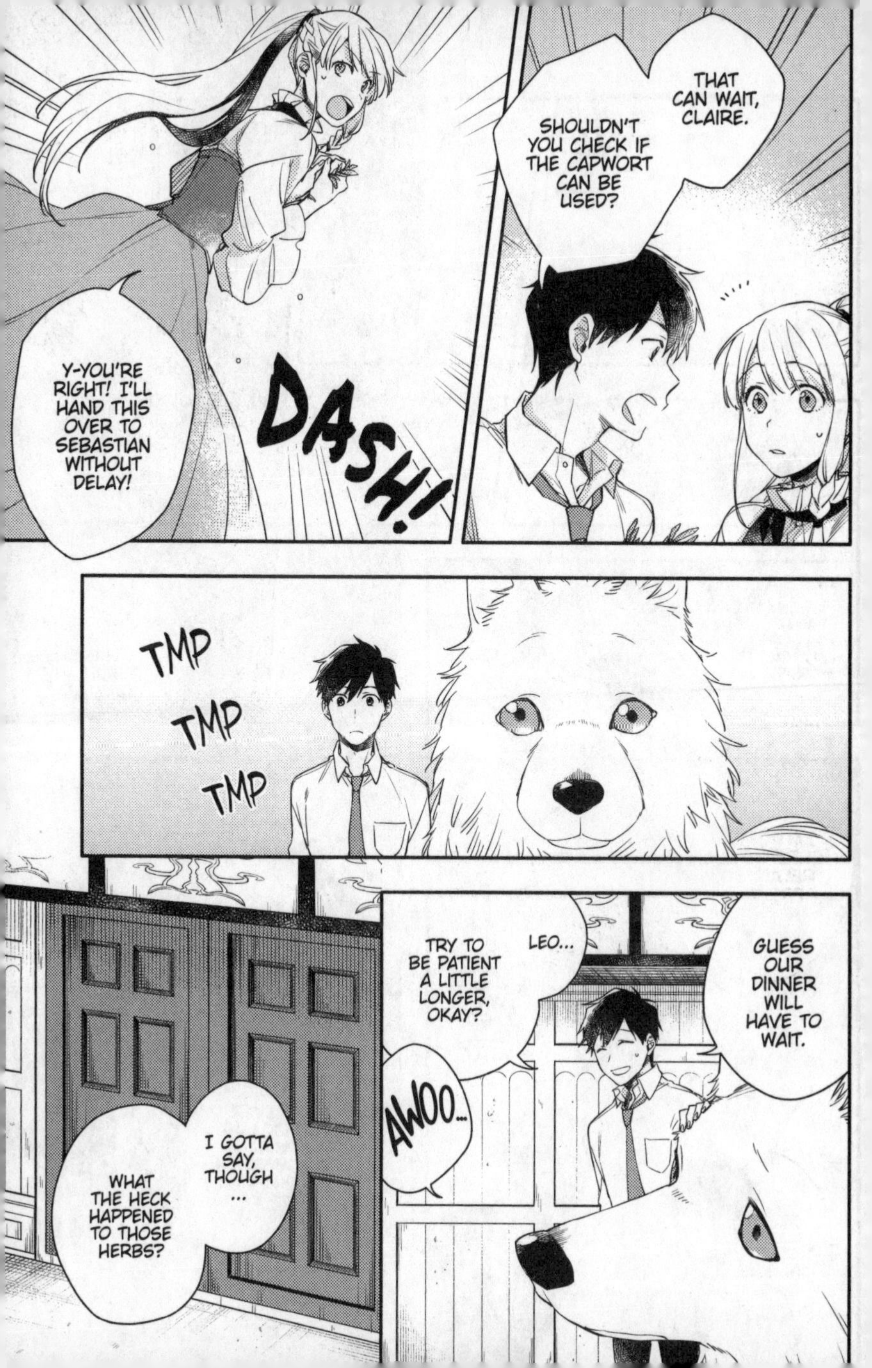
THAT CAN WAIT, CLAIRE.
SHOULDN'T YOU CHECK IF THE CAPWORT CAN BE USED?
...
Y-YOU'RE RIGHT! I'LL HAND THIS OVER TO SEBASTIAN WITHOUT DELAY!
DASH!
TMP
TMP
TMP
GUESS OUR DINNER WILL HAVE TO WAIT.
LEO...
TRY TO BE PATIENT A LITTLE LONGER, OKAY?
AWOO...
I GOTTA SAY, THOUGH ...
WHAT THE HECK HAPPENED TO THOSE HERBS?

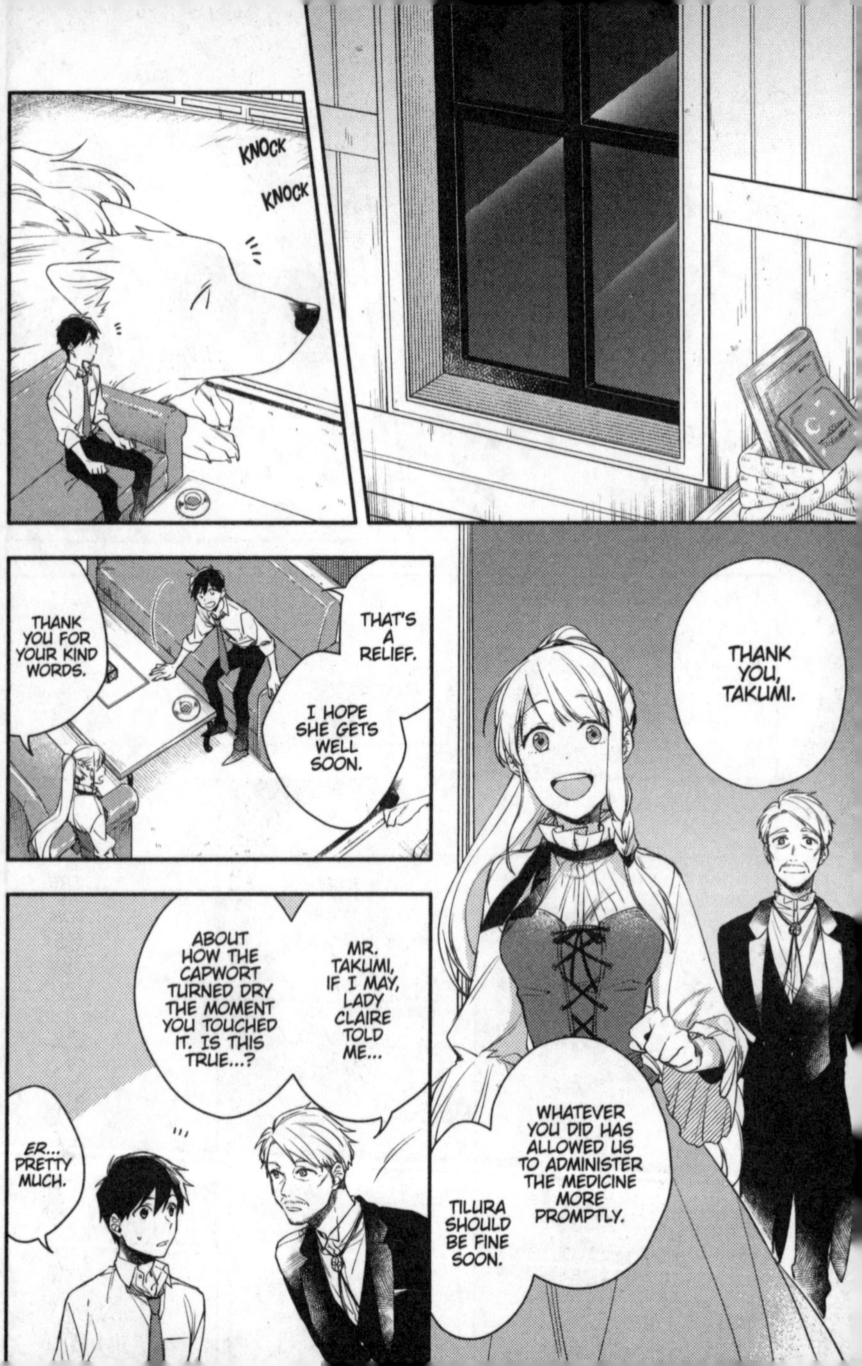
KNOCK
KNOCK
THANK YOU, TAKUMI.
WHATEVER YOU DID HAS ALLOWED US TO ADMINISTER THE MEDICINE MORE PROMPTLY.
TILURA SHOULD BE FINE SOON.
THAT'S A RELIEF.
I HOPE SHE GETS WELL SOON.
THANK YOU FOR YOUR KIND WORDS.
MR. TAKUMI, IF I MAY, LADY CLAIRE TOLD ME...
ABOUT HOW THE CAPWORT TURNED DRY THE MOMENT YOU TOUCHED IT. IS THIS TRUE...?
ER... PRETTY MUCH.

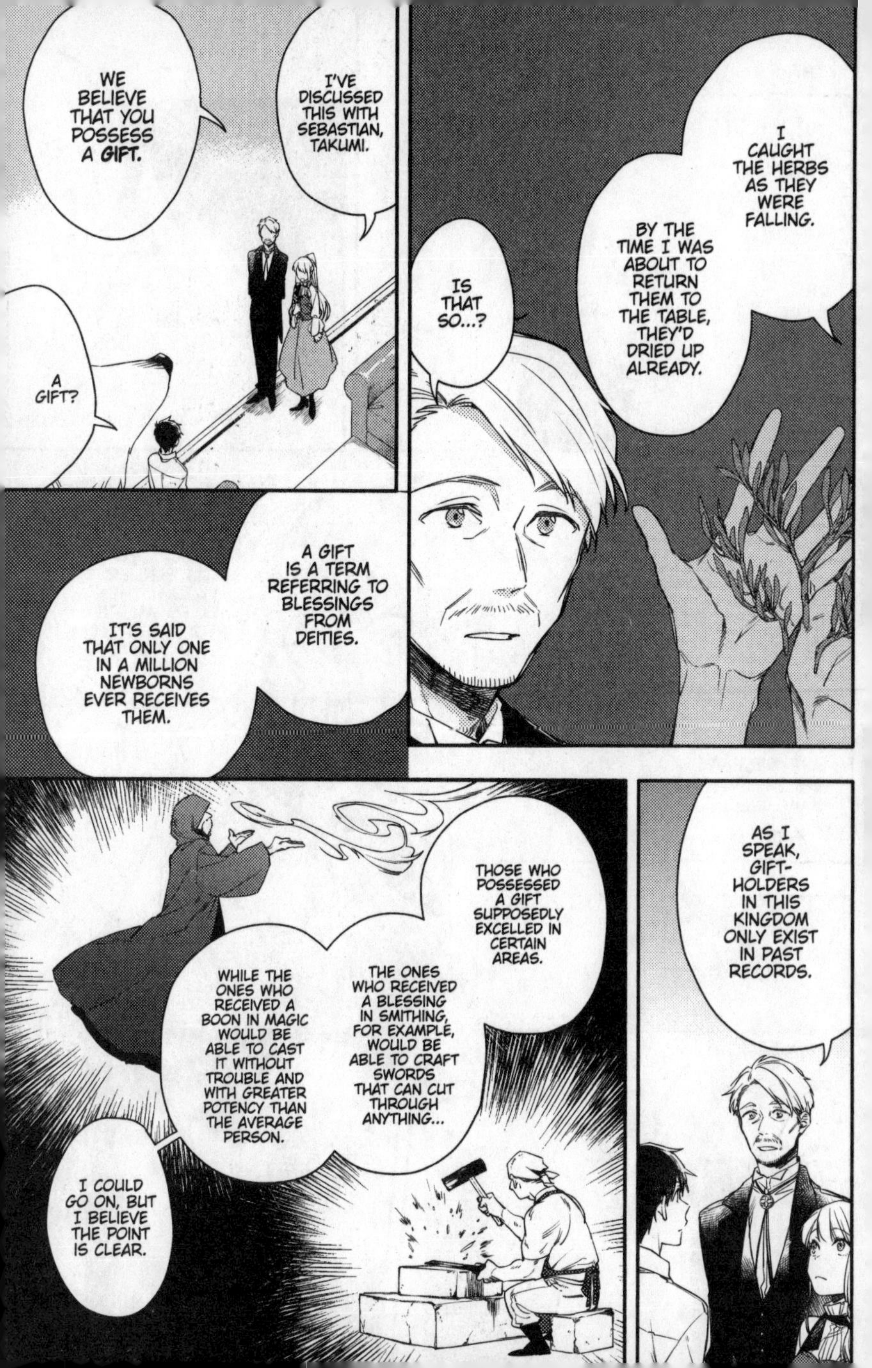
I CAUGHT THE HERBS AS THEY WERE FALLING.
BY THE TIME I WAS ABOUT TO RETURN THEM TO THE TABLE, THEY'D DRIED UP ALREADY.
IS THAT SO...?
I'VE DISCUSSED THIS WITH SEBASTIAN, TAKUMI.
WE BELIEVE THAT YOU POSSESS A **GIFT**.
A GIFT?
A GIFT IS A TERM REFERRING TO BLESSINGS FROM DEITIES.
IT'S SAID THAT ONLY ONE IN A MILLION NEWBORNS EVER RECEIVES THEM.
AS I SPEAK, GIFT-HOLDERS IN THIS KINGDOM ONLY EXIST IN PAST RECORDS.
THOSE WHO POSSESSED A GIFT SUPPOSEDLY EXCELLED IN CERTAIN AREAS.
THE ONES WHO RECEIVED A BLESSING IN SMITHING, FOR EXAMPLE, WOULD BE ABLE TO CRAFT SWORDS THAT CAN CUT THROUGH ANYTHING...
WHILE THE ONES WHO RECEIVED A BOON IN MAGIC WOULD BE ABLE TO CAST IT WITHOUT TROUBLE AND WITH GREATER POTENCY THAN THE AVERAGE PERSON.
I COULD GO ON, BUT I BELIEVE THE POINT IS CLEAR.

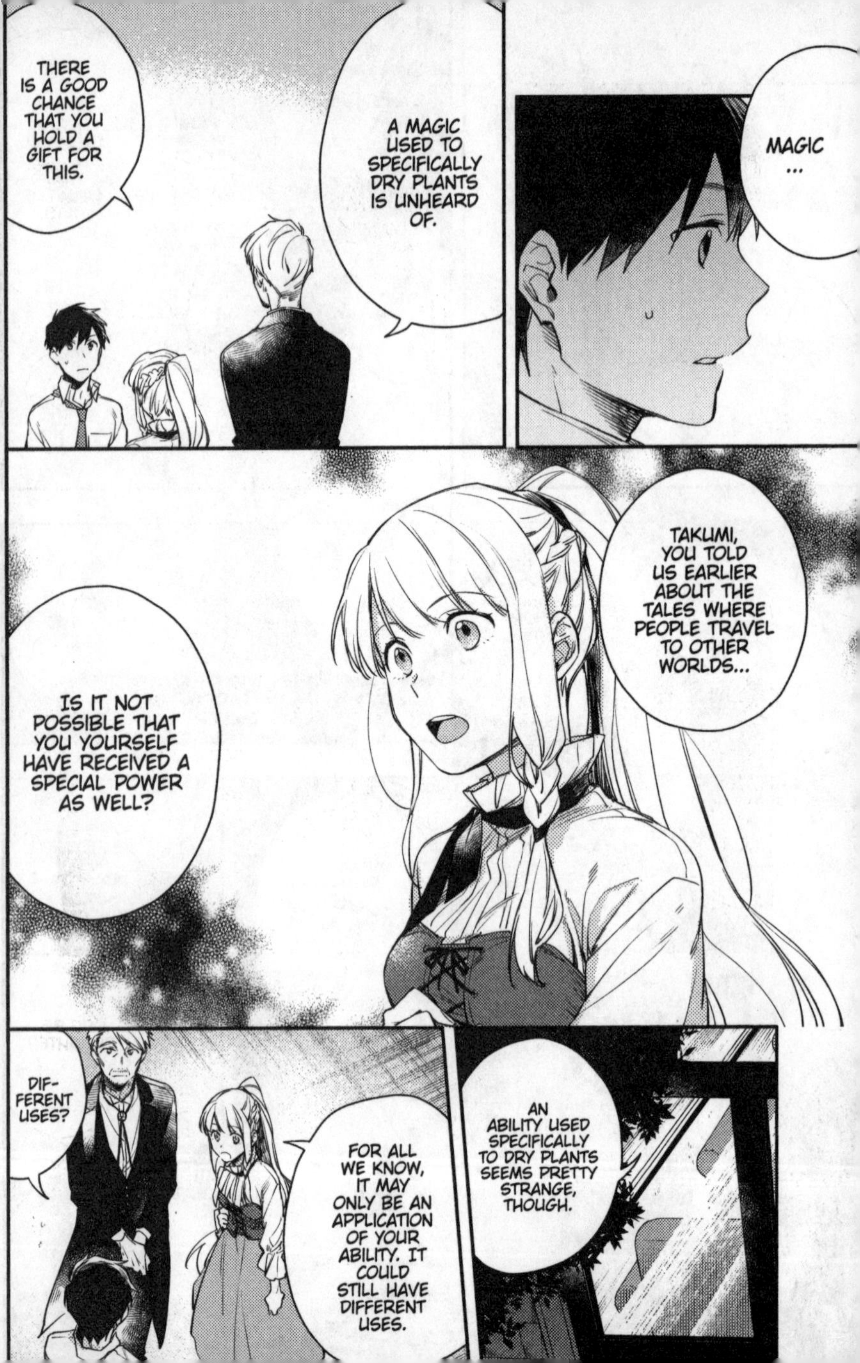
MAGIC ...
A MAGIC USED TO SPECIFICALLY DRY PLANTS IS UNHEARD OF.
THERE IS A GOOD CHANCE THAT YOU HOLD A GIFT FOR THIS.
TAKUMI, YOU TOLD US EARLIER ABOUT THE TALES WHERE PEOPLE TRAVEL TO OTHER WORLDS...
IS IT NOT POSSIBLE THAT YOU YOURSELF HAVE RECEIVED A SPECIAL POWER AS WELL?
AN ABILITY USED SPECIFICALLY TO DRY PLANTS SEEMS PRETTY STRANGE, THOUGH.
FOR ALL WE KNOW, IT MAY ONLY BE AN APPLICATION OF YOUR ABILITY. IT COULD STILL HAVE DIFFERENT USES.
DIF-FERENT USES?

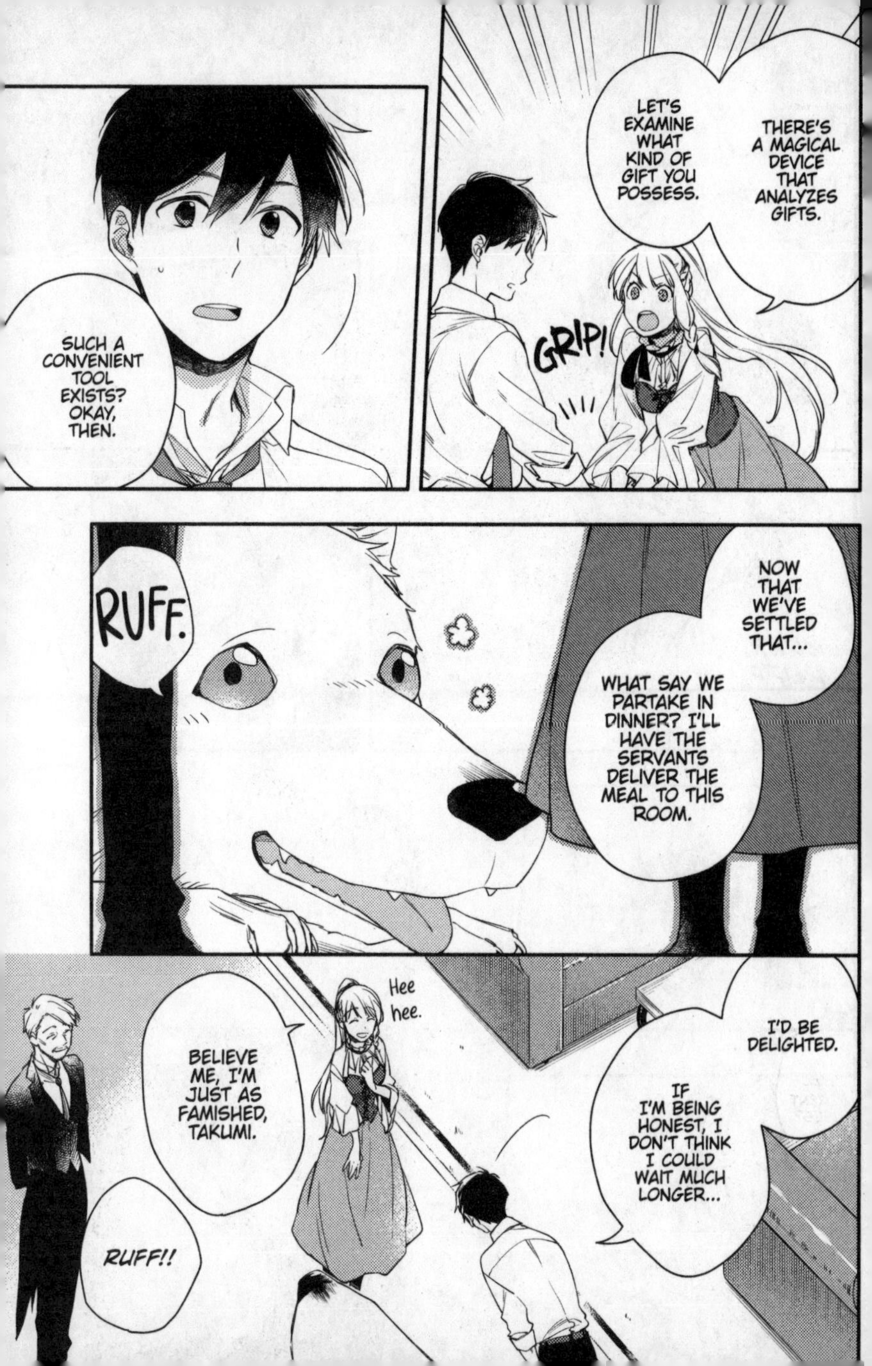
THERE'S A MAGICAL DEVICE THAT ANALYZES GIFTS.
LET'S EXAMINE WHAT KIND OF GIFT YOU POSSESS.
GRIP!
SUCH A CONVENIENT TOOL EXISTS? OKAY, THEN.
NOW THAT WE'VE SETTLED THAT...
WHAT SAY WE PARTAKE IN DINNER? I'LL HAVE THE SERVANTS DELIVER THE MEAL TO THIS ROOM.
RUFF.
I'D BE DELIGHTED.
IF I'M BEING HONEST, I DON'T THINK I COULD WAIT MUCH LONGER...
Hee hee.
BELIEVE ME, I'M JUST AS FAMISHED, TAKUMI.
RUFF!!

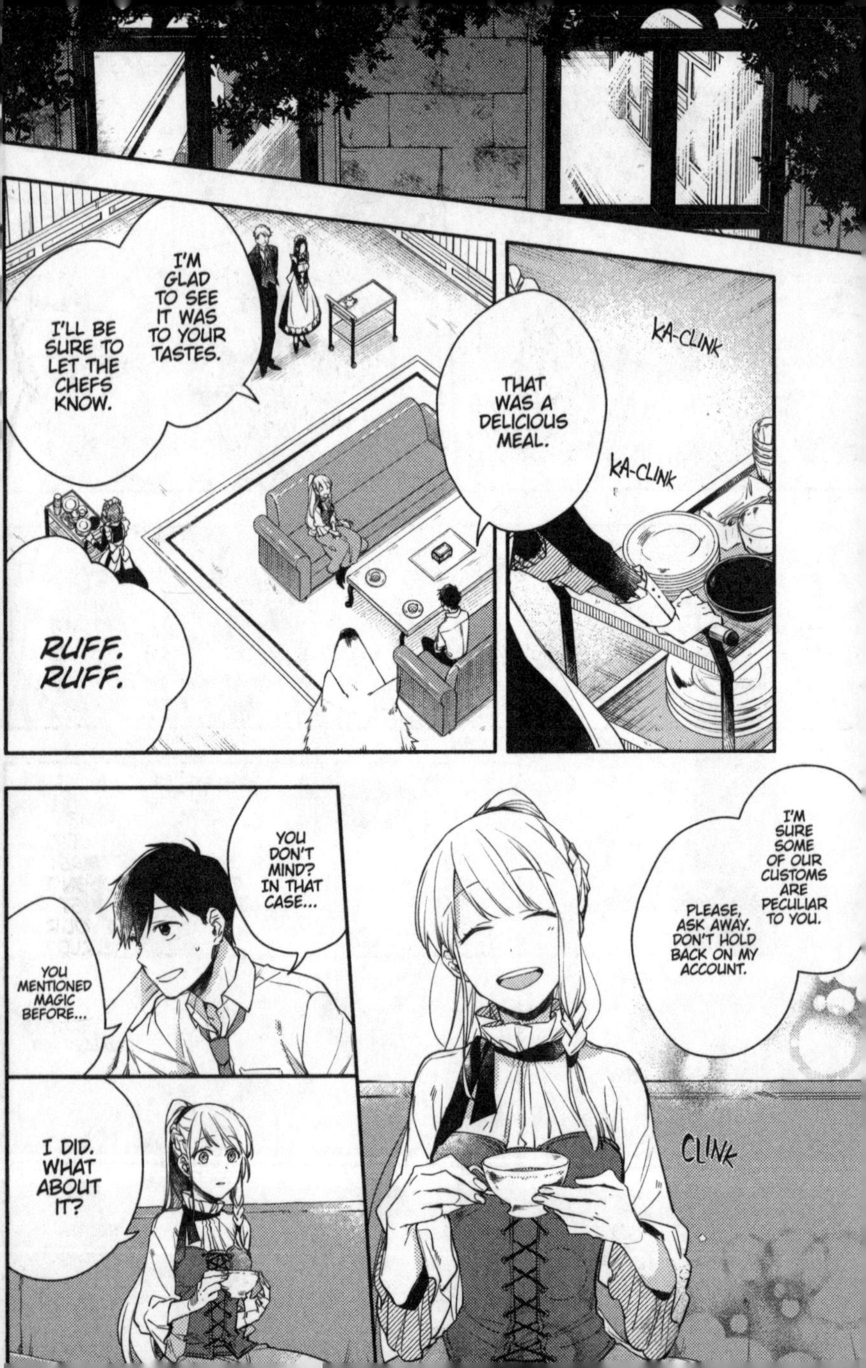
KA-CLINK
THAT WAS A DELICIOUS MEAL.
KA-CLINK
I'M GLAD TO SEE IT WAS TO YOUR TASTES.
I'LL BE SURE TO LET THE CHEFS KNOW.
RUFF. RUFF.
I'M SURE SOME OF OUR CUSTOMS ARE PECULIAR TO YOU.
PLEASE, ASK AWAY. DON'T HOLD BACK ON MY ACCOUNT.
CLINK
YOU DON'T MIND? IN THAT CASE...
YOU MENTIONED MAGIC BEFORE...
I DID. WHAT ABOUT IT?

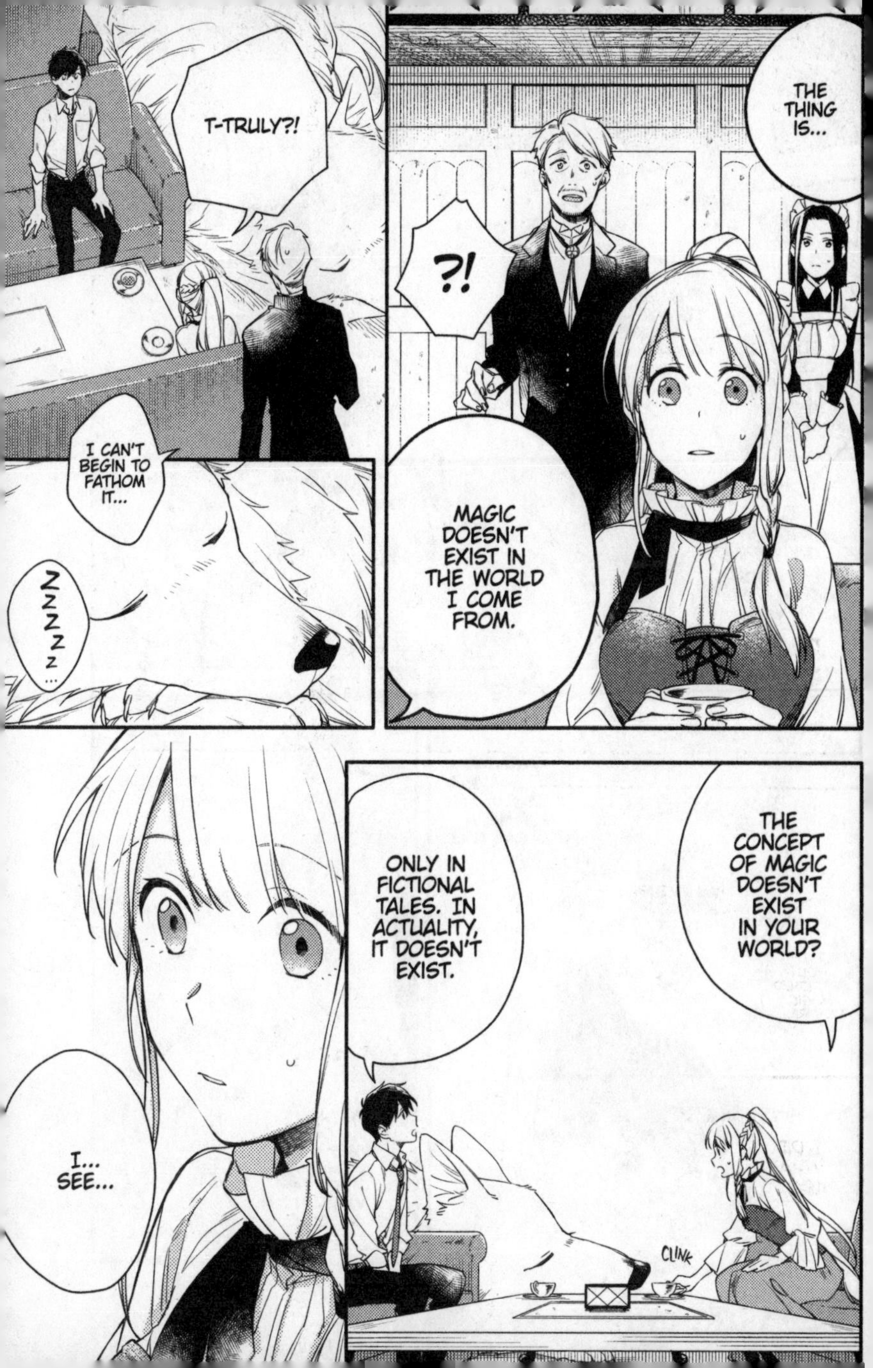
THE THING IS...
?!
MAGIC DOESN'T EXIST IN THE WORLD I COME FROM.
T-TRULY?!
I CAN'T BEGIN TO FATHOM IT...
ZZZZZ...
THE CONCEPT OF MAGIC DOESN'T EXIST IN YOUR WORLD?
ONLY IN FICTIONAL TALES. IN ACTUALITY, IT DOESN'T EXIST.
CLINK
I... SEE...

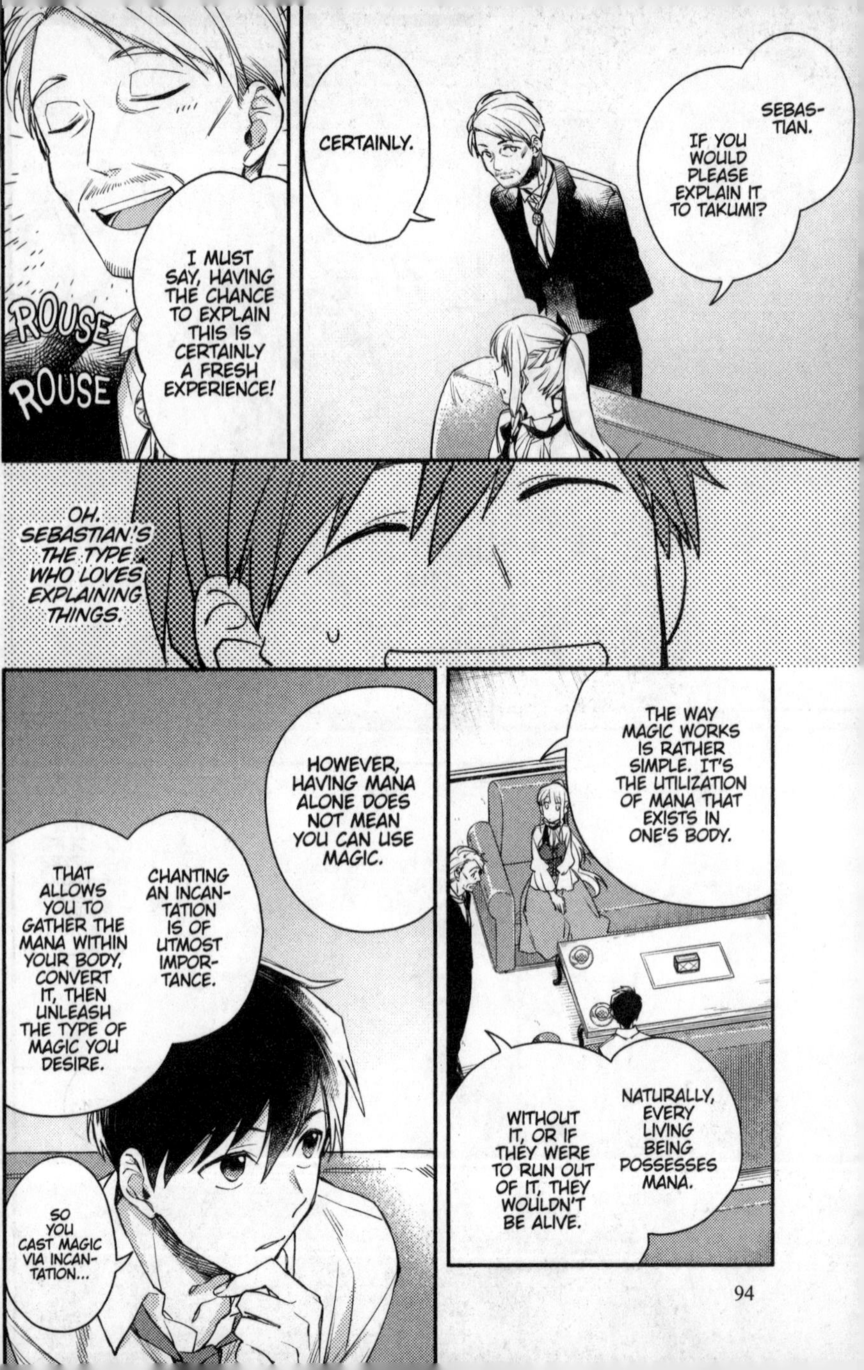
SEBASTIAN.
IF YOU WOULD PLEASE EXPLAIN IT TO TAKUMI?
CERTAINLY.
I MUST SAY, HAVING THE CHANCE TO EXPLAIN THIS IS CERTAINLY A FRESH EXPERIENCE!
ROUSE
ROUSE
OH. SEBASTIAN'S THE TYPE WHO LOVES EXPLAINING THINGS.
THE WAY MAGIC WORKS IS RATHER SIMPLE. IT'S THE UTILIZATION OF MANA THAT EXISTS IN ONE'S BODY.
NATURALLY, EVERY LIVING BEING POSSESSES MANA.
WITHOUT IT, OR IF THEY WERE TO RUN OUT OF IT, THEY WOULDN'T BE ALIVE.
HOWEVER, HAVING MANA ALONE DOES NOT MEAN YOU CAN USE MAGIC.
CHANTING AN INCANTATION IS OF UTMOST IMPORTANCE.
THAT ALLOWS YOU TO GATHER THE MANA WITHIN YOUR BODY, CONVERT IT, THEN UNLEASH THE TYPE OF MAGIC YOU DESIRE.
SO YOU CAST MAGIC VIA INCANTATION...

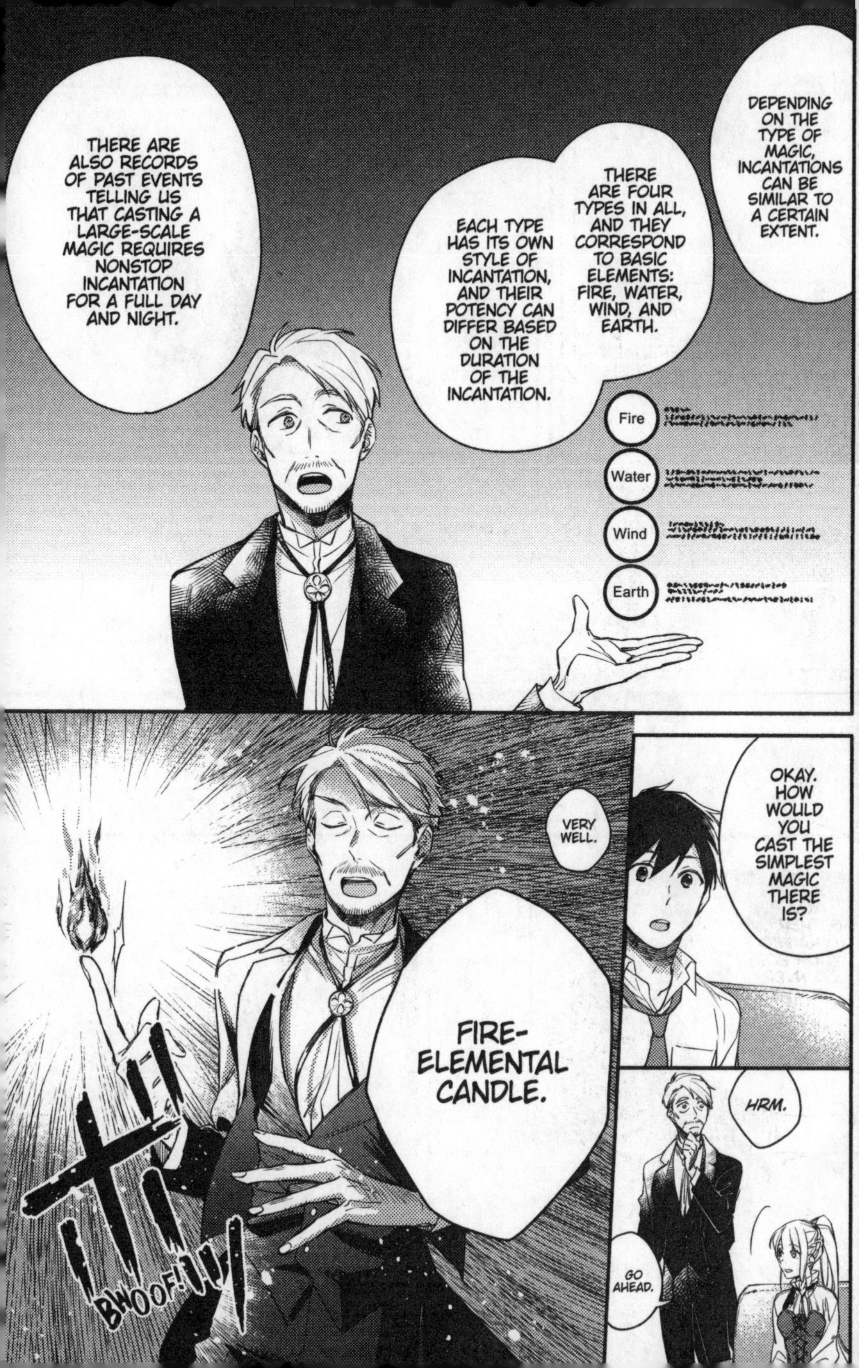
DEPENDING ON THE TYPE OF MAGIC, INCANTATIONS CAN BE SIMILAR TO A CERTAIN EXTENT.
THERE ARE FOUR TYPES IN ALL, AND THEY CORRESPOND TO BASIC ELEMENTS: FIRE, WATER, WIND, AND EARTH.
EACH TYPE HAS ITS OWN STYLE OF INCANTATION, AND THEIR POTENCY CAN DIFFER BASED ON THE DURATION OF THE INCANTATION.
THERE ARE ALSO RECORDS OF PAST EVENTS TELLING US THAT CASTING A LARGE-SCALE MAGIC REQUIRES NONSTOP INCANTATION FOR A FULL DAY AND NIGHT.
Fire
Water
Wind
Earth
OKAY. HOW WOULD YOU CAST THE SIMPLEST MAGIC THERE IS?
HRM.
GO AHEAD.
VERY WELL.
FIRE-ELEMENTAL CANDLE.
BWOOF!

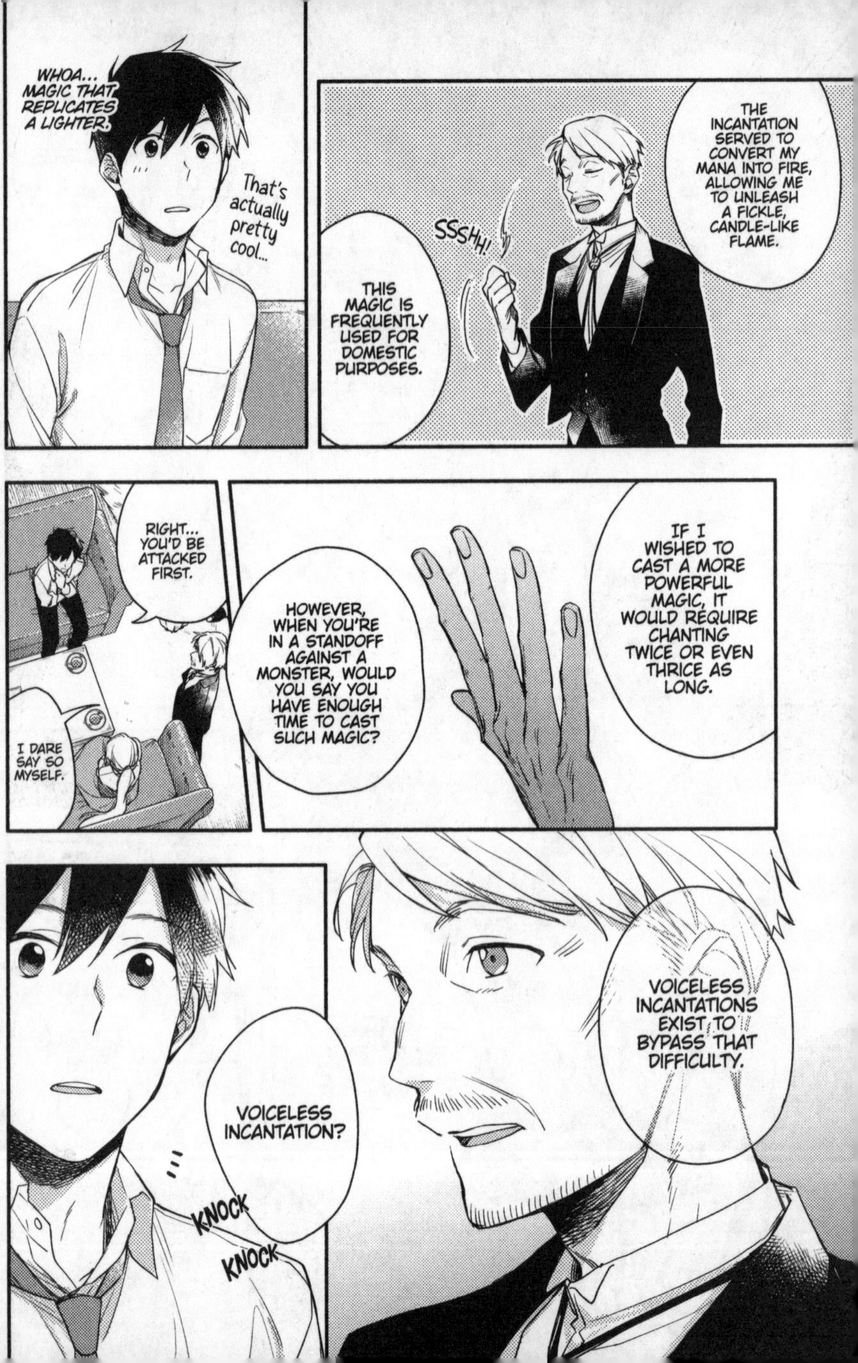
THE INCANTATION SERVED TO CONVERT MY MANA INTO FIRE, ALLOWING ME TO UNLEASH A FICKLE, CANDLE-LIKE FLAME.
SSSHH!
THIS MAGIC IS FREQUENTLY USED FOR DOMESTIC PURPOSES.
WHOA... MAGIC THAT REPLICATES A LIGHTER.
That's actually pretty cool...
IF I WISHED TO CAST A MORE POWERFUL MAGIC, IT WOULD REQUIRE CHANTING TWICE OR EVEN THRICE AS LONG.
HOWEVER, WHEN YOU'RE IN A STANDOFF AGAINST A MONSTER, WOULD YOU SAY YOU HAVE ENOUGH TIME TO CAST SUCH MAGIC?
RIGHT... YOU'D BE ATTACKED FIRST.
I DARE SAY SO MYSELF.
VOICELESS INCANTATIONS EXIST TO BYPASS THAT DIFFICULTY.
VOICELESS INCANTATION?
KNOCK
KNOCK

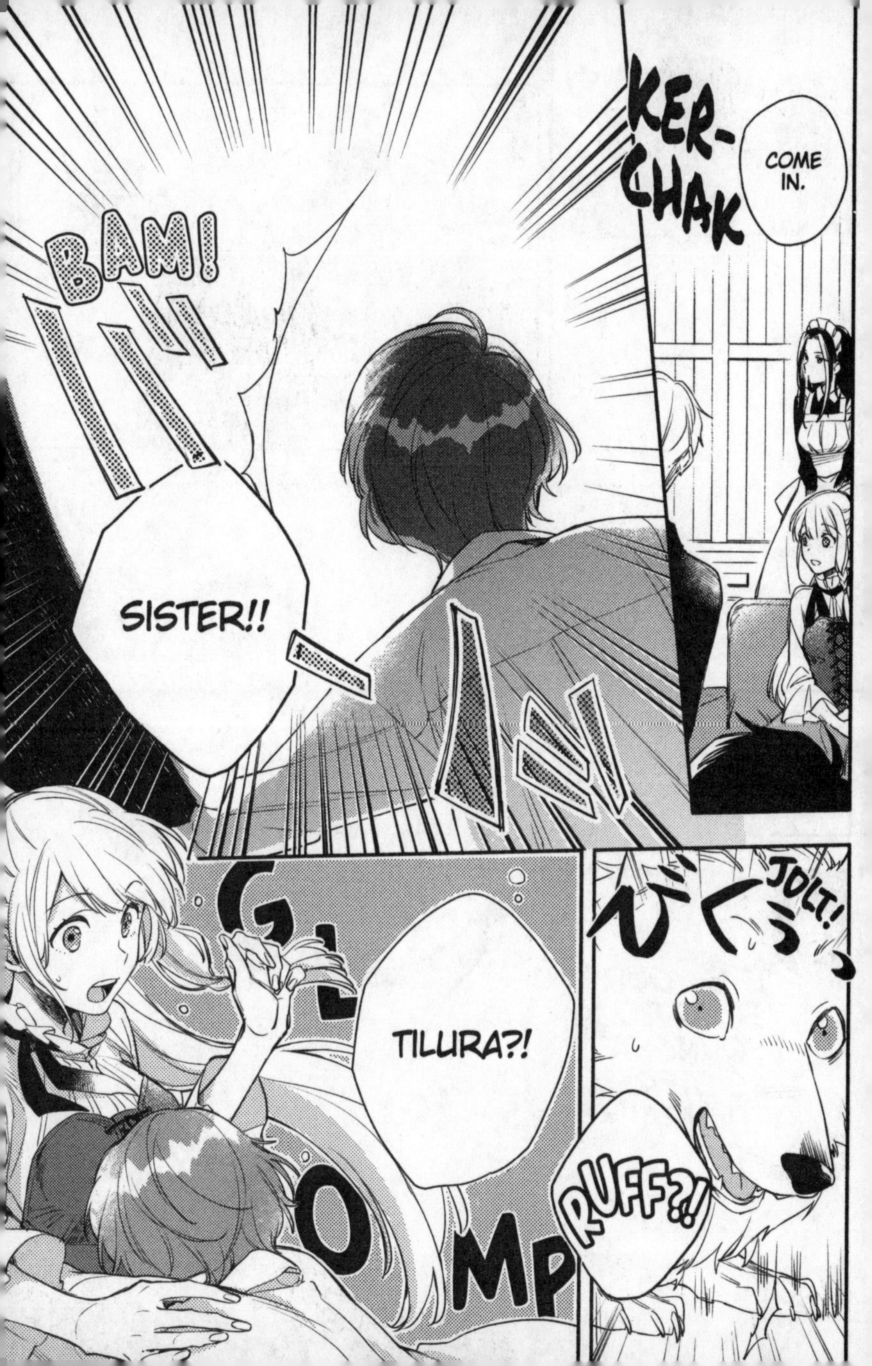
KER-CHAK
COME IN.
BAM!
SISTER!!
びくぅ
JOLT!
RUFF?!
GLOMP
TILURA?!

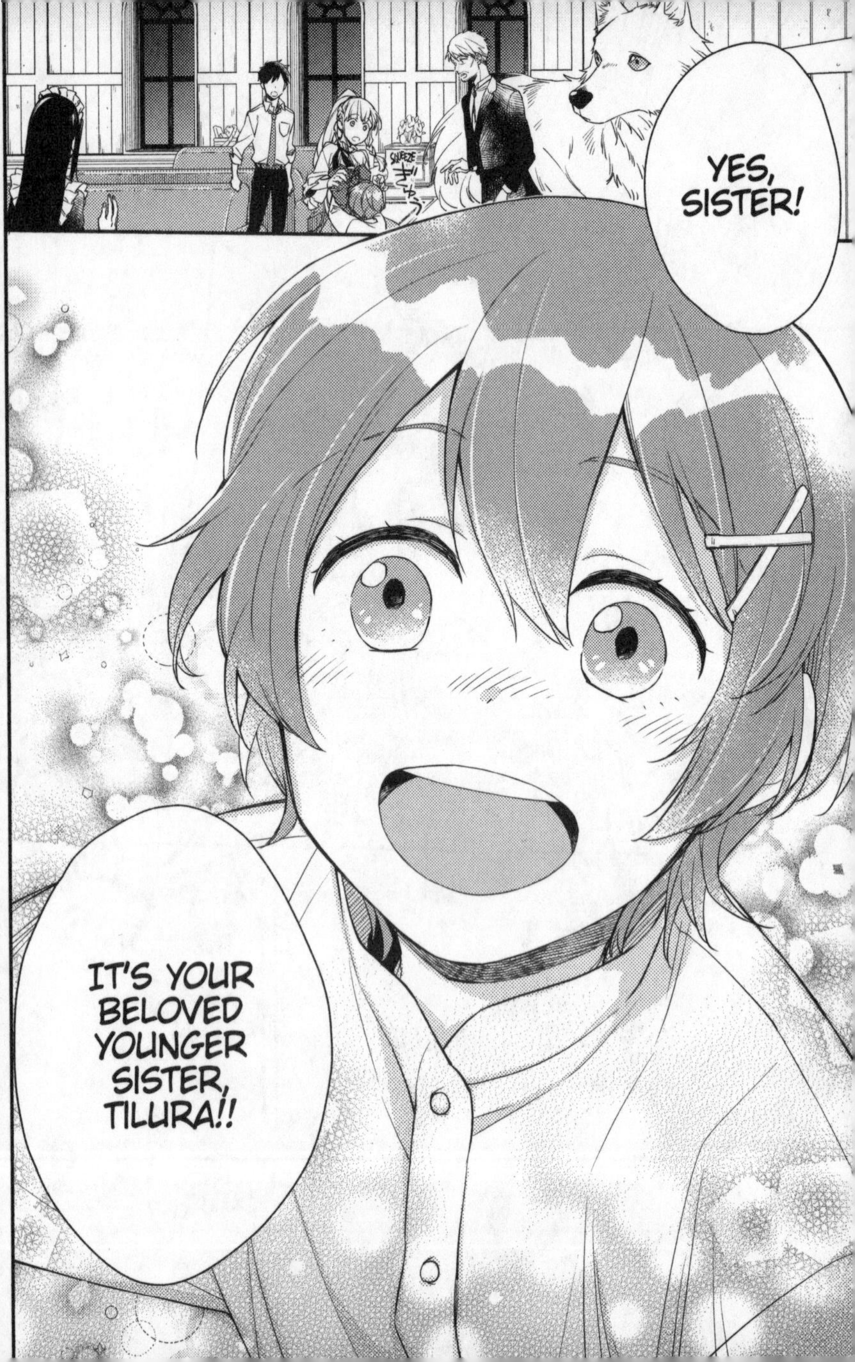
SQUEEZE
YES, SISTER!
IT'S YOUR BELOVED YOUNGER SISTER, TILURA!!

EVEN DOGS GO TO OTHER WORLDS

LIFE IN ANOTHER WORLD WITH MY BELOVED HOUND

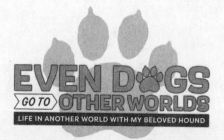

EVEN DOGS GO TO OTHER WORLDS

LIFE IN ANOTHER WORLD WITH MY BELOVED HOUND

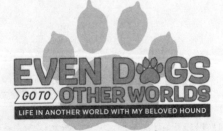

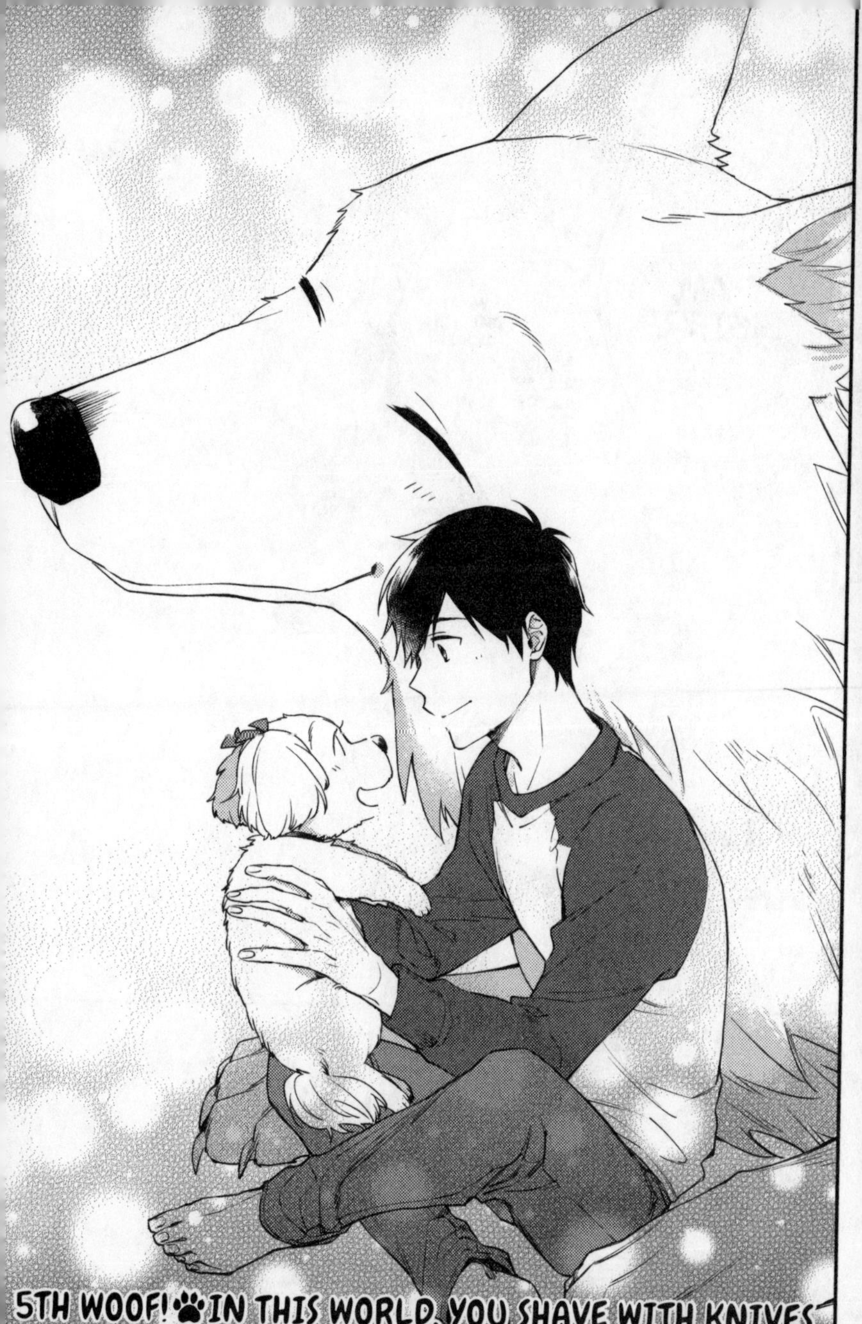

5TH WOOF! IN THIS WORLD, YOU SHAVE WITH KNIVES

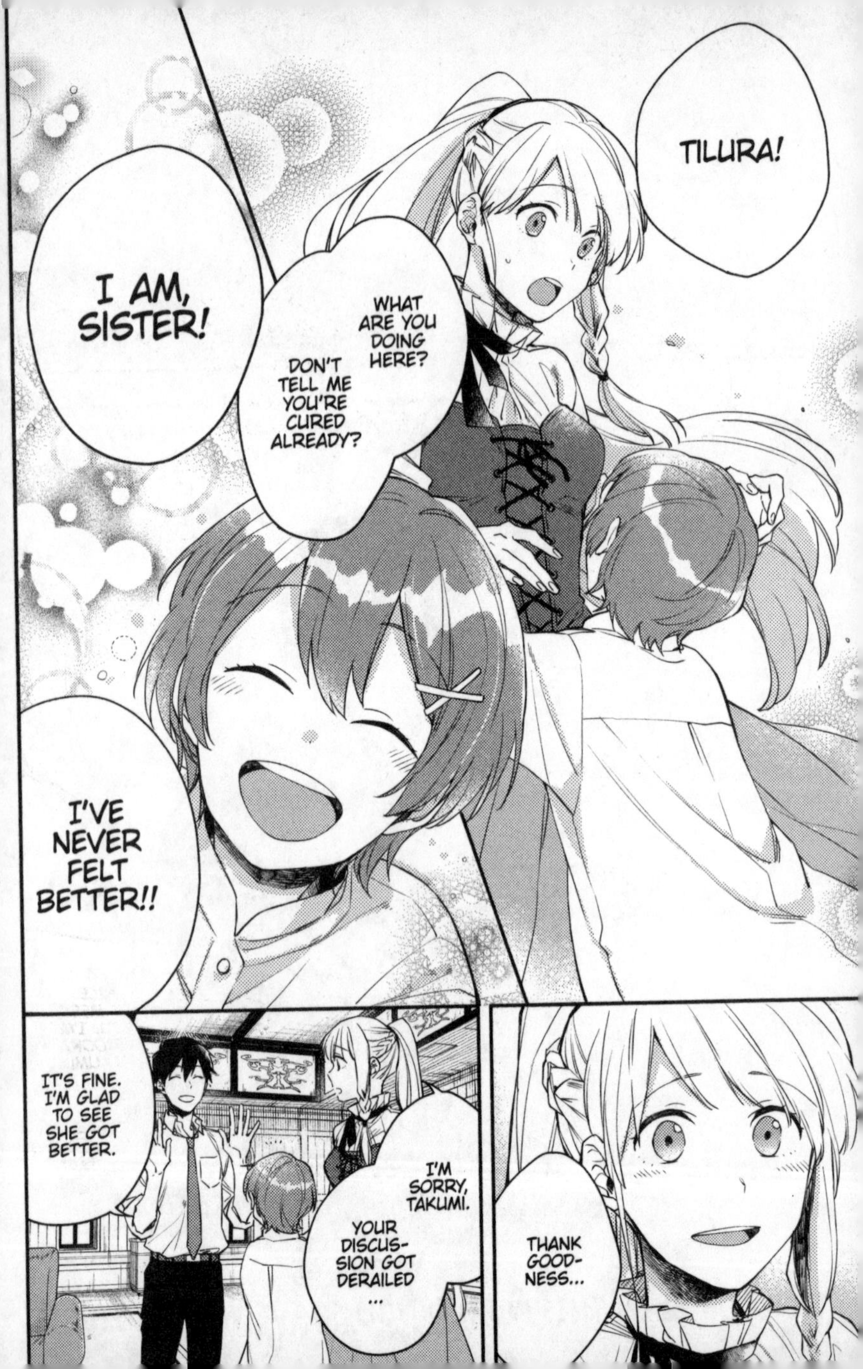
TILURA!
WHAT ARE YOU DOING HERE? DON'T TELL ME YOU'RE CURED ALREADY?
I AM, SISTER!
I'VE NEVER FELT BETTER!!
THANK GOOD-NESS...
I'M SORRY, TAKUMI.
YOUR DISCUS-SION GOT DERAILED ...
IT'S FINE. I'M GLAD TO SEE SHE GOT BETTER.

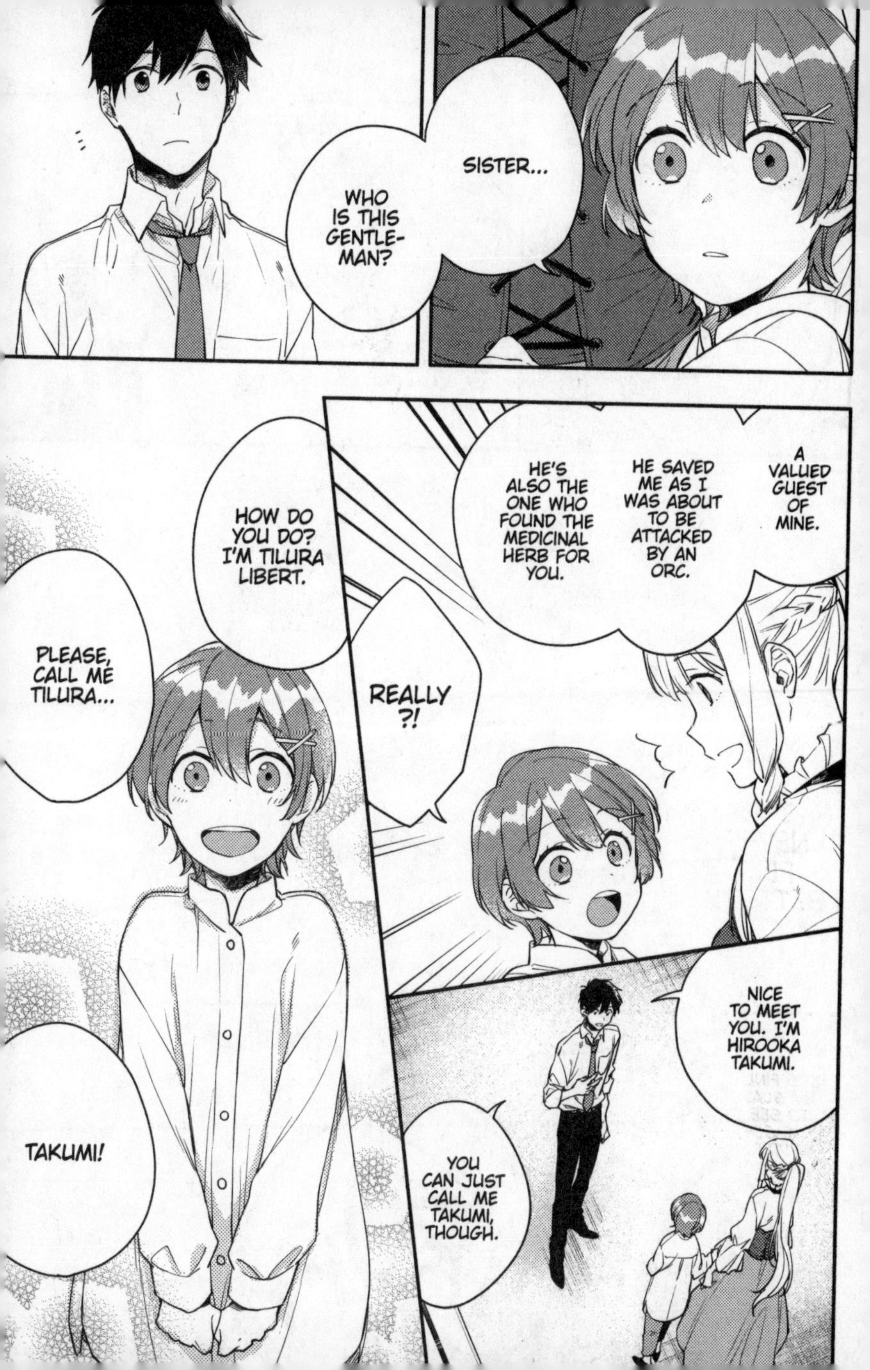
SISTER...
WHO IS THIS GENTLE-MAN?
A VALUED GUEST OF MINE.
HE SAVED ME AS I WAS ABOUT TO BE ATTACKED BY AN ORC.
HE'S ALSO THE ONE WHO FOUND THE MEDICINAL HERB FOR YOU.
REALLY?!
NICE TO MEET YOU. I'M HIROOKA TAKUMI.
YOU CAN JUST CALL ME TAKUMI, THOUGH.
HOW DO YOU DO? I'M TILURA LIBERT.
PLEASE, CALL ME TILURA...
TAKUMI!

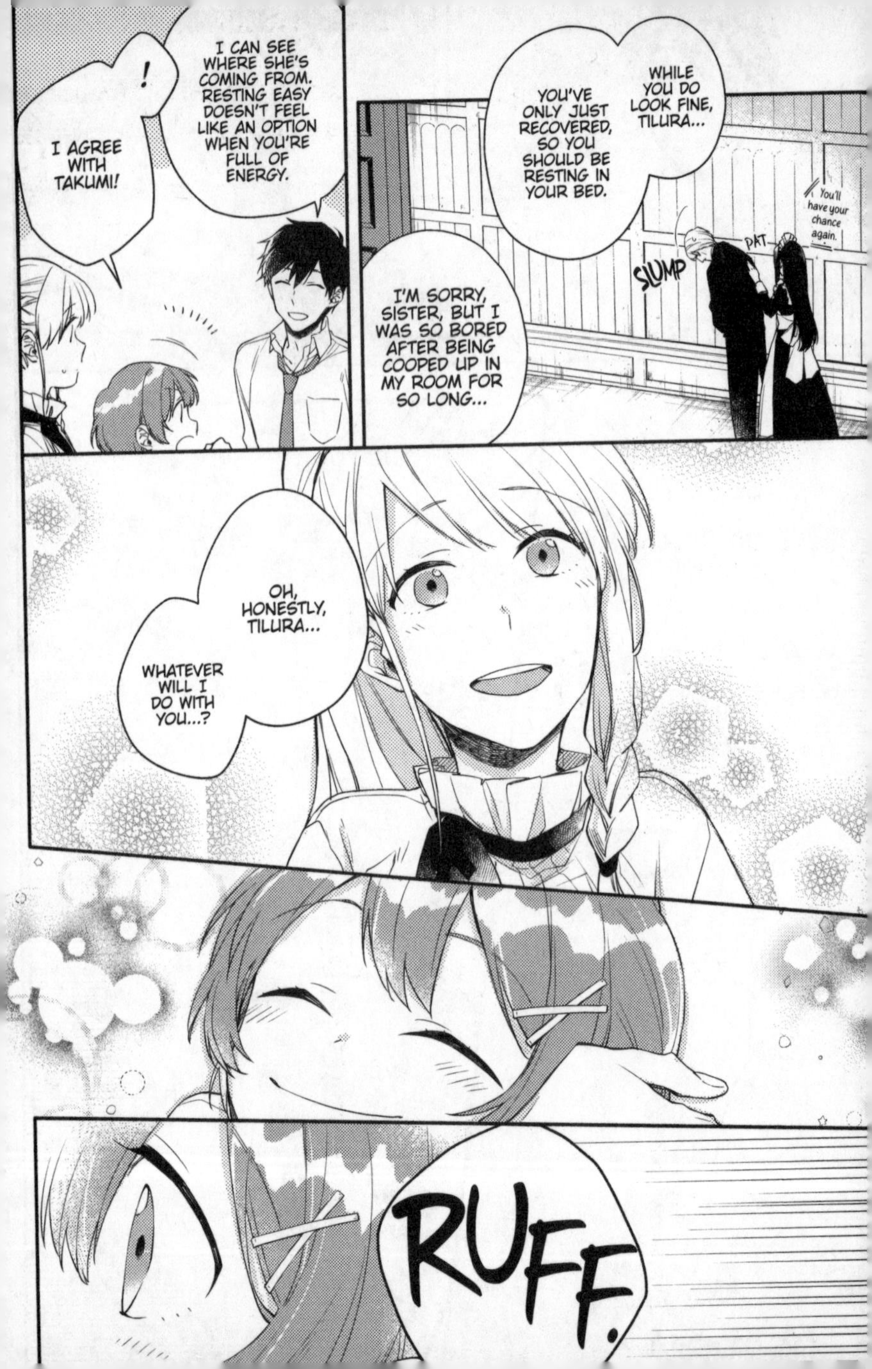
WHILE YOU DO LOOK FINE, TILURA...
YOU'VE ONLY JUST RECOVERED, SO YOU SHOULD BE RESTING IN YOUR BED.
You'll have your chance again.
PAT
SLUMP
I'M SORRY, SISTER, BUT I WAS SO BORED AFTER BEING COOPED UP IN MY ROOM FOR SO LONG...
I CAN SEE WHERE SHE'S COMING FROM. RESTING EASY DOESN'T FEEL LIKE AN OPTION WHEN YOU'RE FULL OF ENERGY.
!
I AGREE WITH TAKUMI!
OH, HONESTLY, TILURA...
WHATEVER WILL I DO WITH YOU...?
RUFF.

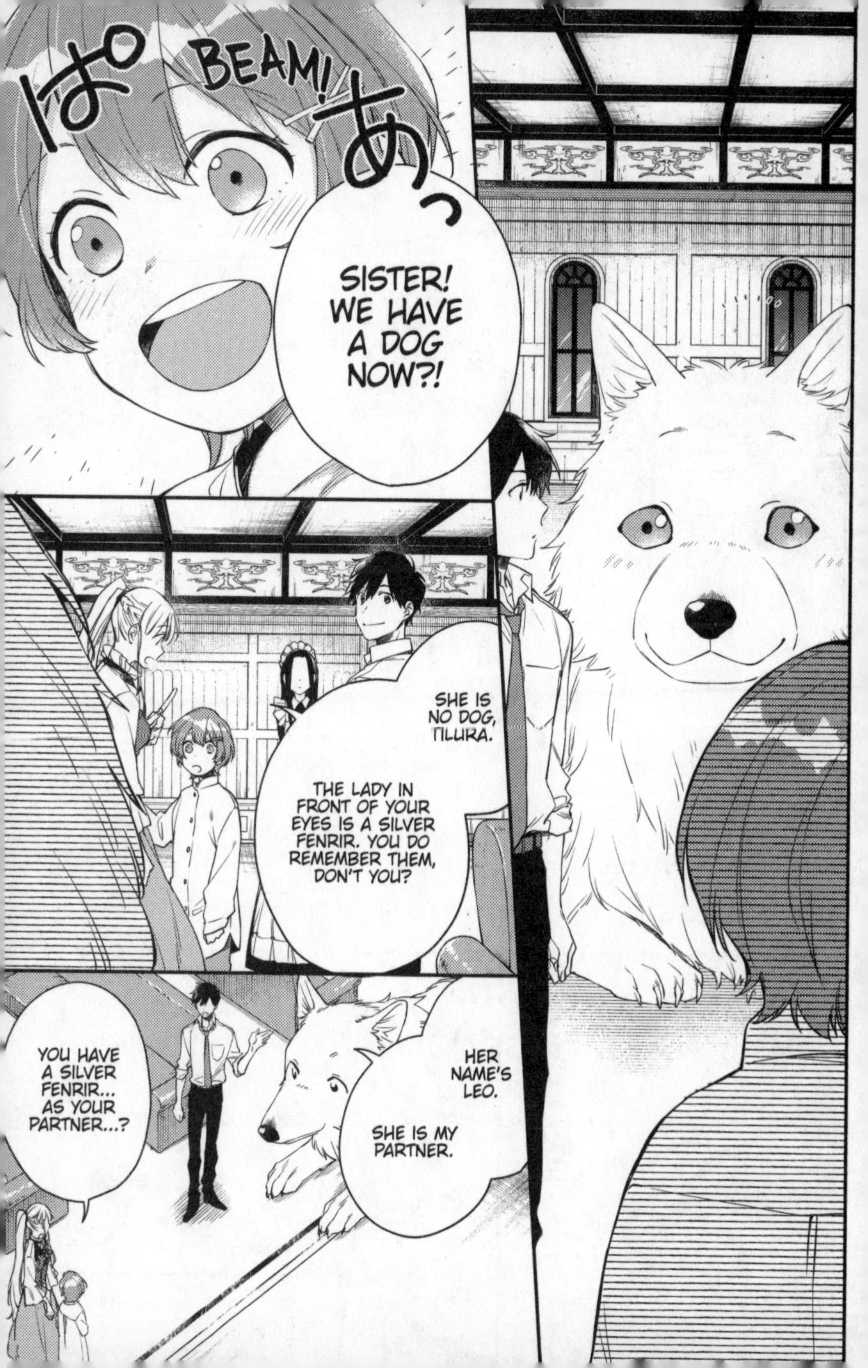
ぱあっ
BEAM!
SISTER! WE HAVE A DOG NOW?!
SHE IS NO DOG, TILURA.
THE LADY IN FRONT OF YOUR EYES IS A SILVER FENRIR. YOU DO REMEMBER THEM, DON'T YOU?
HER NAME'S LEO.
SHE IS MY PARTNER.
YOU HAVE A SILVER FENRIR... AS YOUR PARTNER...?

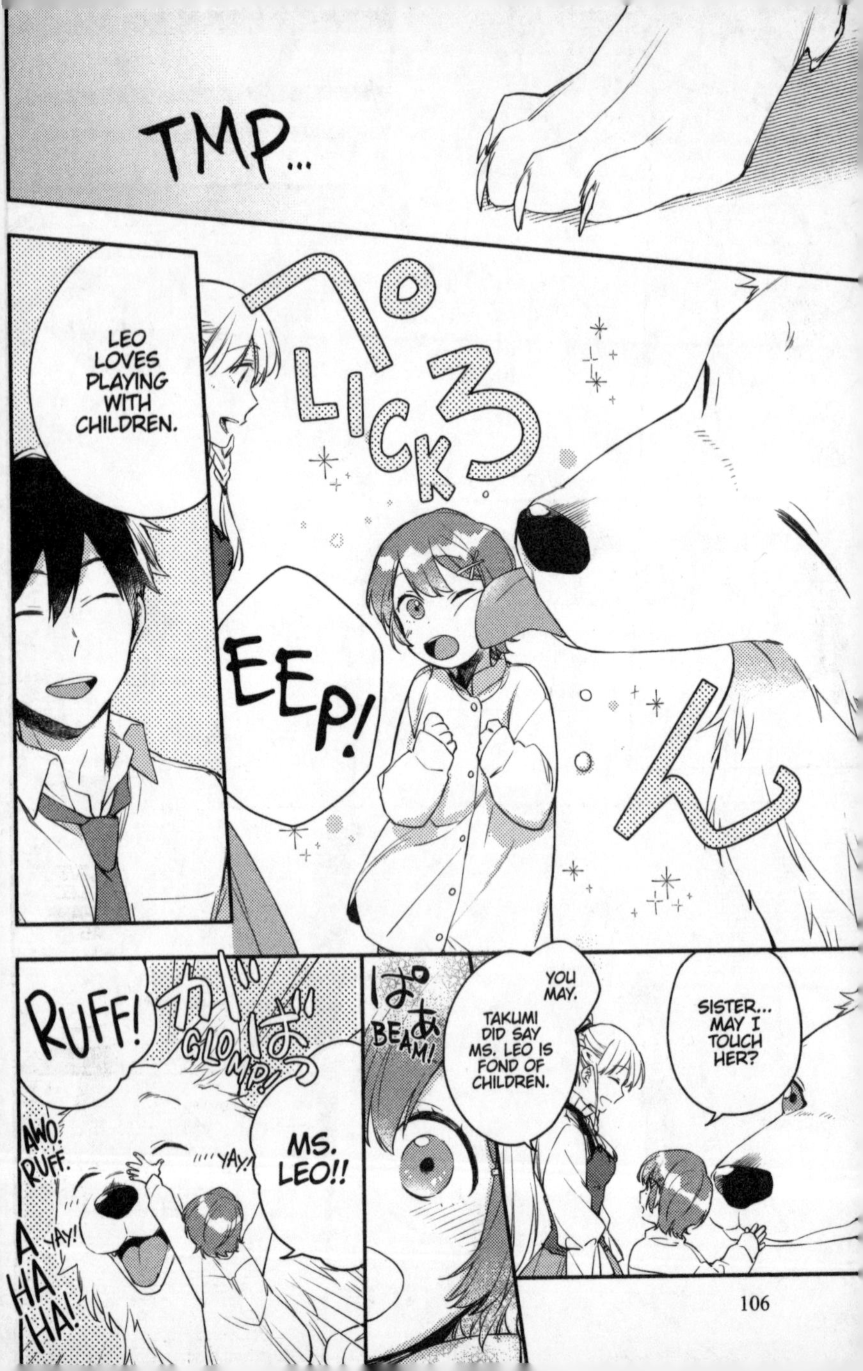
TMP...
ぺろん
LICK
LEO LOVES PLAYING WITH CHILDREN.
EEP!
SISTER... MAY I TOUCH HER?
YOU MAY.
TAKUMI DID SAY MS. LEO IS FOND OF CHILDREN.
ぱあ
BEAM!
がばっ
GLOMP!
MS. LEO!!
RUFF!
YAY!
AWO. RUFF.
YAY!
A HA HA HA!

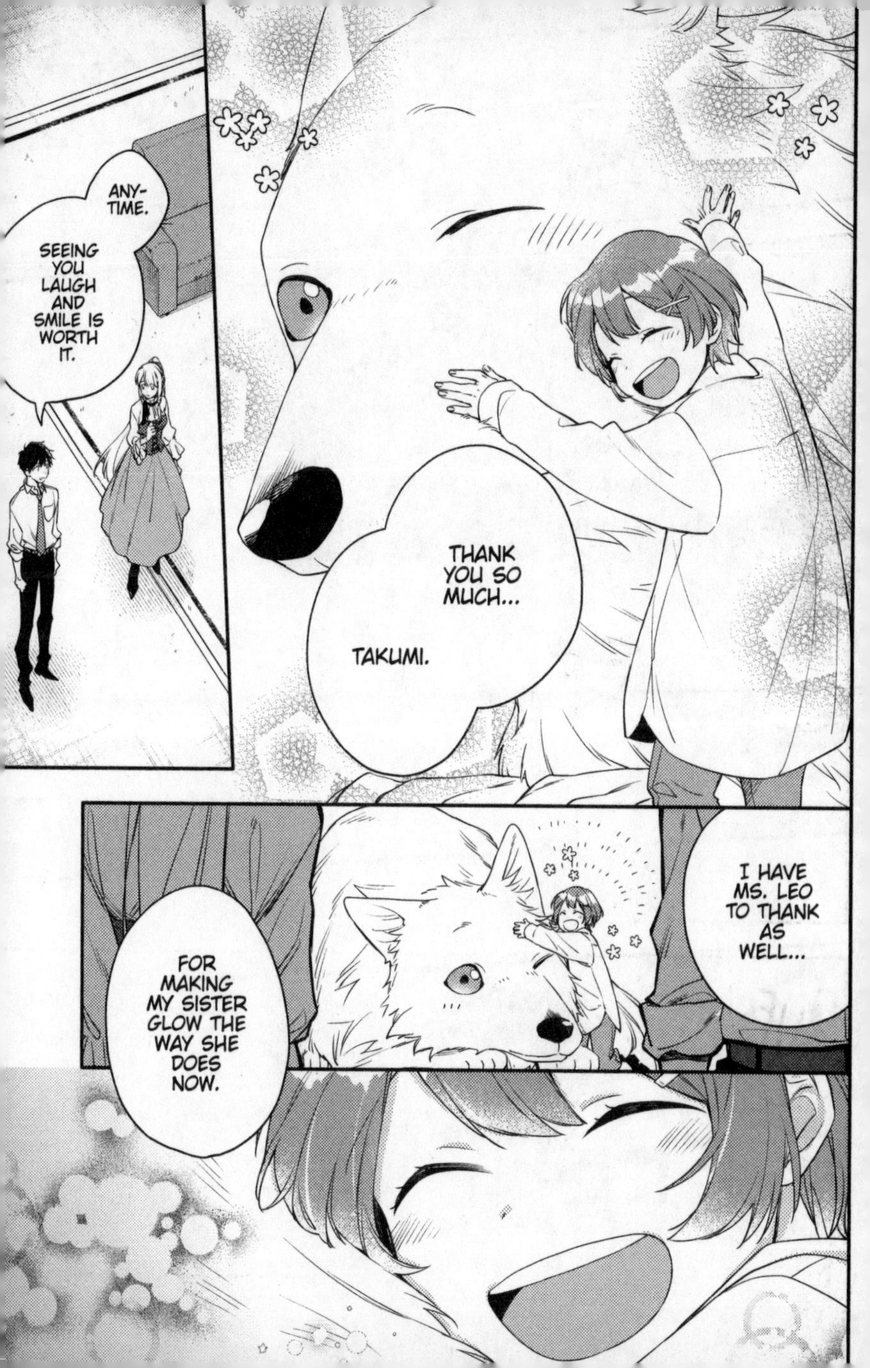
THANK YOU SO MUCH...
TAKUMI.
ANY-TIME.
SEEING YOU LAUGH AND SMILE IS WORTH IT.
I HAVE MS. LEO TO THANK AS WELL...
FOR MAKING MY SISTER GLOW THE WAY SHE DOES NOW.

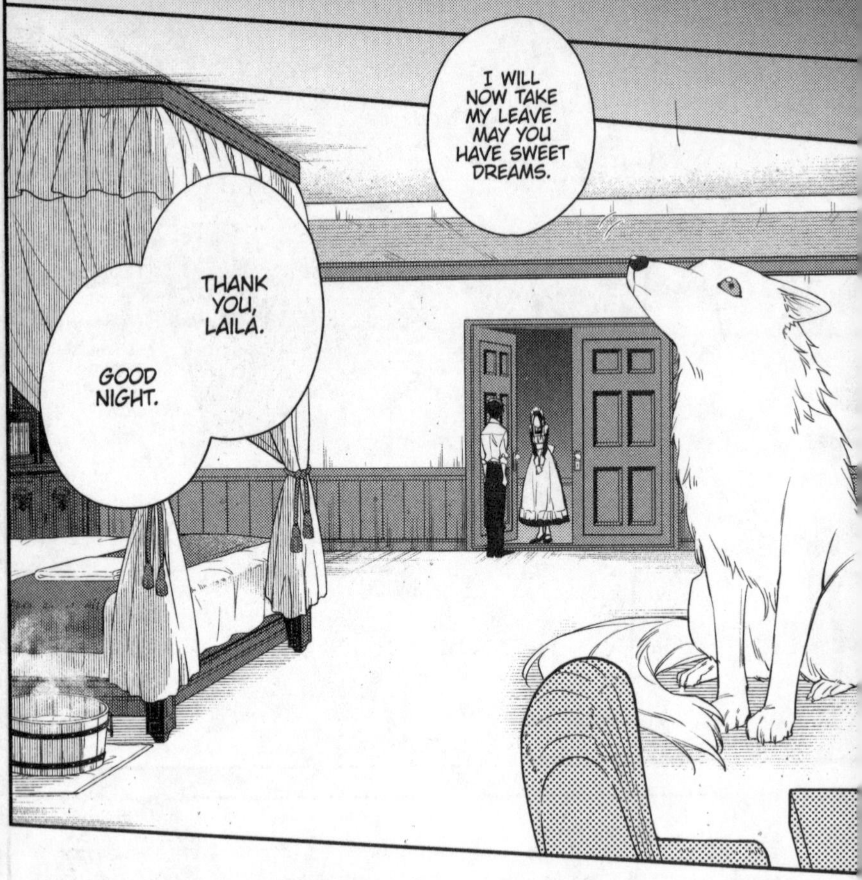
I WILL NOW TAKE MY LEAVE. MAY YOU HAVE SWEET DREAMS.
THANK YOU, LAILA.
GOOD NIGHT.

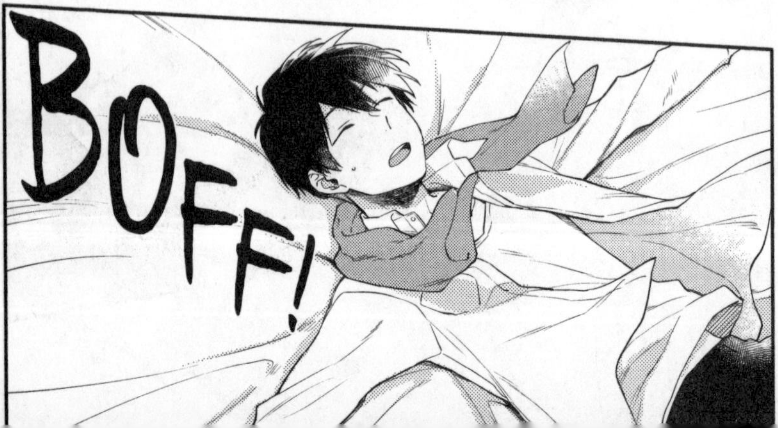
BOFF!

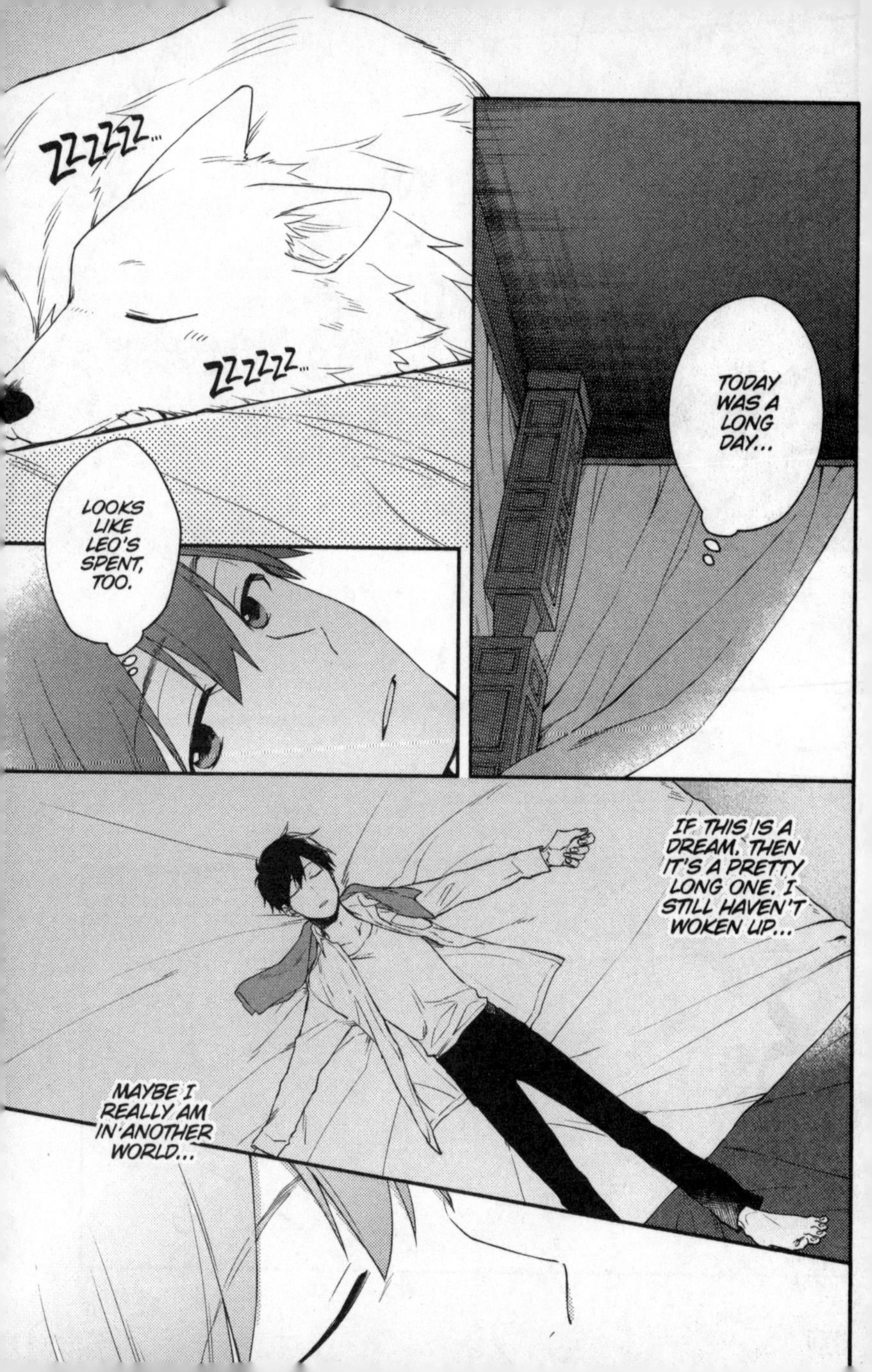
TODAY WAS A LONG DAY...
ZZZZZZ...
ZZZZZZ...
LOOKS LIKE LEO'S SPENT, TOO.
IF THIS IS A DREAM, THEN IT'S A PRETTY LONG ONE. I STILL HAVEN'T WOKEN UP...
MAYBE I REALLY AM IN ANOTHER WORLD...

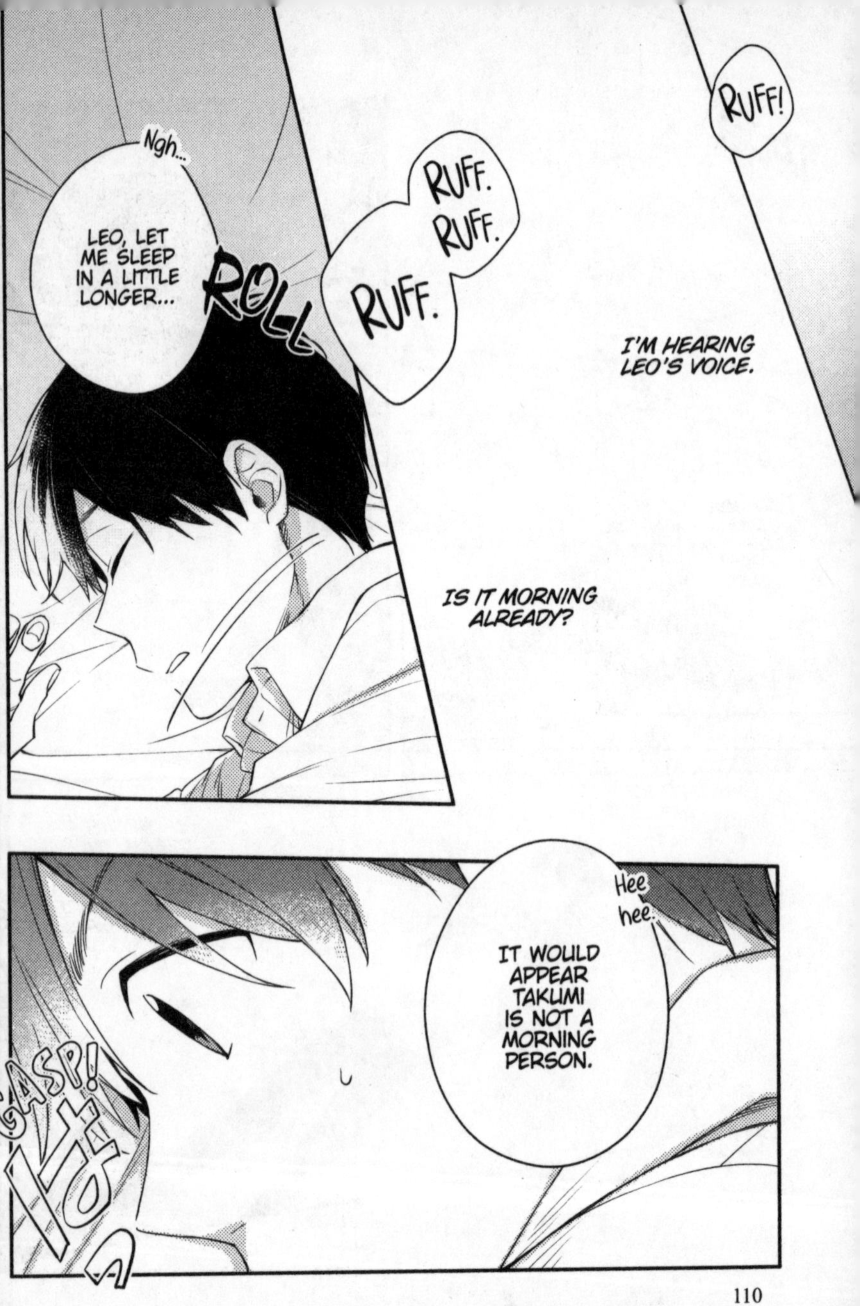
RUFF!
I'M HEARING LEO'S VOICE.
IS IT MORNING ALREADY?
RUFF. RUFF. RUFF.
ROLL
Ngh...
LEO, LET ME SLEEP IN A LITTLE LONGER...
Hee hee.
IT WOULD APPEAR TAKUMI IS NOT A MORNING PERSON.
GASP!

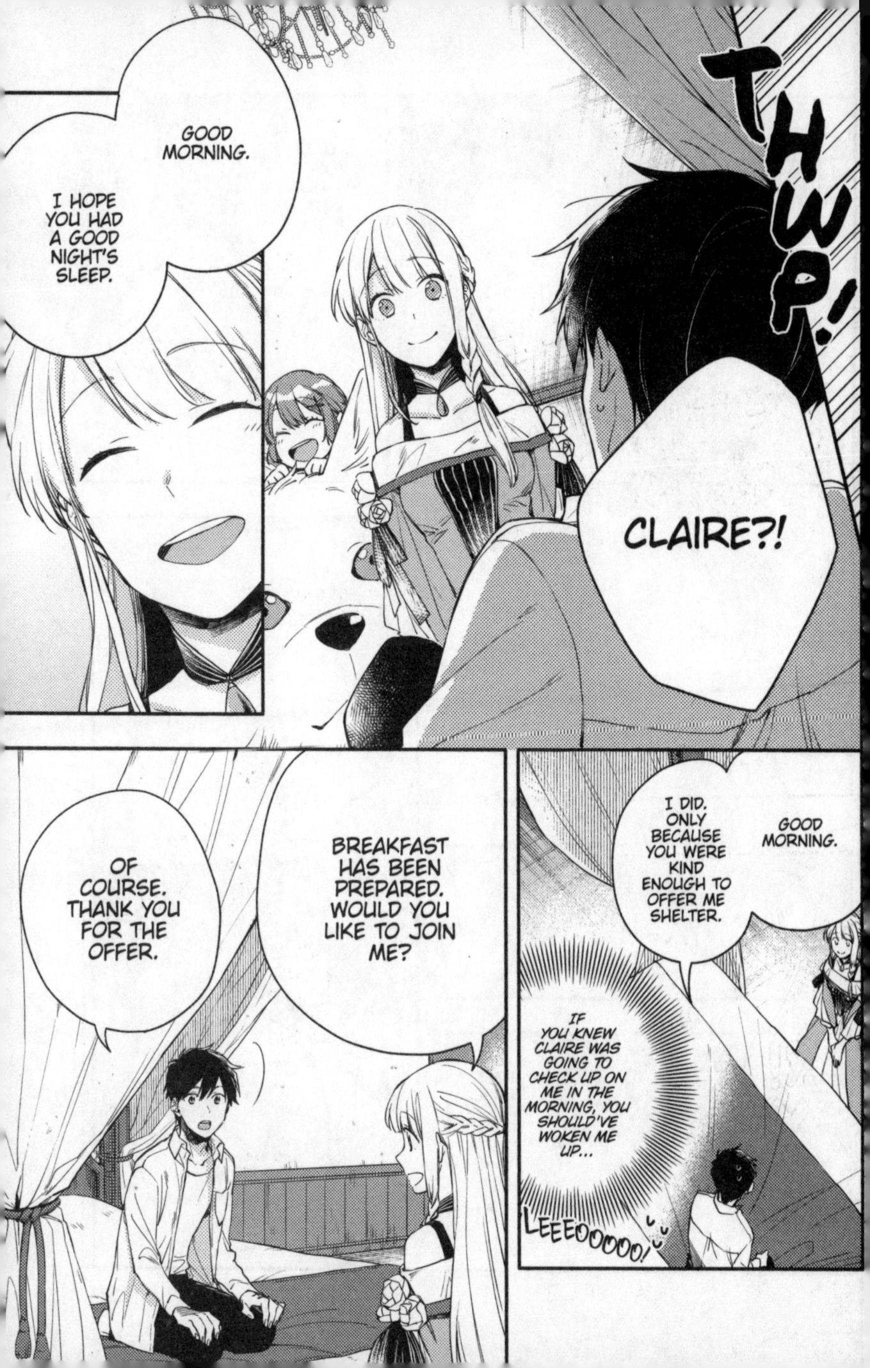
THWP!
CLAIRE?!
GOOD MORNING.
I HOPE YOU HAD A GOOD NIGHT'S SLEEP.
GOOD MORNING.
I DID. ONLY BECAUSE YOU WERE KIND ENOUGH TO OFFER ME SHELTER.
IF YOU KNEW CLAIRE WAS GOING TO CHECK UP ON ME IN THE MORNING, YOU SHOULD'VE WOKEN ME UP...
LEEEOOOOOO!
BREAKFAST HAS BEEN PREPARED. WOULD YOU LIKE TO JOIN ME?
OF COURSE. THANK YOU FOR THE OFFER.

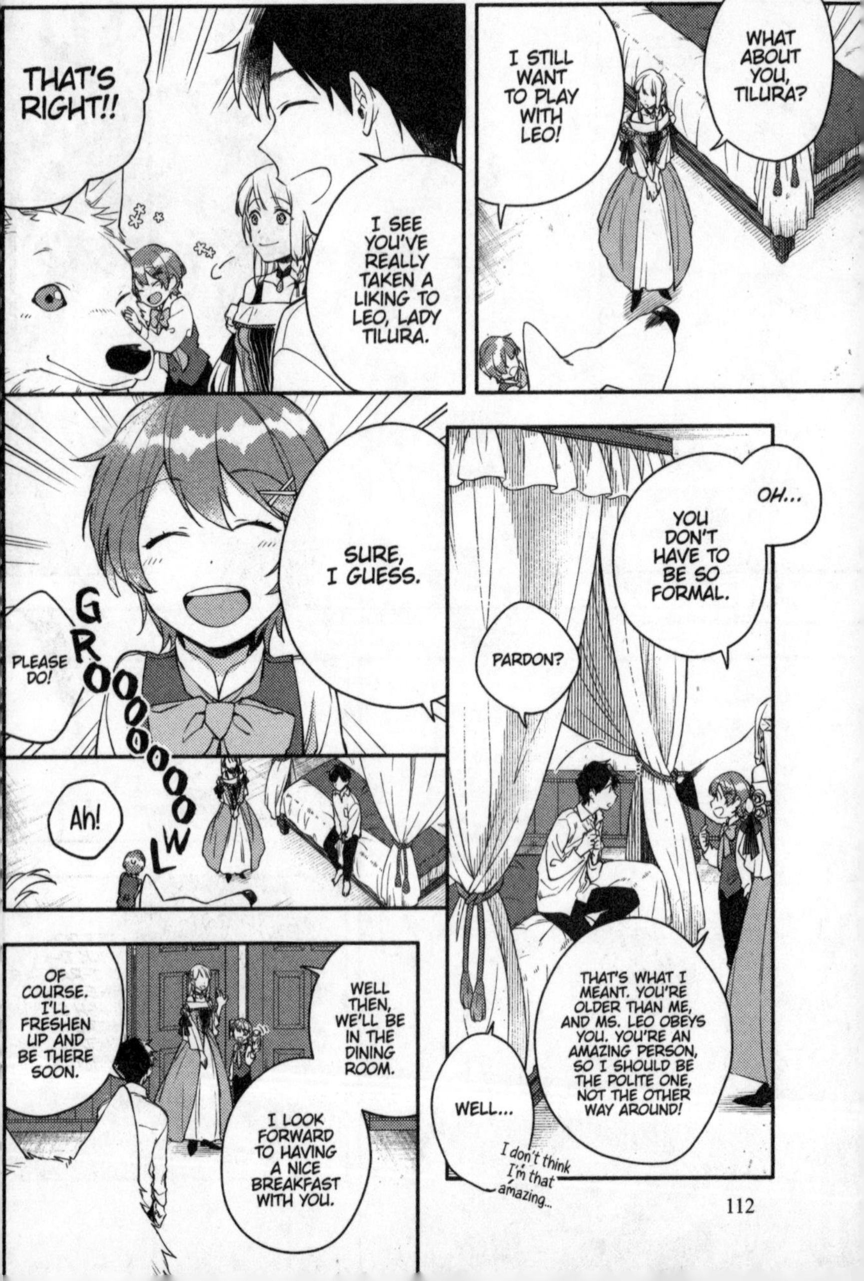
WHAT ABOUT YOU, TILURA?
I STILL WANT TO PLAY WITH LEO!
I SEE YOU'VE REALLY TAKEN A LIKING TO LEO, LADY TILURA.
THAT'S RIGHT!!
OH...
YOU DON'T HAVE TO BE SO FORMAL.
PARDON?
THAT'S WHAT I MEANT. YOU'RE OLDER THAN ME, AND MS. LEO OBEYS YOU. YOU'RE AN AMAZING PERSON, SO I SHOULD BE THE POLITE ONE, NOT THE OTHER WAY AROUND!
WELL...
I don't think I'm that amazing...
SURE, I GUESS.
PLEASE DO!
GROOOOOOOOWL
Ah!
WELL THEN, WE'LL BE IN THE DINING ROOM.
OF COURSE. I'LL FRESHEN UP AND BE THERE SOON.
I LOOK FORWARD TO HAVING A NICE BREAKFAST WITH YOU.

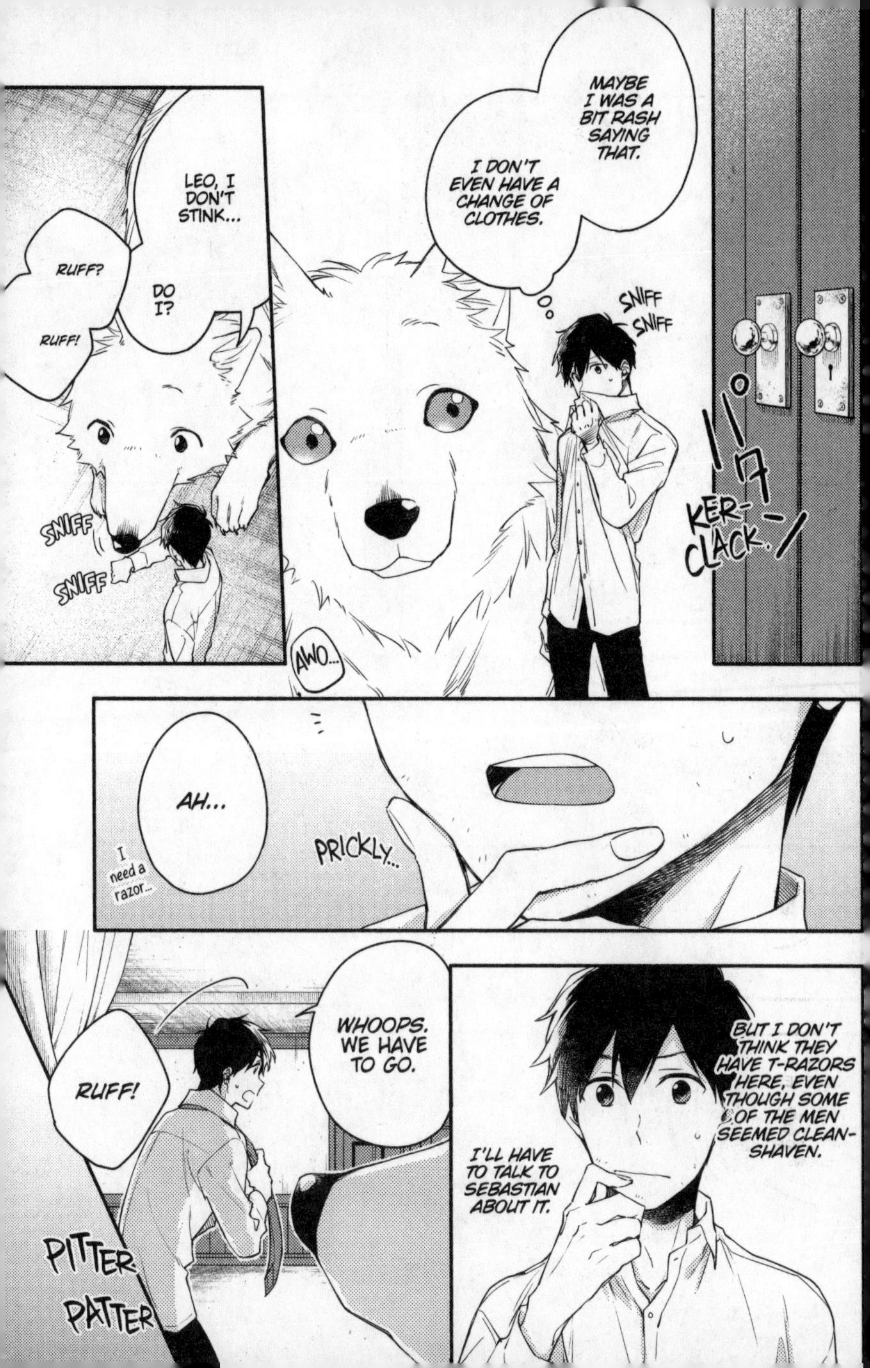
MAYBE I WAS A BIT RASH SAYING THAT.
I DON'T EVEN HAVE A CHANGE OF CLOTHES.
SNIFF SNIFF
KER-CLACK
AWO...
LEO, I DON'T STINK...
DO I?
RUFF?
RUFF!
SNIFF
SNIFF
AH...
PRICKLY...
I need a razor...
BUT I DON'T THINK THEY HAVE T-RAZORS HERE, EVEN THOUGH SOME OF THE MEN SEEMED CLEAN-SHAVEN.
I'LL HAVE TO TALK TO SEBASTIAN ABOUT IT.
WHOOPS. WE HAVE TO GO.
RUFF!
PITTER PATTER

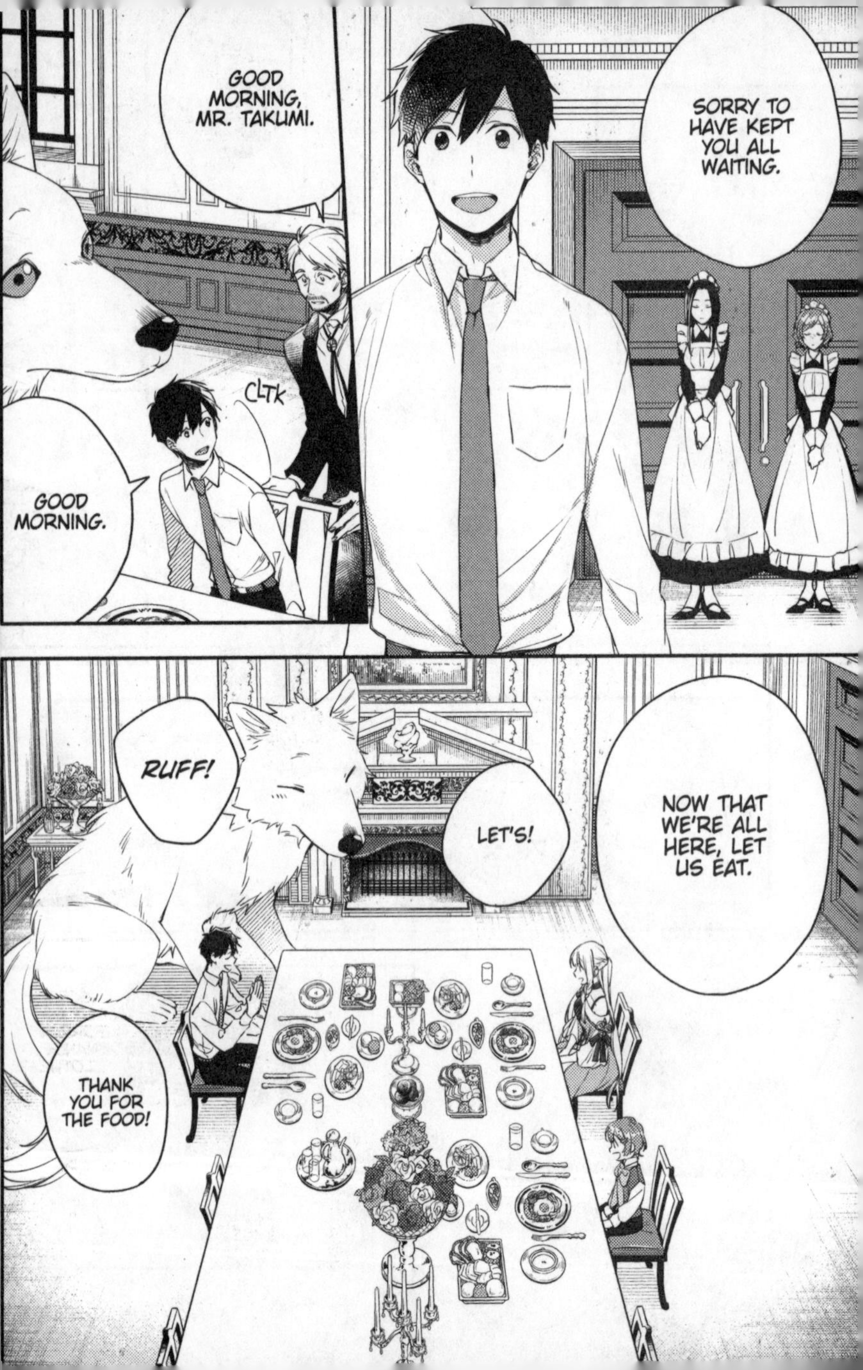
SORRY TO HAVE KEPT YOU ALL WAITING.
GOOD MORNING, MR. TAKUMI.
CLTK
GOOD MORNING.
NOW THAT WE'RE ALL HERE, LET US EAT.
LET'S!
RUFF!
THANK YOU FOR THE FOOD!

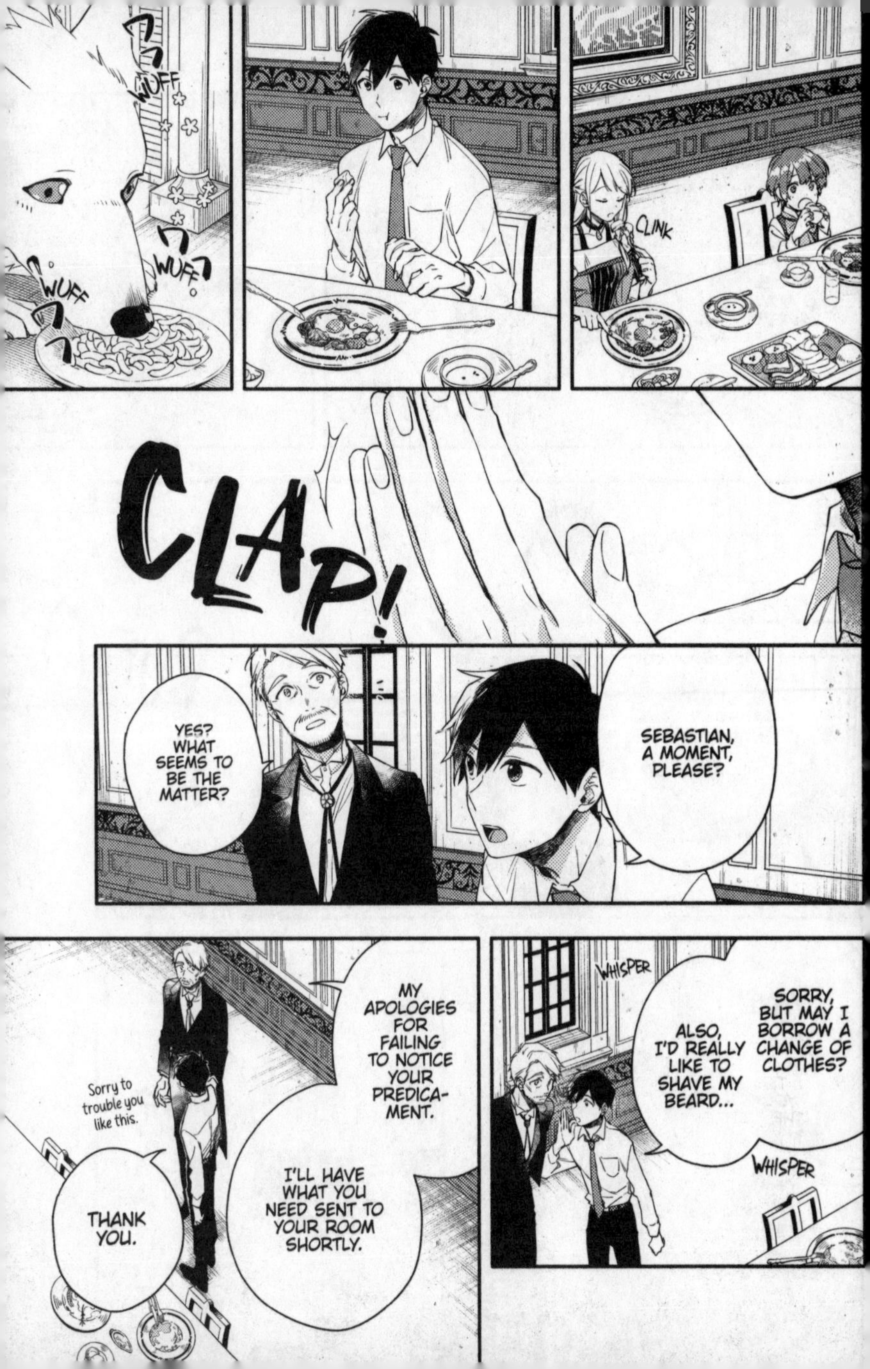
CLINK
WUFF
WUFF
WUFF
CLAP!
SEBASTIAN, A MOMENT, PLEASE?
YES? WHAT SEEMS TO BE THE MATTER?
WHISPER
SORRY, BUT MAY I BORROW A CHANGE OF CLOTHES?
ALSO, I'D REALLY LIKE TO SHAVE MY BEARD...
WHISPER
MY APOLOGIES FOR FAILING TO NOTICE YOUR PREDICAMENT.
I'LL HAVE WHAT YOU NEED SENT TO YOUR ROOM SHORTLY.
Sorry to trouble you like this.
THANK YOU.

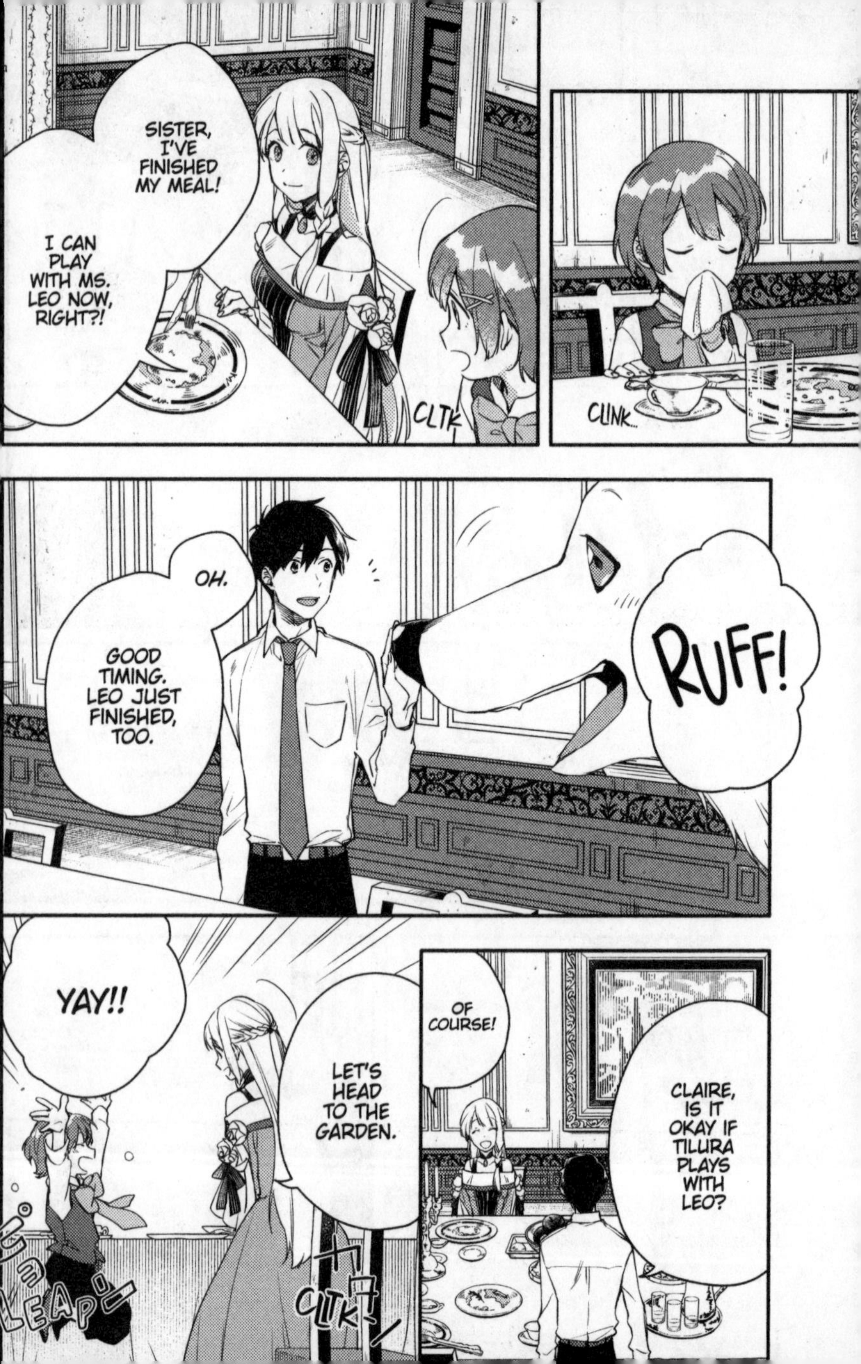
CLINK...
SISTER, I'VE FINISHED MY MEAL!
I CAN PLAY WITH MS. LEO NOW, RIGHT?!
CLTK
RUFF!
OH.
GOOD TIMING. LEO JUST FINISHED, TOO.
CLAIRE, IS IT OKAY IF TILURA PLAYS WITH LEO?
OF COURSE!
LET'S HEAD TO THE GARDEN.
YAY!!
CLTK
LEAP

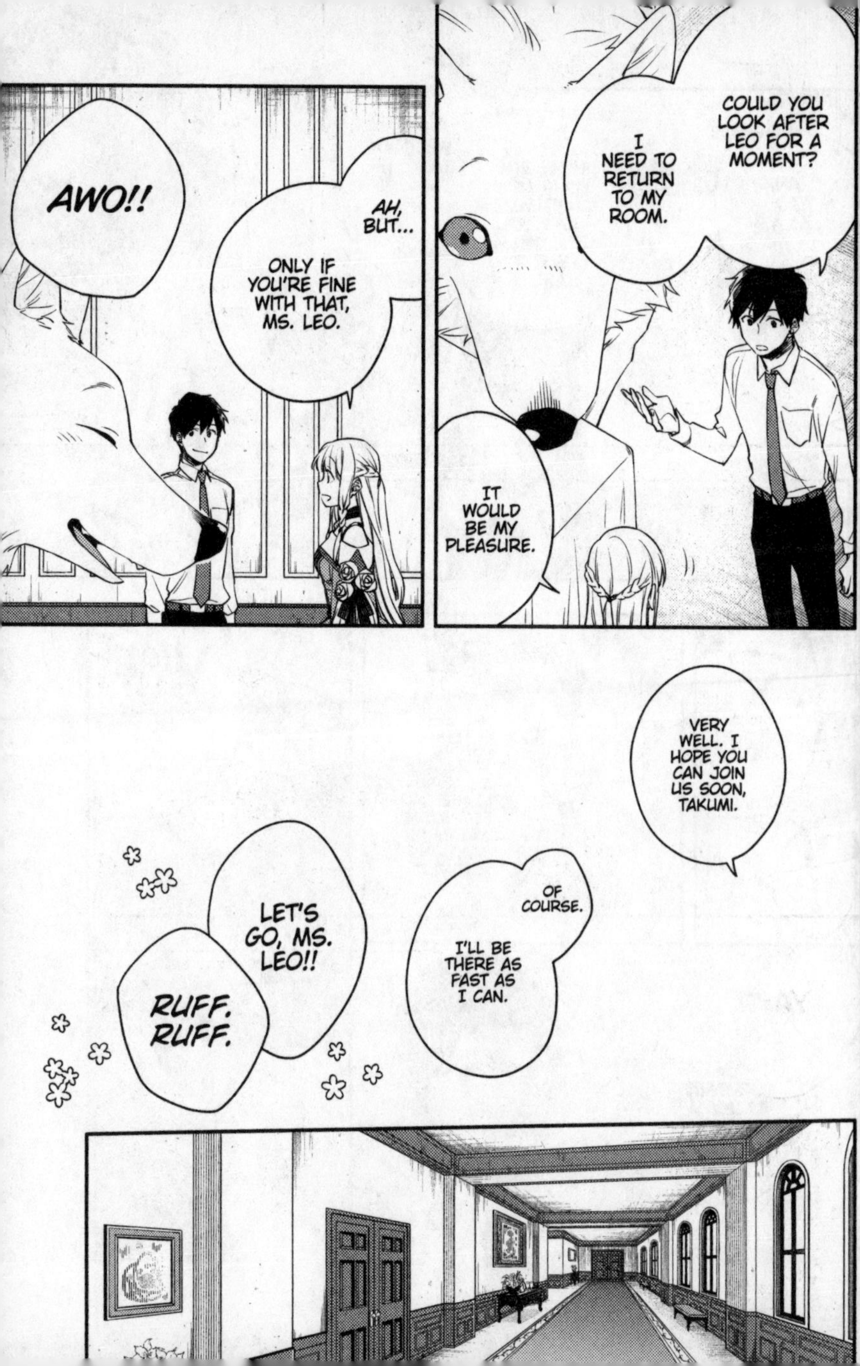
COULD YOU LOOK AFTER LEO FOR A MOMENT?
I NEED TO RETURN TO MY ROOM.
IT WOULD BE MY PLEASURE.
AH, BUT...
ONLY IF YOU'RE FINE WITH THAT, MS. LEO.
AWO!!
VERY WELL. I HOPE YOU CAN JOIN US SOON, TAKUMI.
OF COURSE.
I'LL BE THERE AS FAST AS I CAN.
LET'S GO, MS. LEO!!
RUFF. RUFF.

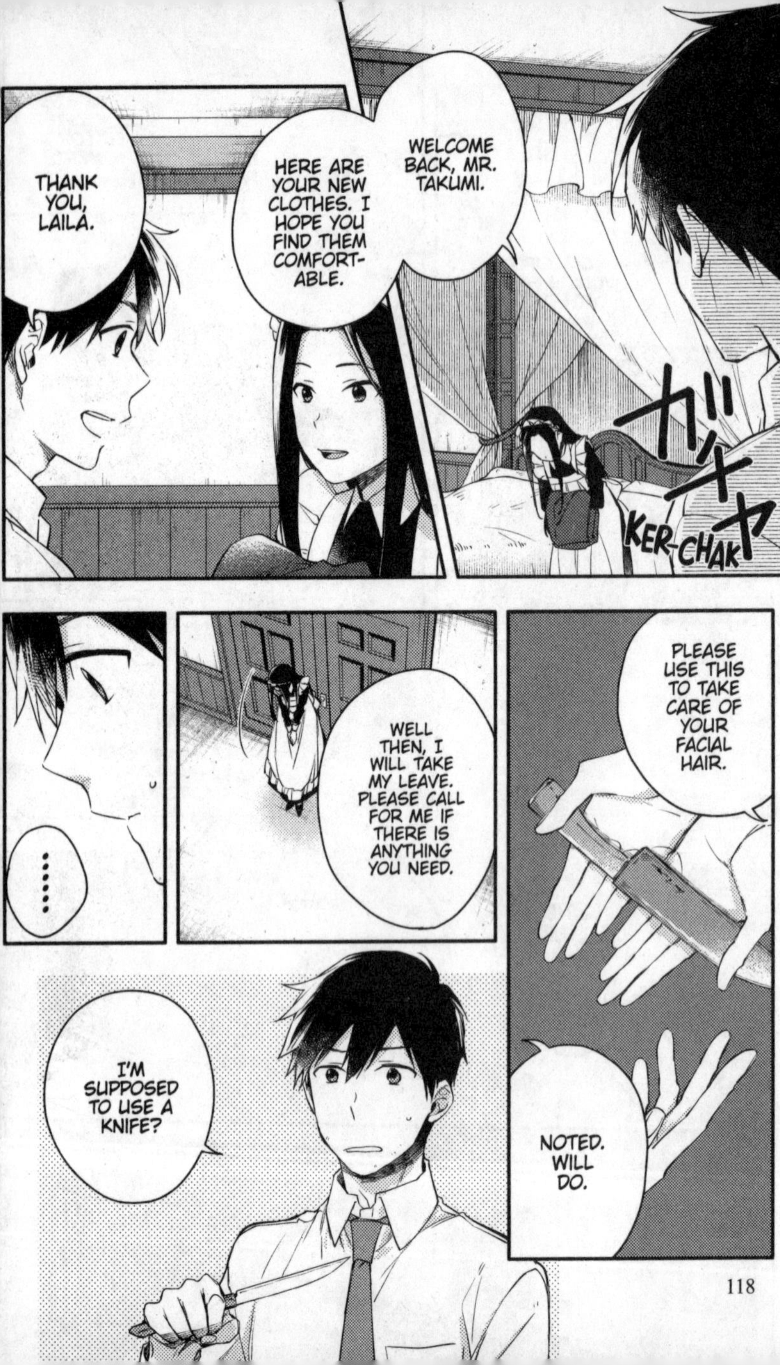
ガチャ
KER-CHAK
WELCOME BACK, MR. TAKUMI.
HERE ARE YOUR NEW CLOTHES. I HOPE YOU FIND THEM COMFORT-ABLE.
THANK YOU, LAILA.
PLEASE USE THIS TO TAKE CARE OF YOUR FACIAL HAIR.
NOTED. WILL DO.
WELL THEN, I WILL TAKE MY LEAVE. PLEASE CALL FOR ME IF THERE IS ANYTHING YOU NEED.
......
I'M SUPPOSED TO USE A KNIFE?

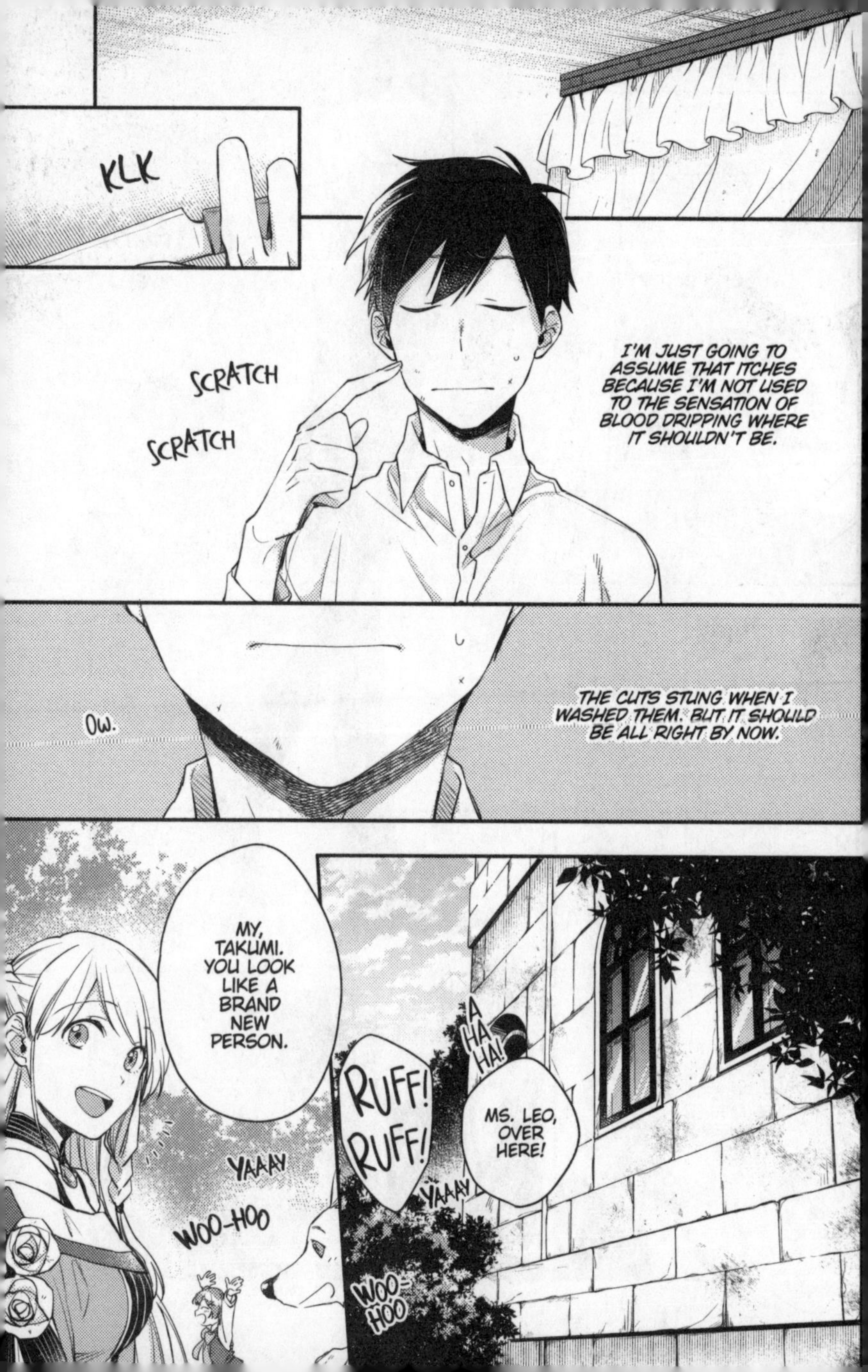
KLK
I'M JUST GOING TO ASSUME THAT ITCHES BECAUSE I'M NOT USED TO THE SENSATION OF BLOOD DRIPPING WHERE IT SHOULDN'T BE.
SCRATCH
SCRATCH
THE CUTS STUNG WHEN I WASHED THEM. BUT IT SHOULD BE ALL RIGHT BY NOW.
OW.
AHAHA!
MS. LEO, OVER HERE!
RUFF! RUFF!
YAAAY
WOO-HOO
MY, TAKUMI. YOU LOOK LIKE A BRAND NEW PERSON.
YAAAY
WOO-HOO

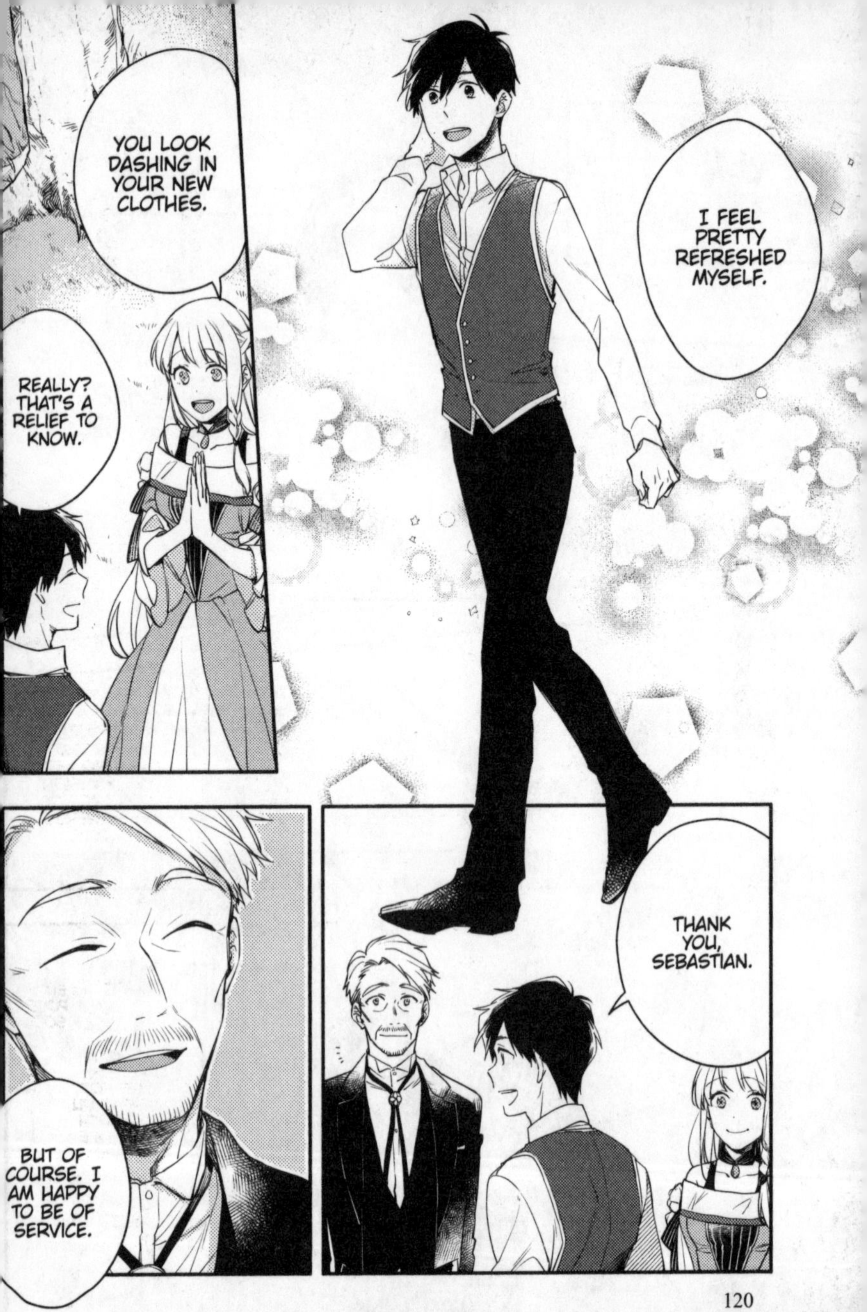
I FEEL PRETTY REFRESHED MYSELF.
YOU LOOK DASHING IN YOUR NEW CLOTHES.
REALLY? THAT'S A RELIEF TO KNOW.
THANK YOU, SEBASTIAN.
BUT OF COURSE. I AM HAPPY TO BE OF SERVICE.

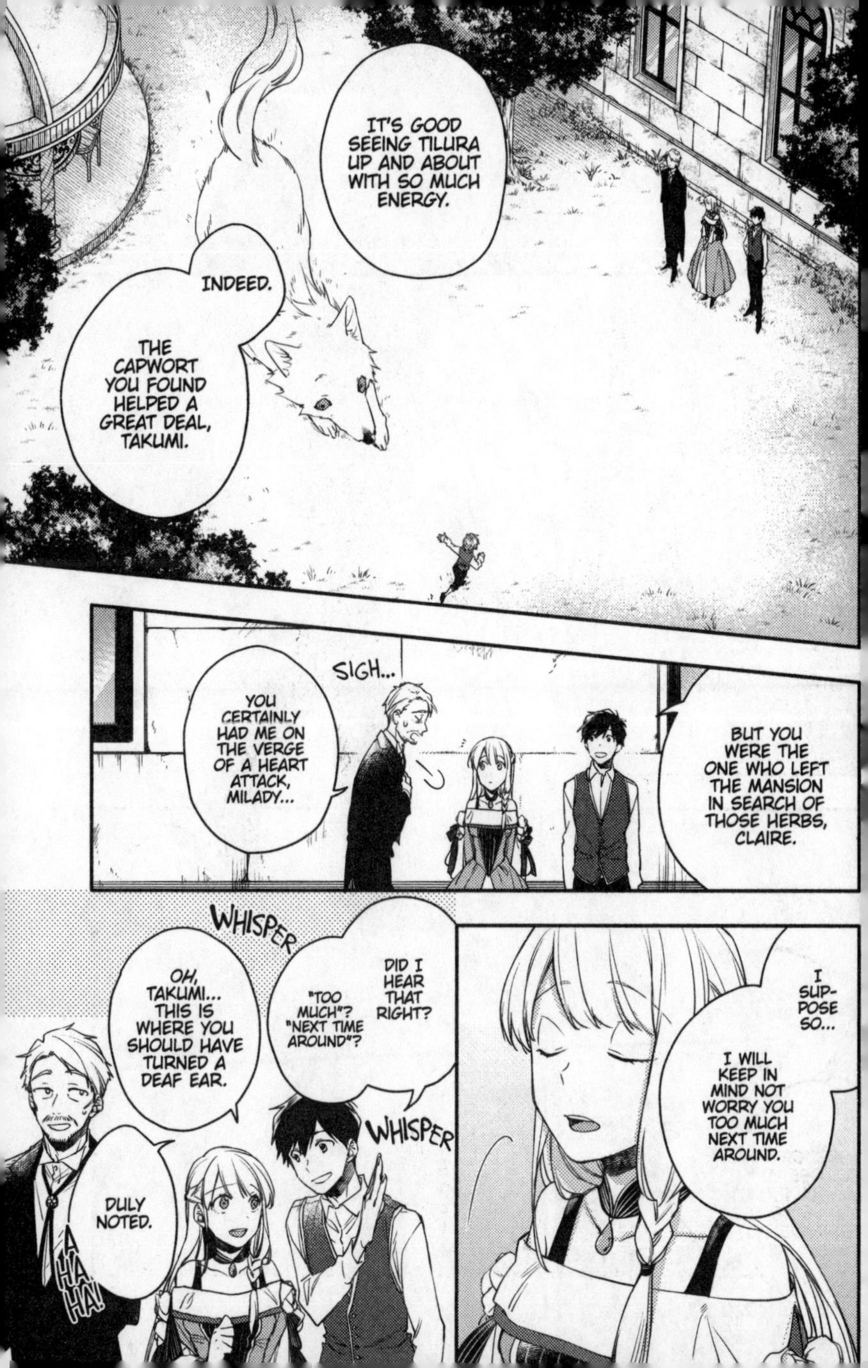
IT'S GOOD SEEING TILURA UP AND ABOUT WITH SO MUCH ENERGY.
INDEED.
THE CAPWORT YOU FOUND HELPED A GREAT DEAL, TAKUMI.
BUT YOU WERE THE ONE WHO LEFT THE MANSION IN SEARCH OF THOSE HERBS, CLAIRE.
SIGH...
YOU CERTAINLY HAD ME ON THE VERGE OF A HEART ATTACK, MILADY...
I SUP-POSE SO...
I WILL KEEP IN MIND NOT WORRY YOU TOO MUCH NEXT TIME AROUND.
DID I HEAR THAT RIGHT?
"TOO MUCH"? "NEXT TIME AROUND"?
WHISPER
OH, TAKUMI... THIS IS WHERE YOU SHOULD HAVE TURNED A DEAF EAR.
WHISPER
DULY NOTED.
AHAHA!

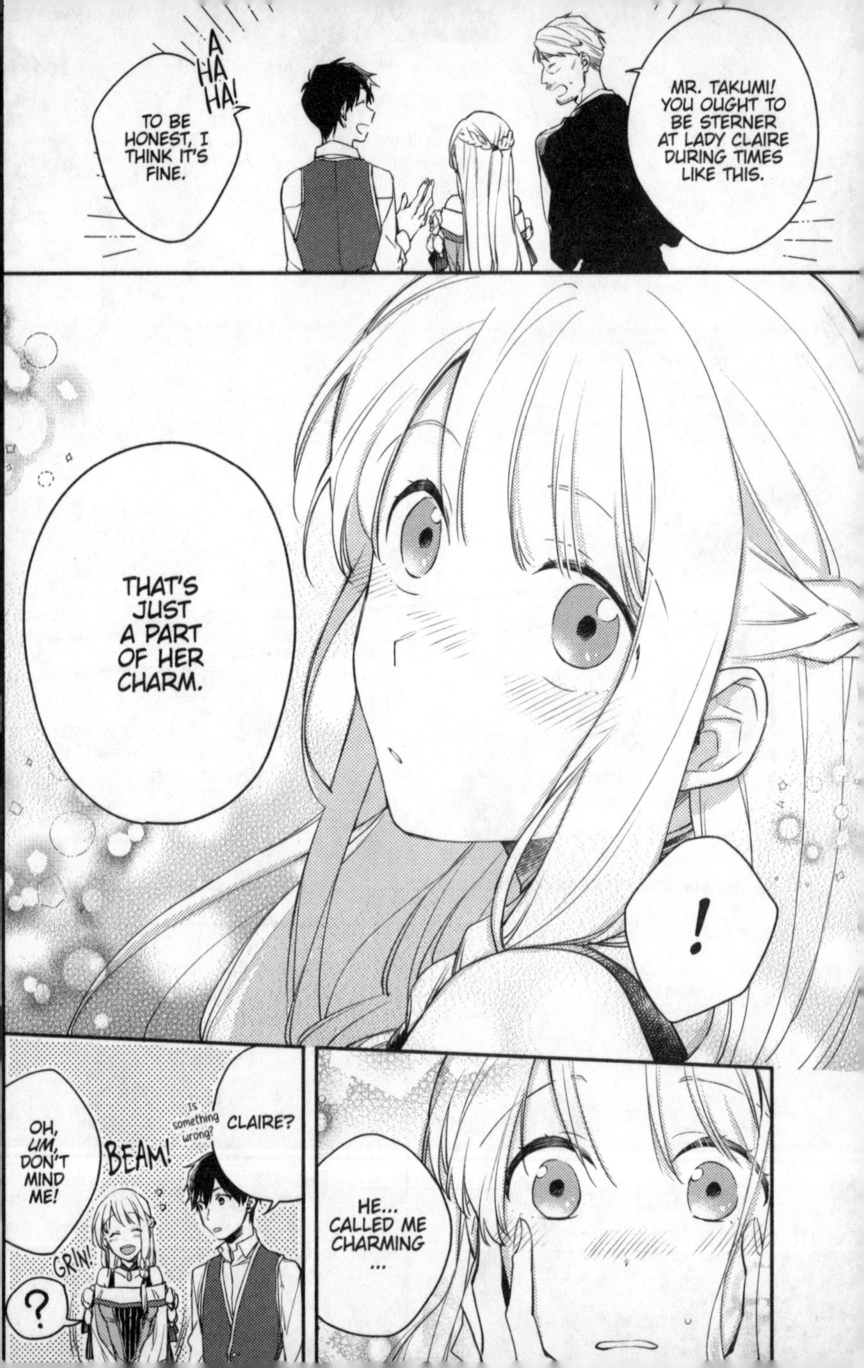
MR. TAKUMI! YOU OUGHT TO BE STERNER AT LADY CLAIRE DURING TIMES LIKE THIS.
A HA HA!
TO BE HONEST, I THINK IT'S FINE.
THAT'S JUST A PART OF HER CHARM.
!
HE... CALLED ME CHARMING ...
CLAIRE?
Is something wrong?
BEAM!
OH, UM, DON'T MIND ME!
GRIN!
?

EVEN DOGS GO TO OTHER WORLDS

LIFE IN ANOTHER WORLD WITH MY BELOVED HOUND

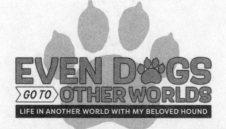

EVEN DOGS GO TO OTHER WORLDS

LIFE IN ANOTHER WORLD WITH MY BELOVED HOUND

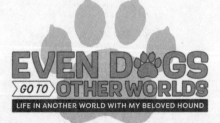

6TH WOOF! THE BOISTEROUS TOWN OF RACTOS

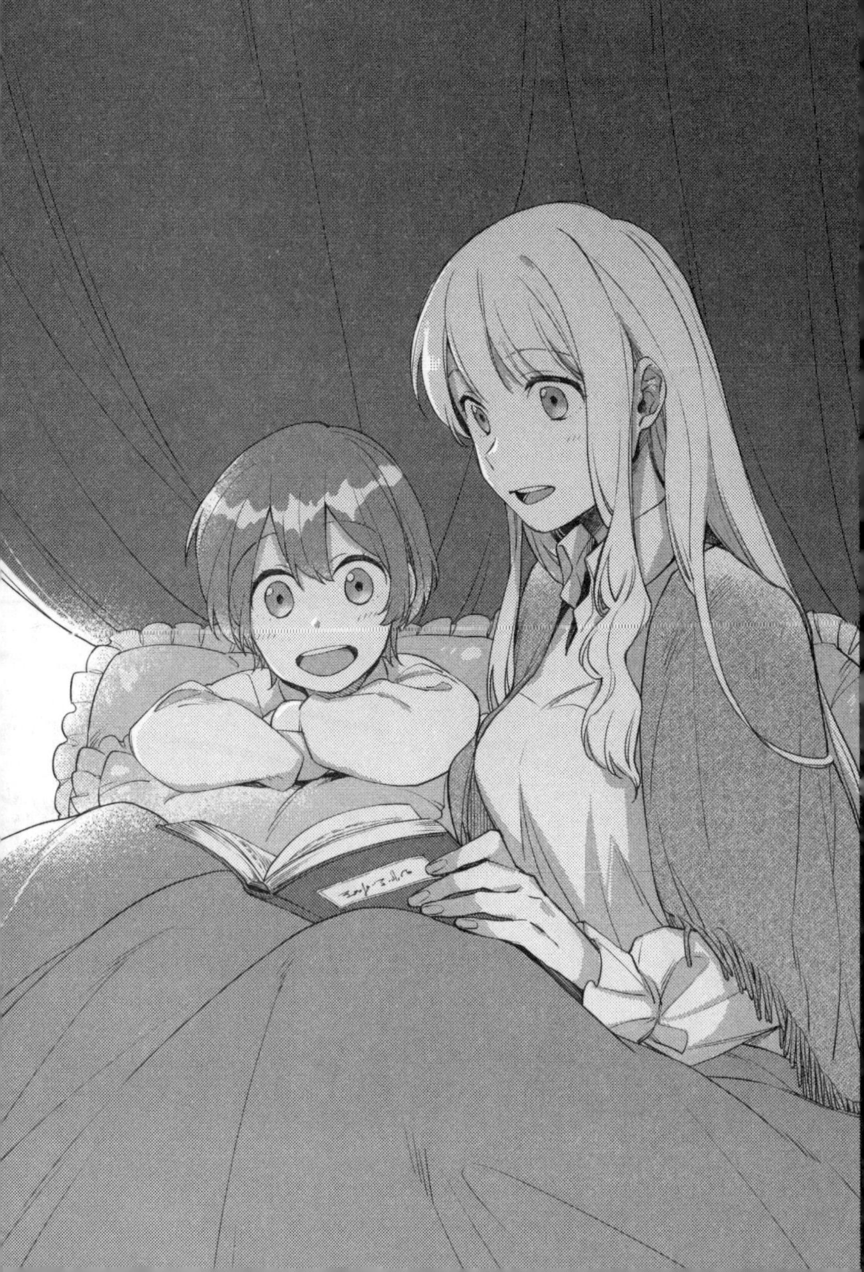

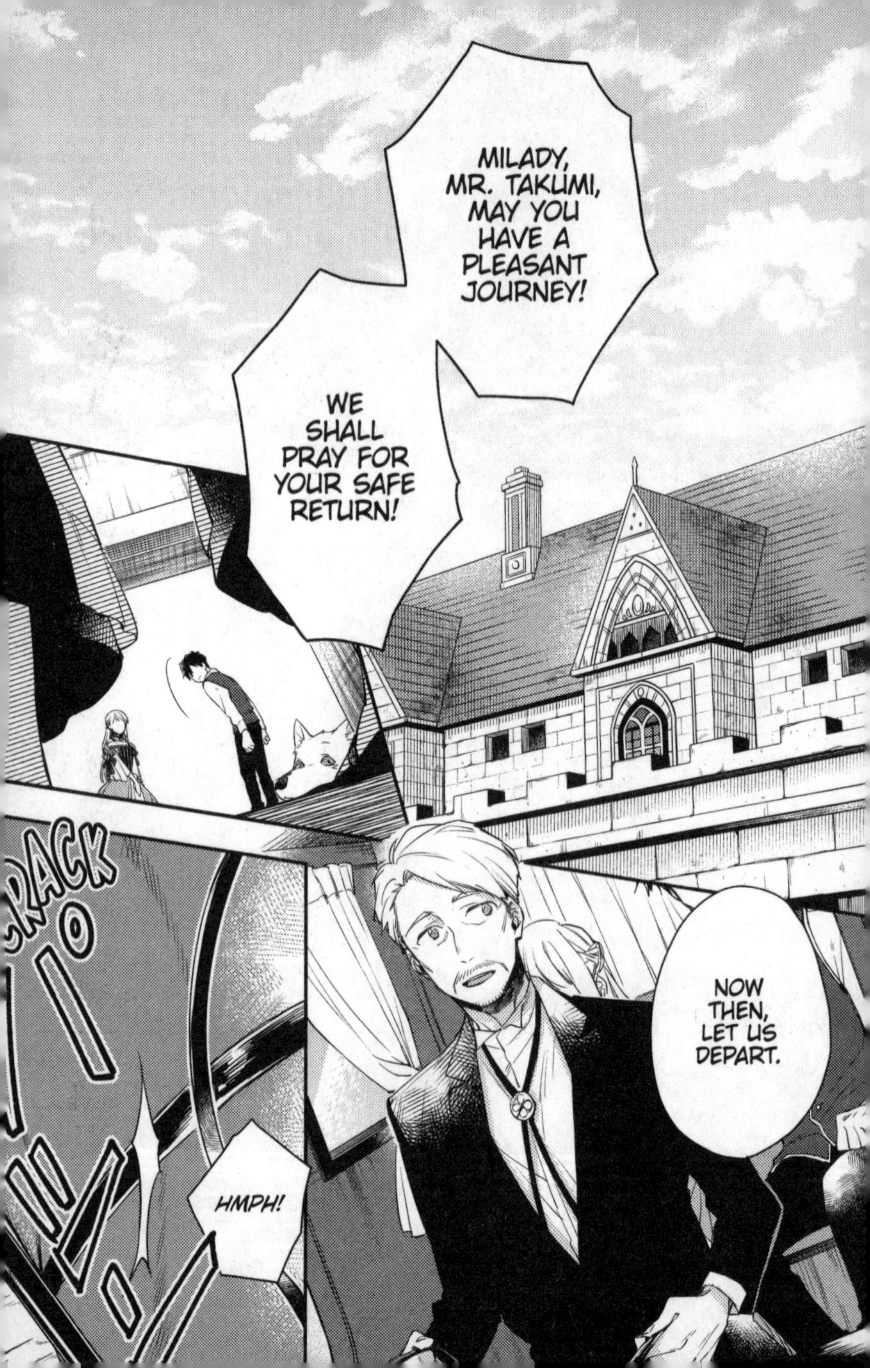
MILADY, MR. TAKUMI, MAY YOU HAVE A PLEASANT JOURNEY!
WE SHALL PRAY FOR YOUR SAFE RETURN!
NOW THEN, LET US DEPART.
HMPH!
CRACK

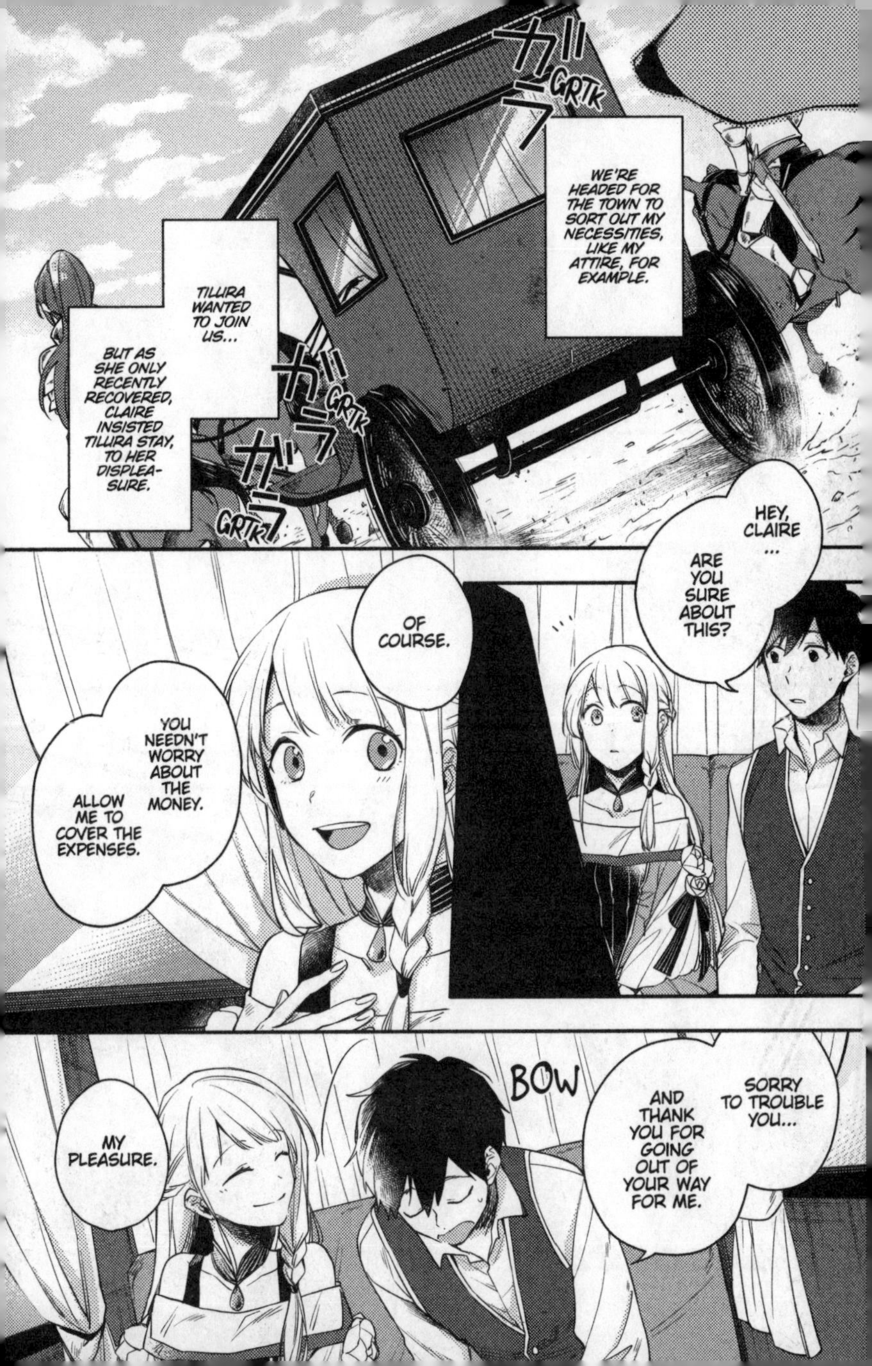

GRTK
WE'RE HEADED FOR THE TOWN TO SORT OUT MY NECESSITIES, LIKE MY ATTIRE, FOR EXAMPLE.
GRTK
GRTK
TILURA WANTED TO JOIN US...
BUT AS SHE ONLY RECENTLY RECOVERED, CLAIRE INSISTED TILURA STAY, TO HER DISPLEASURE.
HEY, CLAIRE ...
ARE YOU SURE ABOUT THIS?
...
OF COURSE.
YOU NEEDN'T WORRY ABOUT THE MONEY.
ALLOW ME TO COVER THE EXPENSES.
SORRY TO TROUBLE YOU...
AND THANK YOU FOR GOING OUT OF YOUR WAY FOR ME.
BOW
MY PLEASURE.

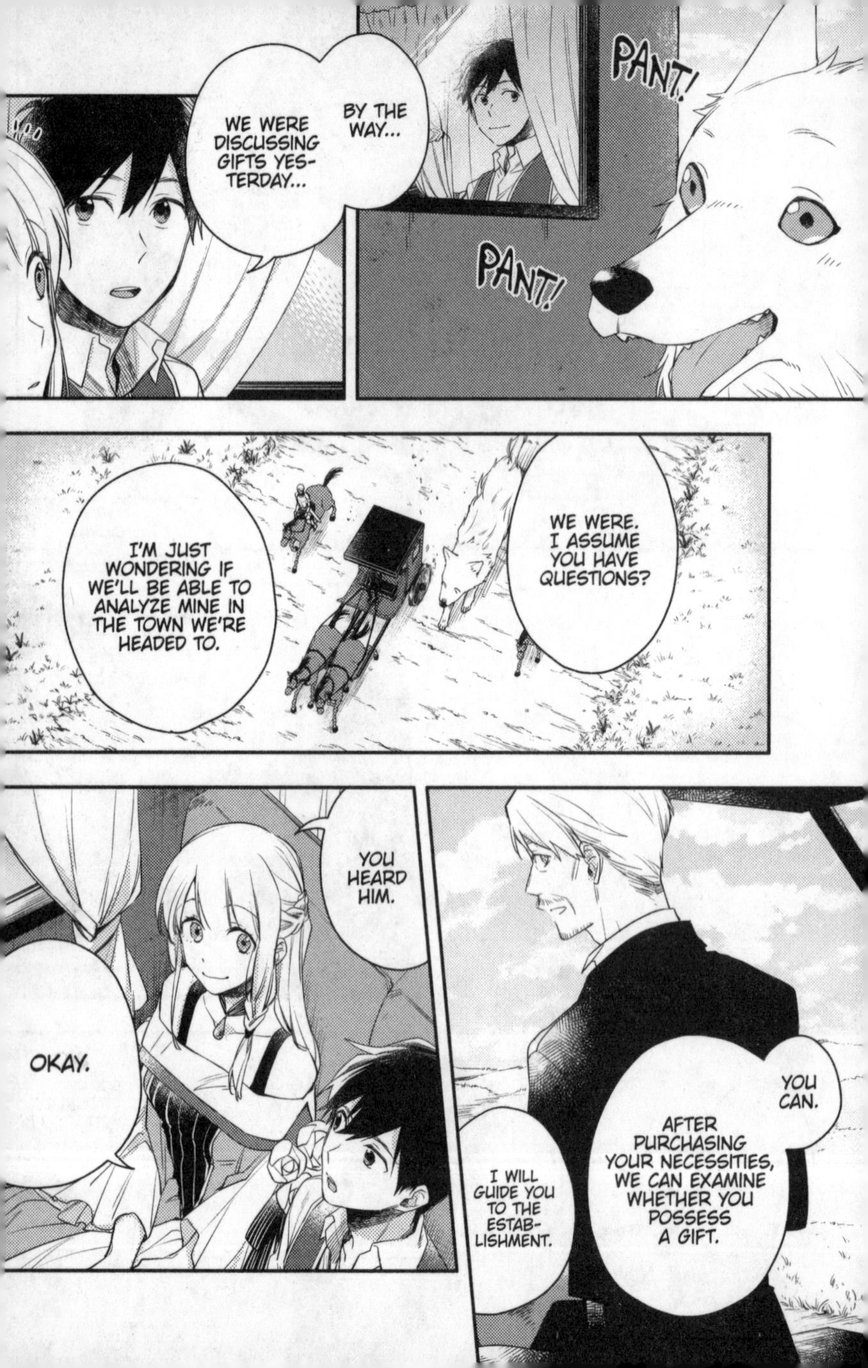
PANT!
PANT!
BY THE WAY...
WE WERE DISCUSSING GIFTS YESTERDAY...
WE WERE. I ASSUME YOU HAVE QUESTIONS?
I'M JUST WONDERING IF WE'LL BE ABLE TO ANALYZE MINE IN THE TOWN WE'RE HEADED TO.
YOU CAN.
AFTER PURCHASING YOUR NECESSITIES, WE CAN EXAMINE WHETHER YOU POSSESS A GIFT.
I WILL GUIDE YOU TO THE ESTAB-LISHMENT.
YOU HEARD HIM.
OKAY.

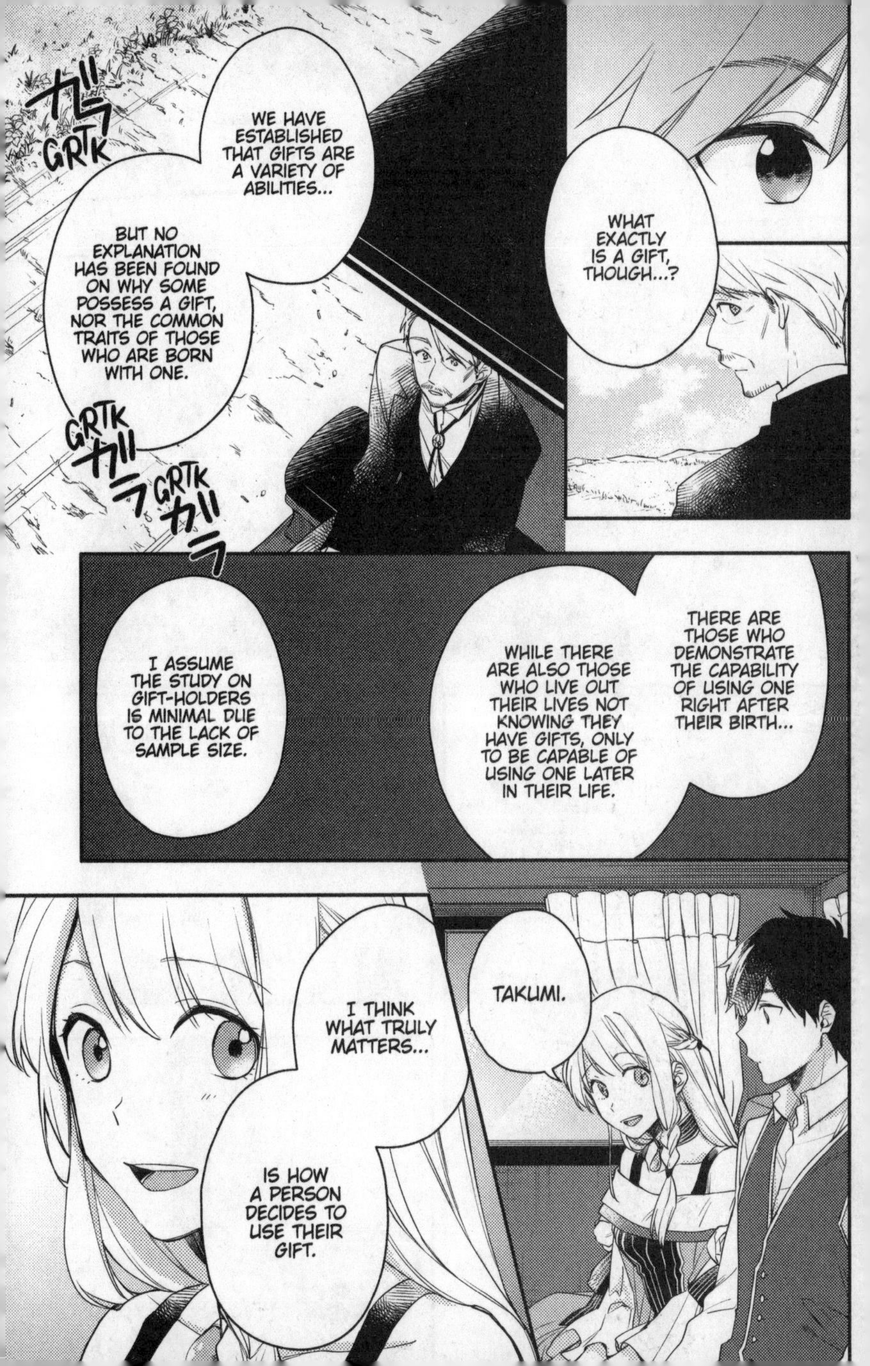
WHAT EXACTLY IS A GIFT, THOUGH...?
ガラ GRTK
WE HAVE ESTABLISHED THAT GIFTS ARE A VARIETY OF ABILITIES...
BUT NO EXPLANATION HAS BEEN FOUND ON WHY SOME POSSESS A GIFT, NOR THE COMMON TRAITS OF THOSE WHO ARE BORN WITH ONE.
GRTK ガラ
GRTK ガラ
THERE ARE THOSE WHO DEMONSTRATE THE CAPABILITY OF USING ONE RIGHT AFTER THEIR BIRTH...
WHILE THERE ARE ALSO THOSE WHO LIVE OUT THEIR LIVES NOT KNOWING THEY HAVE GIFTS, ONLY TO BE CAPABLE OF USING ONE LATER IN THEIR LIFE.
I ASSUME THE STUDY ON GIFT-HOLDERS IS MINIMAL DUE TO THE LACK OF SAMPLE SIZE.
TAKUMI.
I THINK WHAT TRULY MATTERS...
IS HOW A PERSON DECIDES TO USE THEIR GIFT.

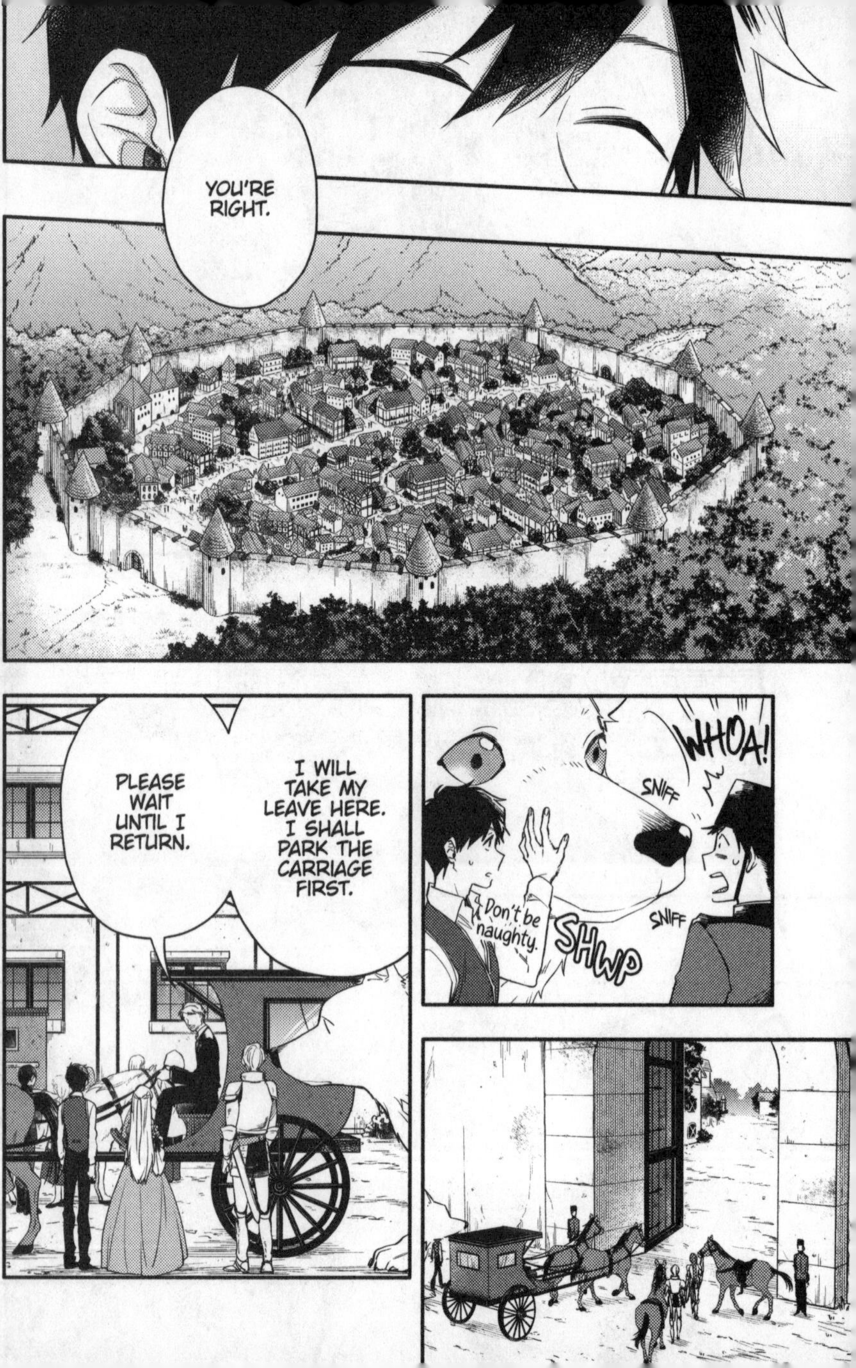
YOU'RE RIGHT.
WHOA!
SNIFF
SNIFF
SHWP
Don't be naughty.
I WILL TAKE MY LEAVE HERE. I SHALL PARK THE CARRIAGE FIRST.
PLEASE WAIT UNTIL I RETURN.

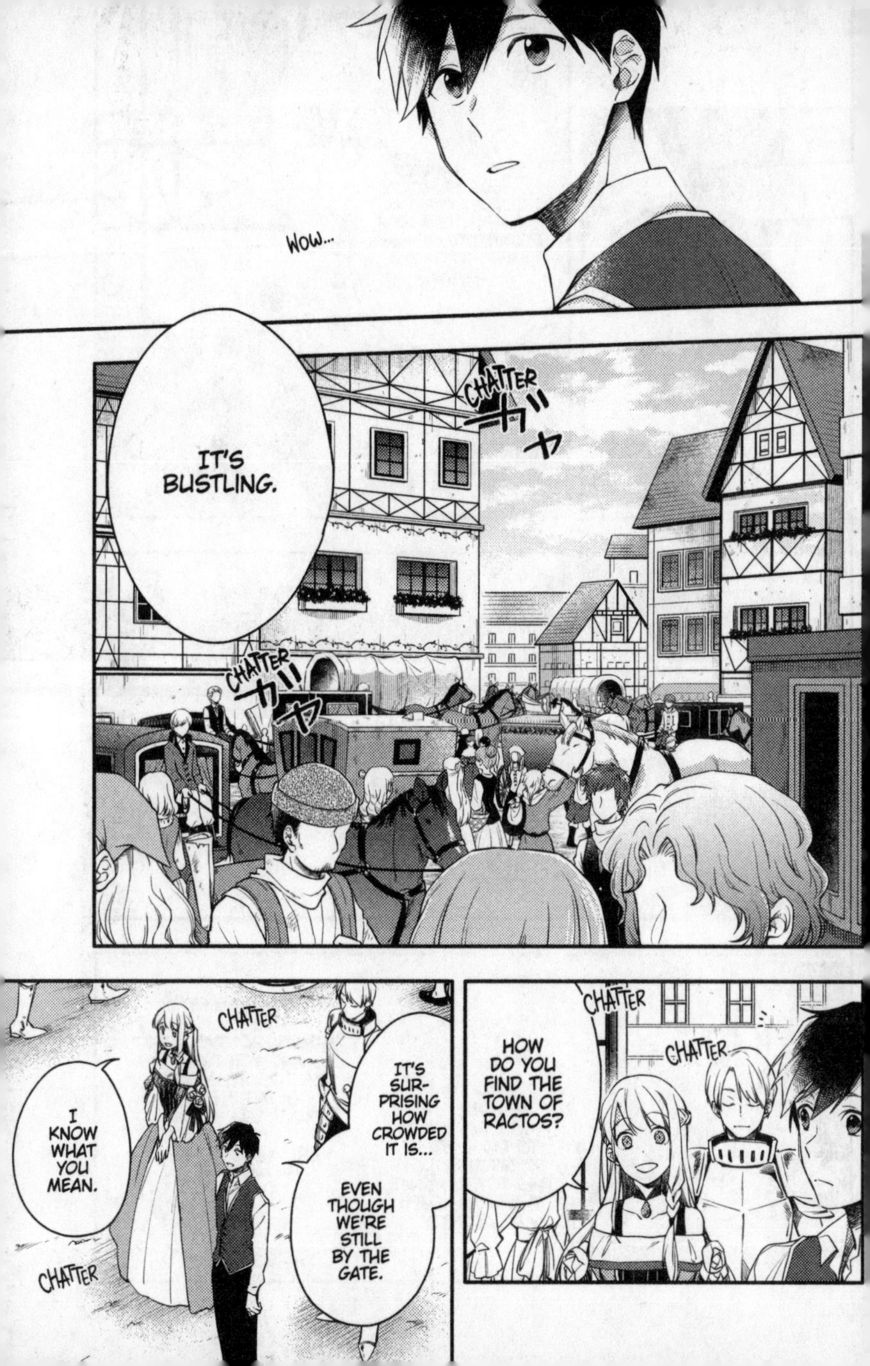
WOW...
CHATTER
ガヤ
IT'S BUSTLING.
CHATTER
ガヤ
CHATTER
CHATTER
HOW DO YOU FIND THE TOWN OF RACTOS?
IT'S SURPRISING HOW CROWDED IT IS...
EVEN THOUGH WE'RE STILL BY THE GATE.
CHATTER
I KNOW WHAT YOU MEAN.
CHATTER

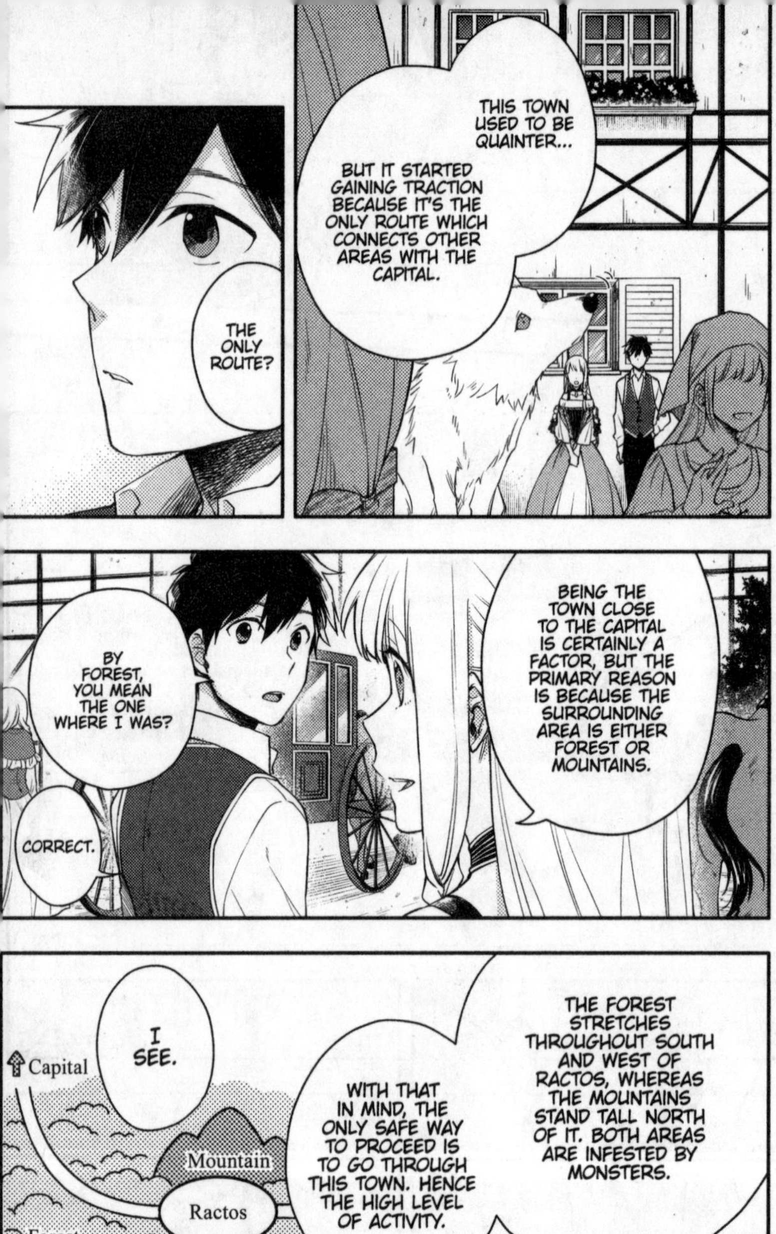
THIS TOWN USED TO BE QUAINTER...
BUT IT STARTED GAINING TRACTION BECAUSE IT'S THE ONLY ROUTE WHICH CONNECTS OTHER AREAS WITH THE CAPITAL.
THE ONLY ROUTE?
BEING THE TOWN CLOSE TO THE CAPITAL IS CERTAINLY A FACTOR, BUT THE PRIMARY REASON IS BECAUSE THE SURROUNDING AREA IS EITHER FOREST OR MOUNTAINS.
BY FOREST, YOU MEAN THE ONE WHERE I WAS?
CORRECT.
THE FOREST STRETCHES THROUGHOUT SOUTH AND WEST OF RACTOS, WHEREAS THE MOUNTAINS STAND TALL NORTH OF IT. BOTH AREAS ARE INFESTED BY MONSTERS.
WITH THAT IN MIND, THE ONLY SAFE WAY TO PROCEED IS TO GO THROUGH THIS TOWN. HENCE THE HIGH LEVEL OF ACTIVITY.
I SEE.
Capital
Mountain
Ractos
Forest

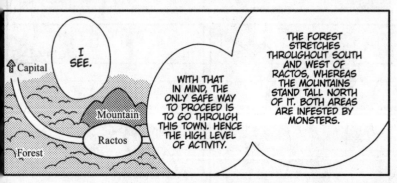

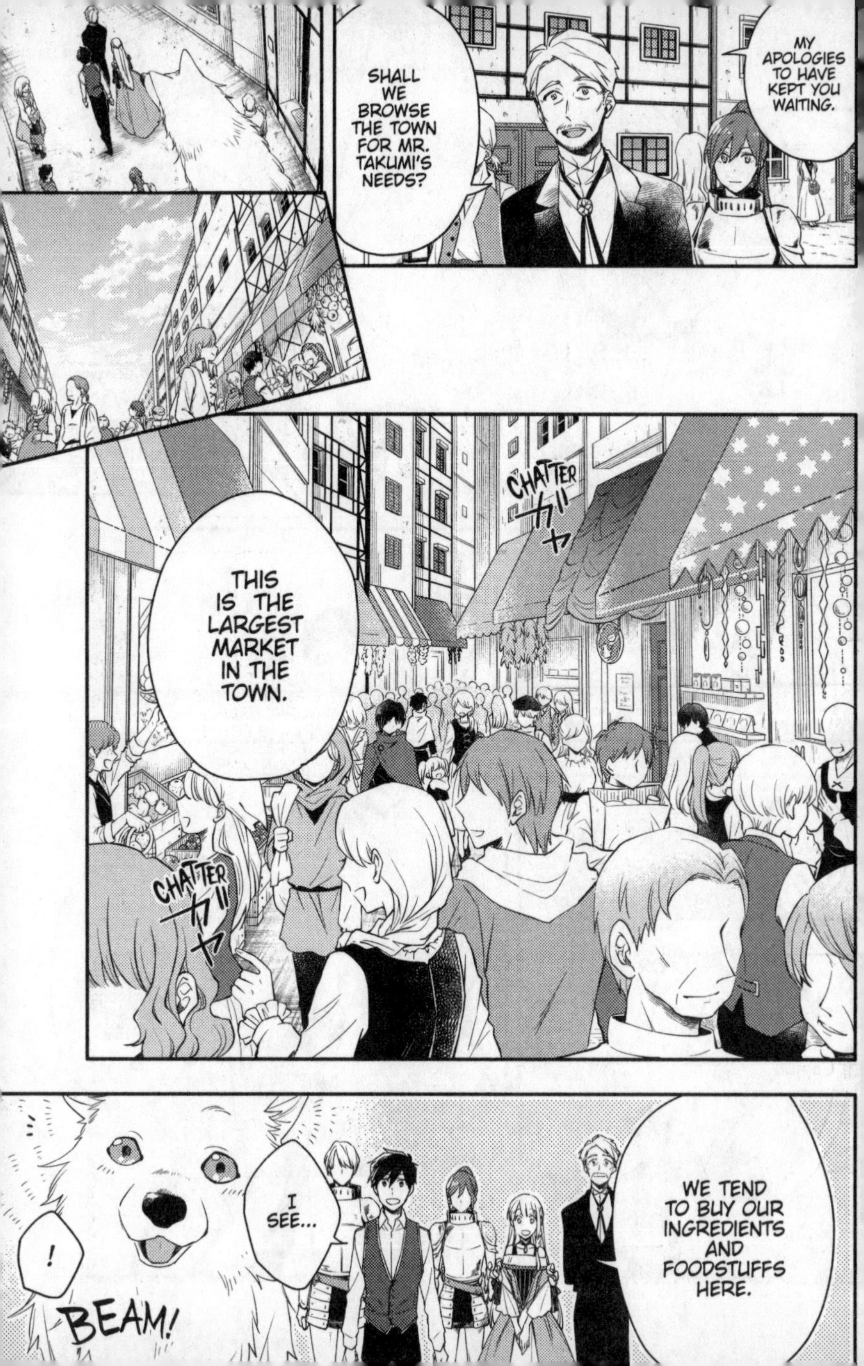

MY APOLOGIES TO HAVE KEPT YOU WAITING.
SHALL WE BROWSE THE TOWN FOR MR. TAKUMI'S NEEDS?
CHATTER ガヤ
THIS IS THE LARGEST MARKET IN THE TOWN.
CHATTER ガヤ
WE TEND TO BUY OUR INGREDIENTS AND FOODSTUFFS HERE.
I SEE...
!
BEAM!

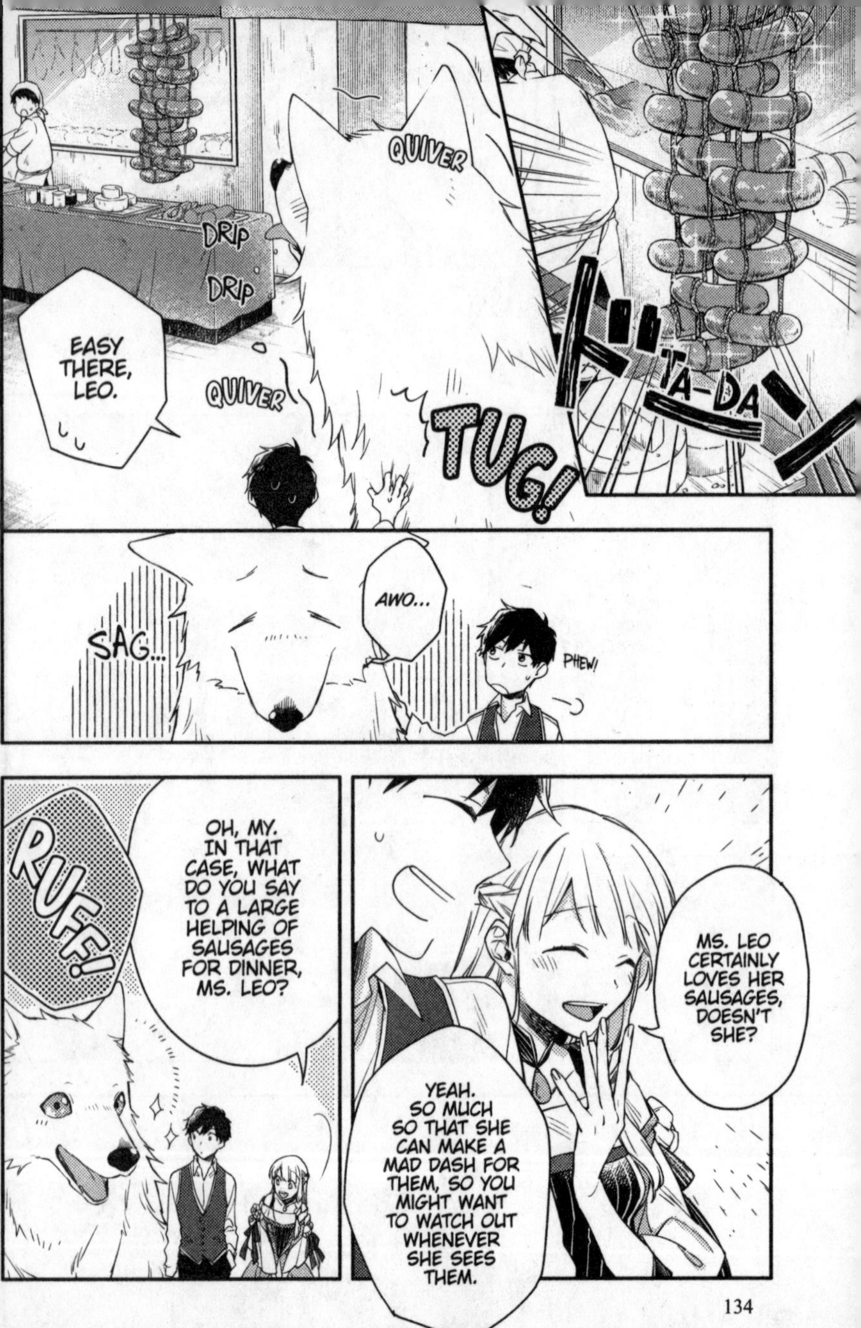
TA-DA
QUIVER
DRIP
DRIP
EASY THERE, LEO.
QUIVER
TUG!
PHEW!
AWO...
SAG...
MS. LEO CERTAINLY LOVES HER SAUSAGES, DOESN'T SHE?
YEAH. SO MUCH SO THAT SHE CAN MAKE A MAD DASH FOR THEM, SO YOU MIGHT WANT TO WATCH OUT WHENEVER SHE SEES THEM.
OH, MY. IN THAT CASE, WHAT DO YOU SAY TO A LARGE HELPING OF SAUSAGES FOR DINNER, MS. LEO?
RUFF!

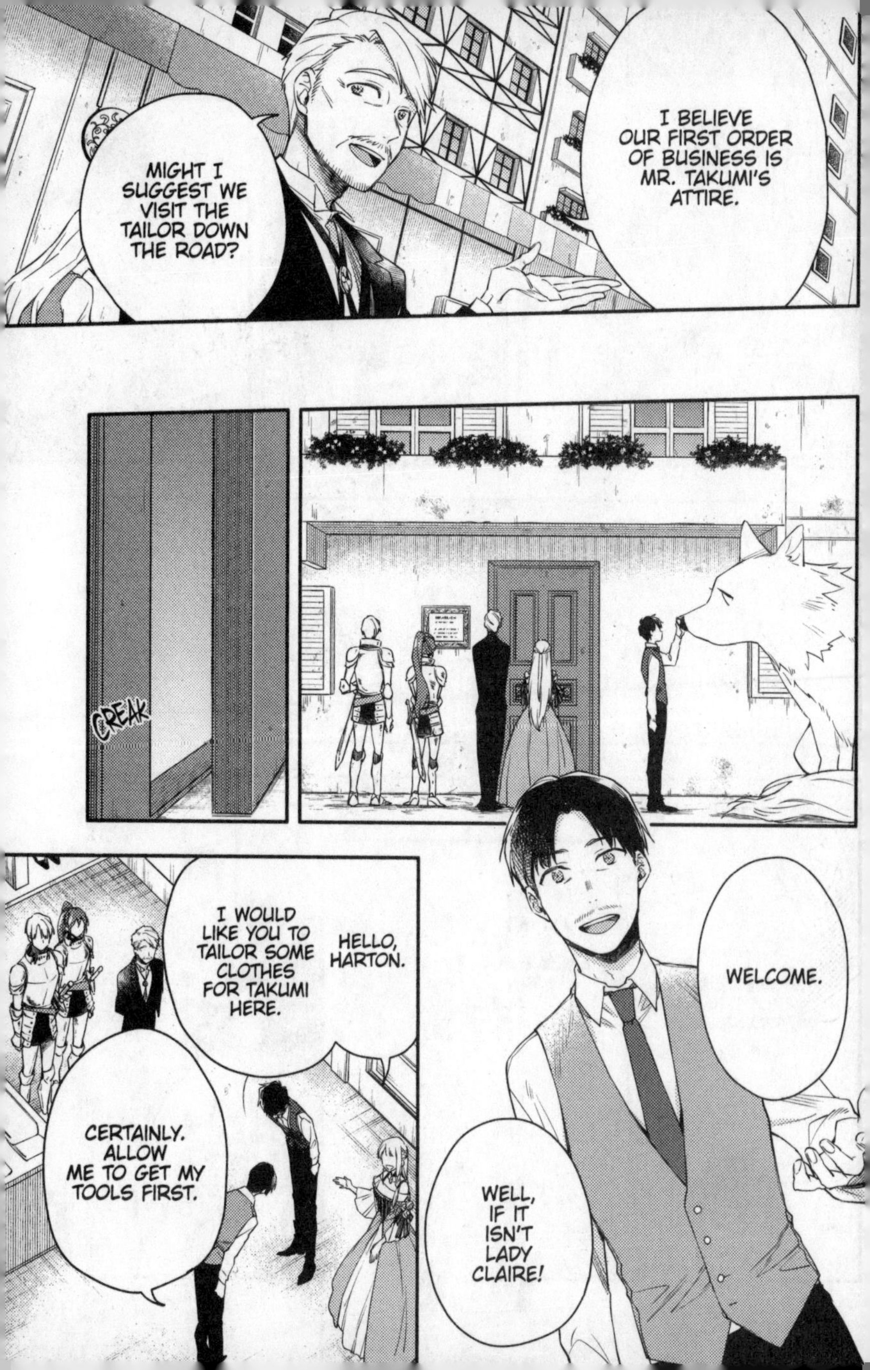
I BELIEVE OUR FIRST ORDER OF BUSINESS IS MR. TAKUMI'S ATTIRE.
MIGHT I SUGGEST WE VISIT THE TAILOR DOWN THE ROAD?
CREAK
WELCOME.
WELL, IF IT ISN'T LADY CLAIRE!
HELLO, HARTON.
I WOULD LIKE YOU TO TAILOR SOME CLOTHES FOR TAKUMI HERE.
CERTAINLY. ALLOW ME TO GET MY TOOLS FIRST.

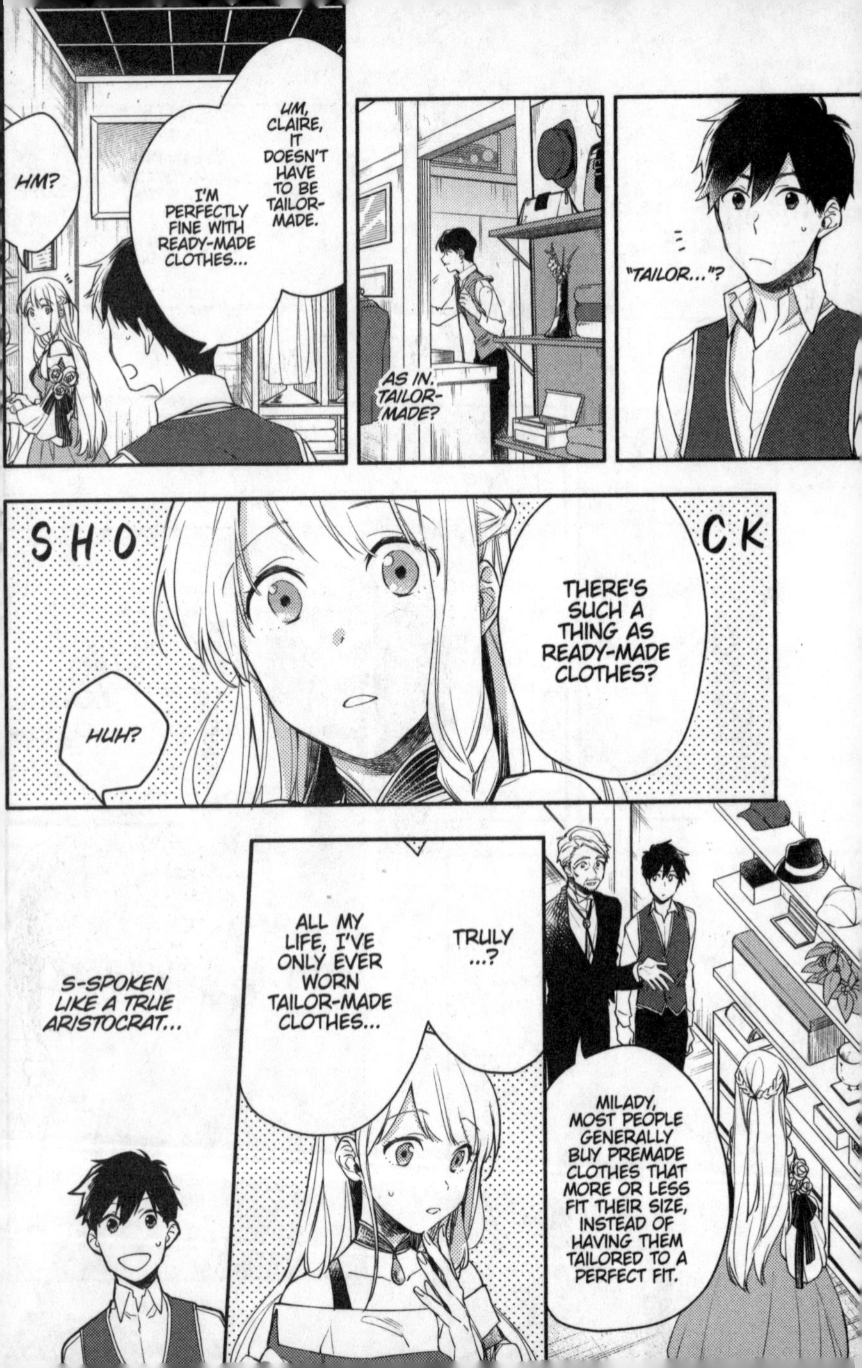
"TAILOR..."?
AS IN. TAILOR-MADE?
UM, CLAIRE, IT DOESN'T HAVE TO BE TAILOR-MADE.
I'M PERFECTLY FINE WITH READY-MADE CLOTHES...
HM?
SHOCK
THERE'S SUCH A THING AS READY-MADE CLOTHES?
HUH?
MILADY, MOST PEOPLE GENERALLY BUY PREMADE CLOTHES THAT MORE OR LESS FIT THEIR SIZE, INSTEAD OF HAVING THEM TAILORED TO A PERFECT FIT.
TRULY ...?
ALL MY LIFE, I'VE ONLY EVER WORN TAILOR-MADE CLOTHES...
S-SPOKEN LIKE A TRUE ARISTOCRAT...

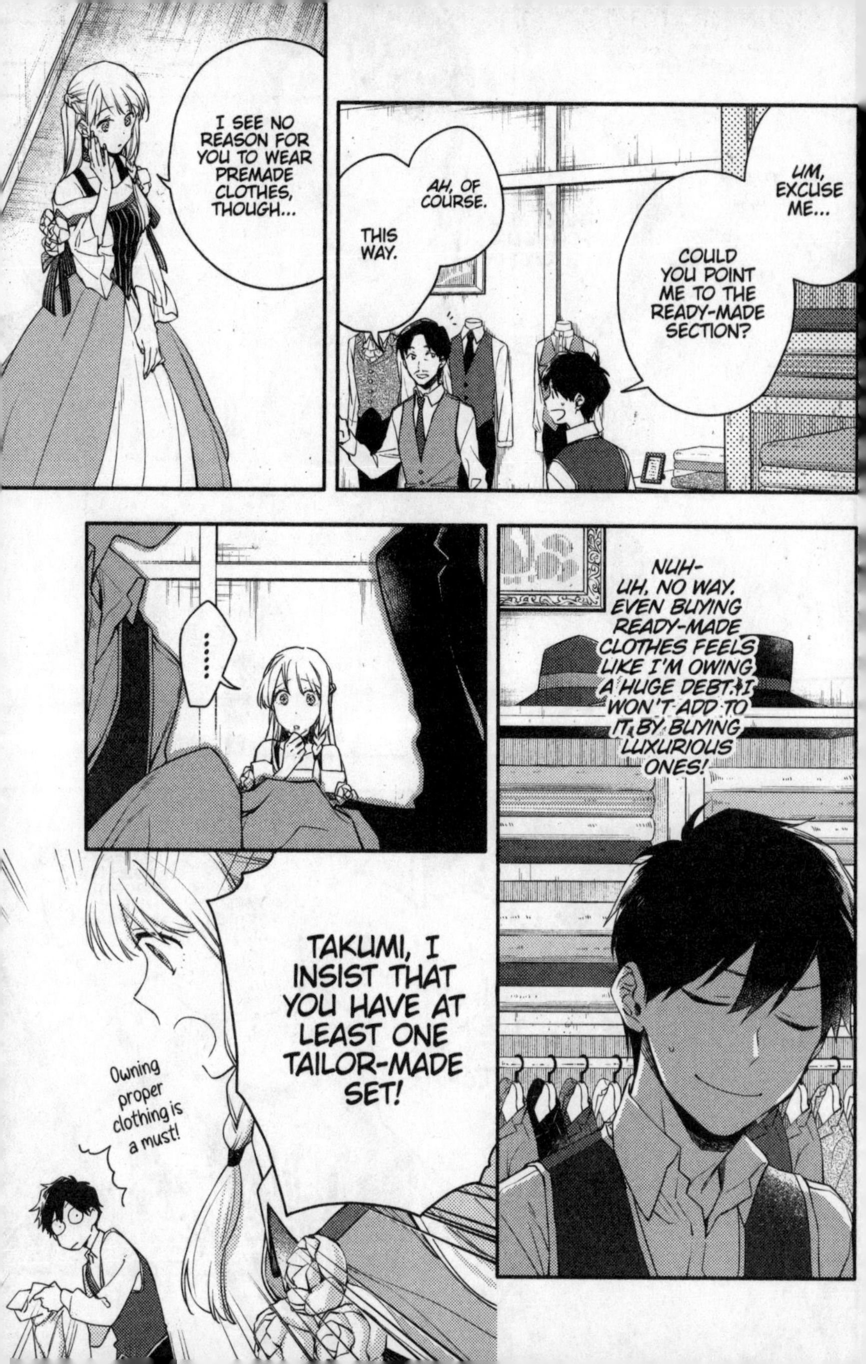
UM, EXCUSE ME...
COULD YOU POINT ME TO THE READY-MADE SECTION?
AH, OF COURSE.
THIS WAY.
I SEE NO REASON FOR YOU TO WEAR PREMADE CLOTHES, THOUGH...
NUH-UH. NO WAY. EVEN BUYING READY-MADE CLOTHES FEELS LIKE I'M OWING A HUGE DEBT. I WON'T ADD TO IT BY BUYING LUXURIOUS ONES!
......
TAKUMI, I INSIST THAT YOU HAVE AT LEAST ONE TAILOR-MADE SET!
Owning proper clothing is a must!

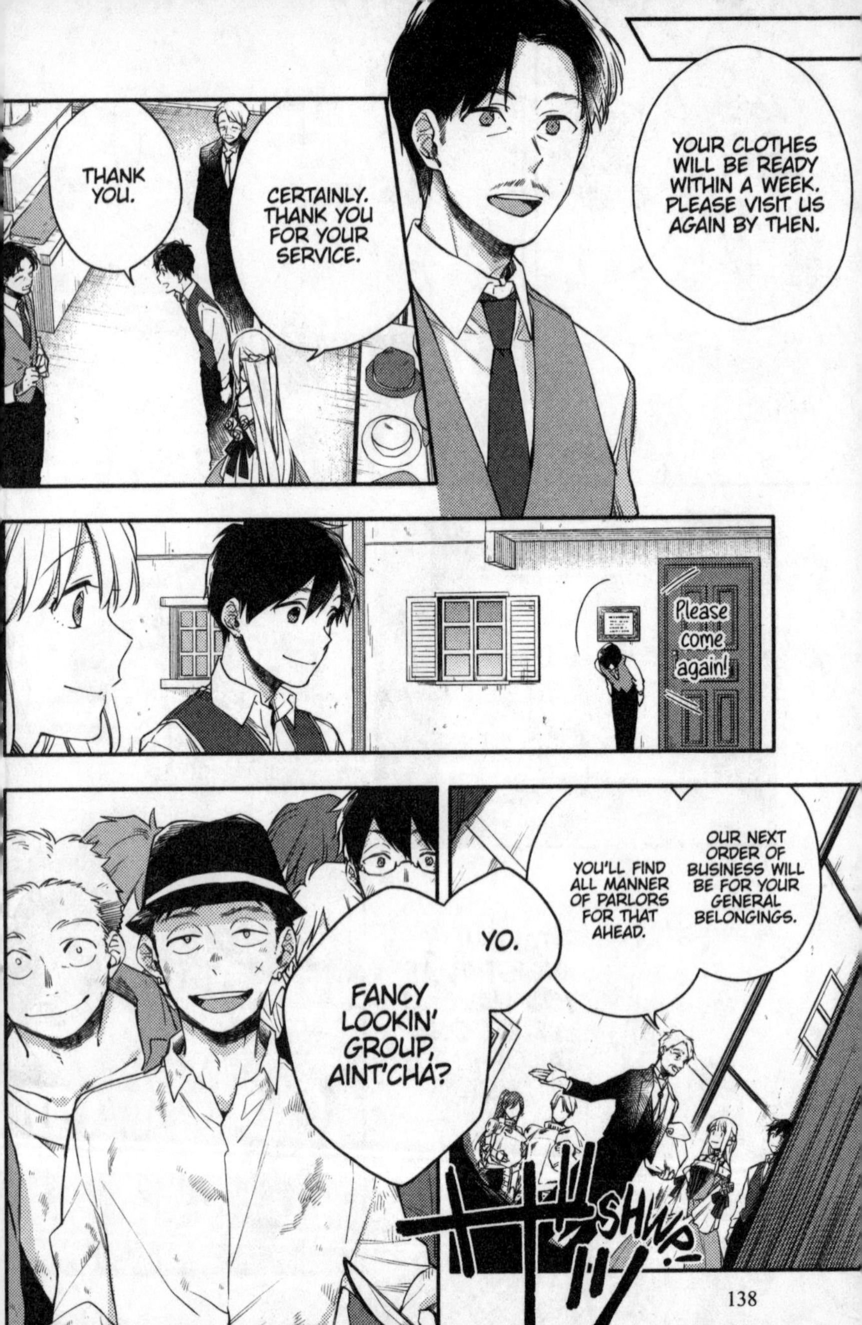
YOUR CLOTHES WILL BE READY WITHIN A WEEK. PLEASE VISIT US AGAIN BY THEN.
CERTAINLY. THANK YOU FOR YOUR SERVICE.
THANK YOU.
Please come again!
OUR NEXT ORDER OF BUSINESS WILL BE FOR YOUR GENERAL BELONGINGS.
YOU'LL FIND ALL MANNER OF PARLORS FOR THAT AHEAD.
SHWP!
YO.
FANCY LOOKIN' GROUP, AINT'CHA?

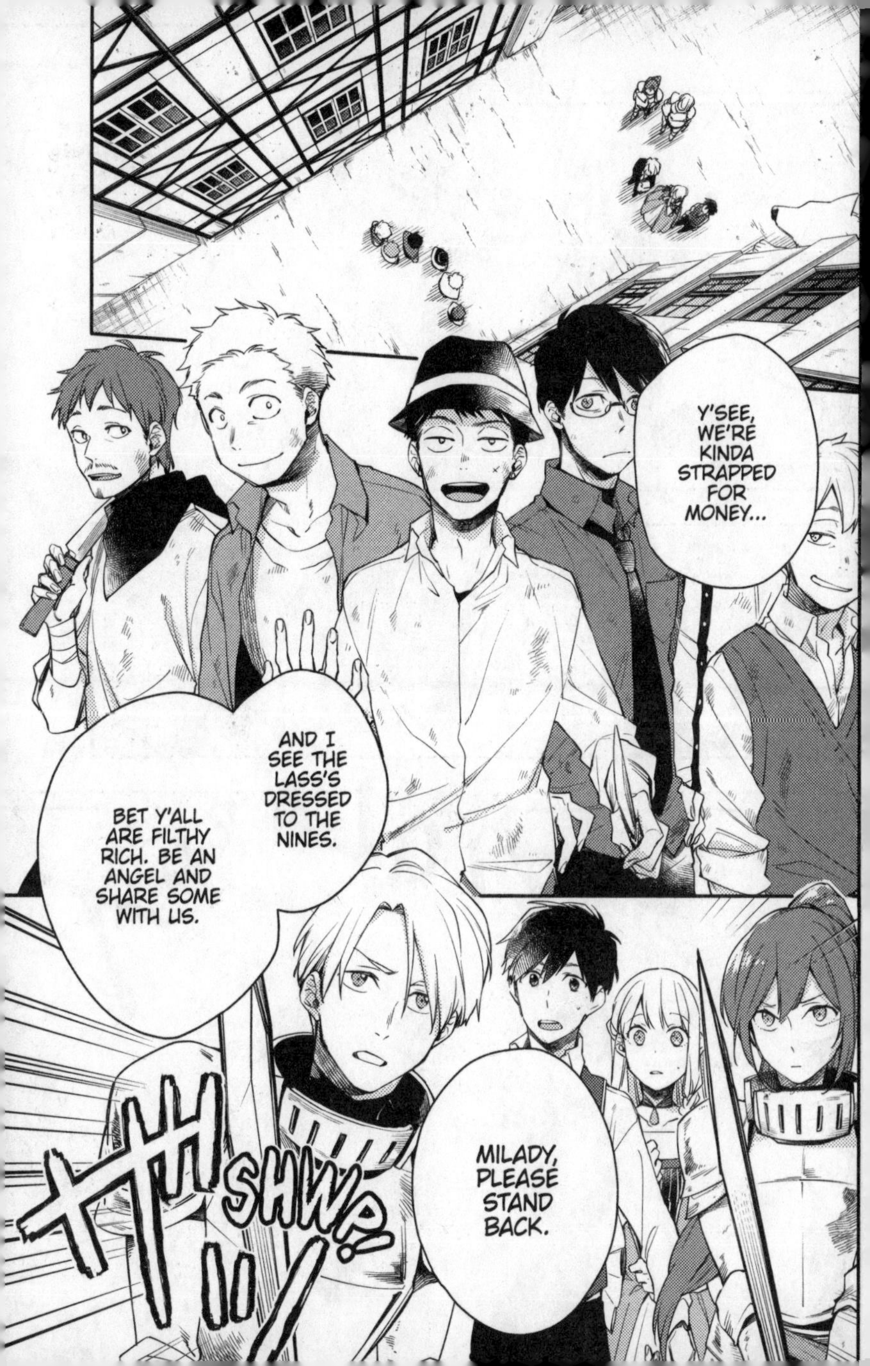

Y'SEE, WE'RE KINDA STRAPPED FOR MONEY...
AND I SEE THE LASS'S DRESSED TO THE NINES.
BET Y'ALL ARE FILTHY RICH. BE AN ANGEL AND SHARE SOME WITH US.
MILADY, PLEASE STAND BACK.
SHWP!

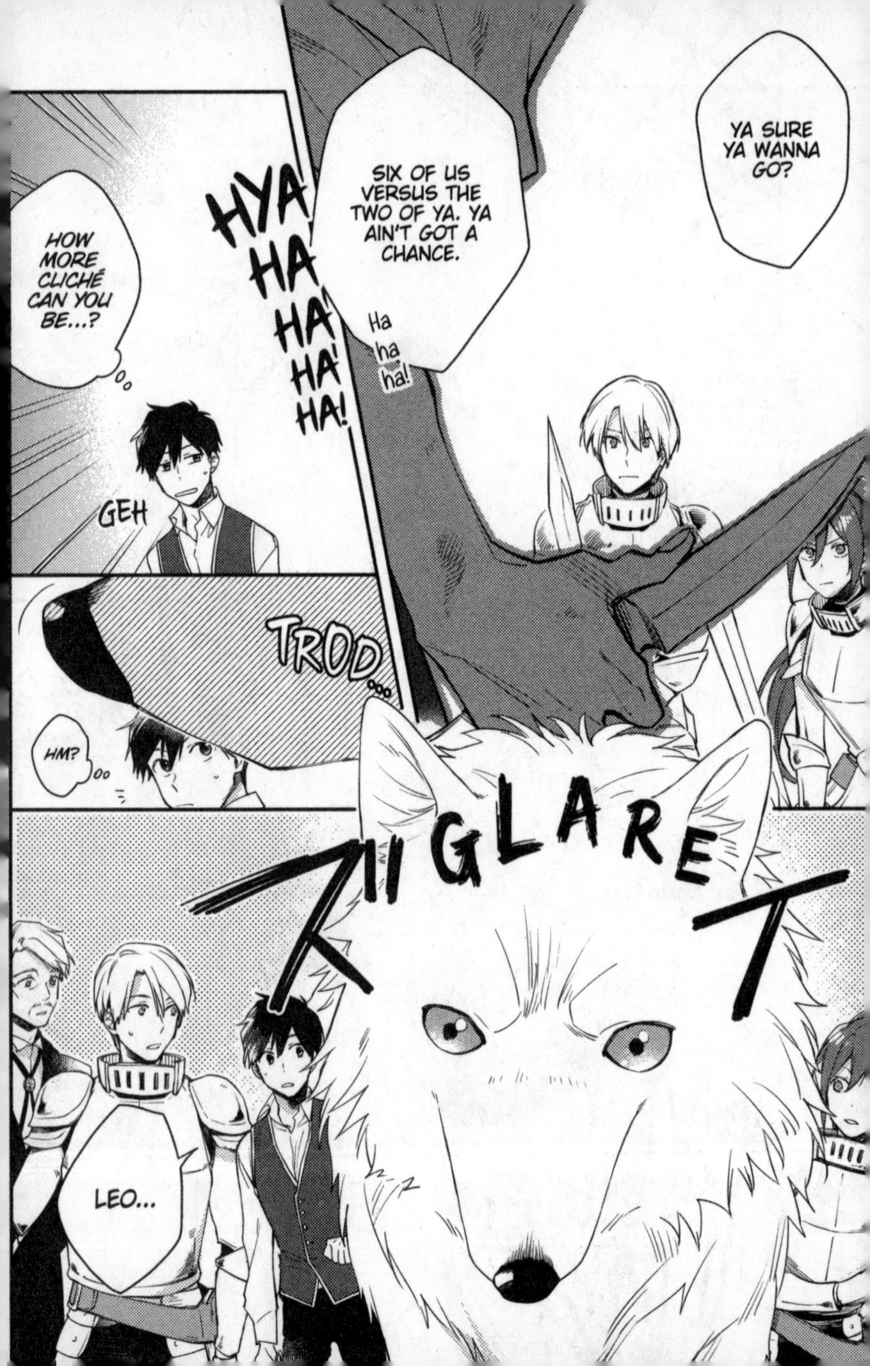
YA SURE YA WANNA GO?
SIX OF US VERSUS THE TWO OF YA. YA AIN'T GOT A CHANCE.
Ha ha ha!
HYA HA HA HA HA!
HOW MORE CLICHÉ CAN YOU BE...?
GEH
TROD...
HM?
GLARE
LEO...

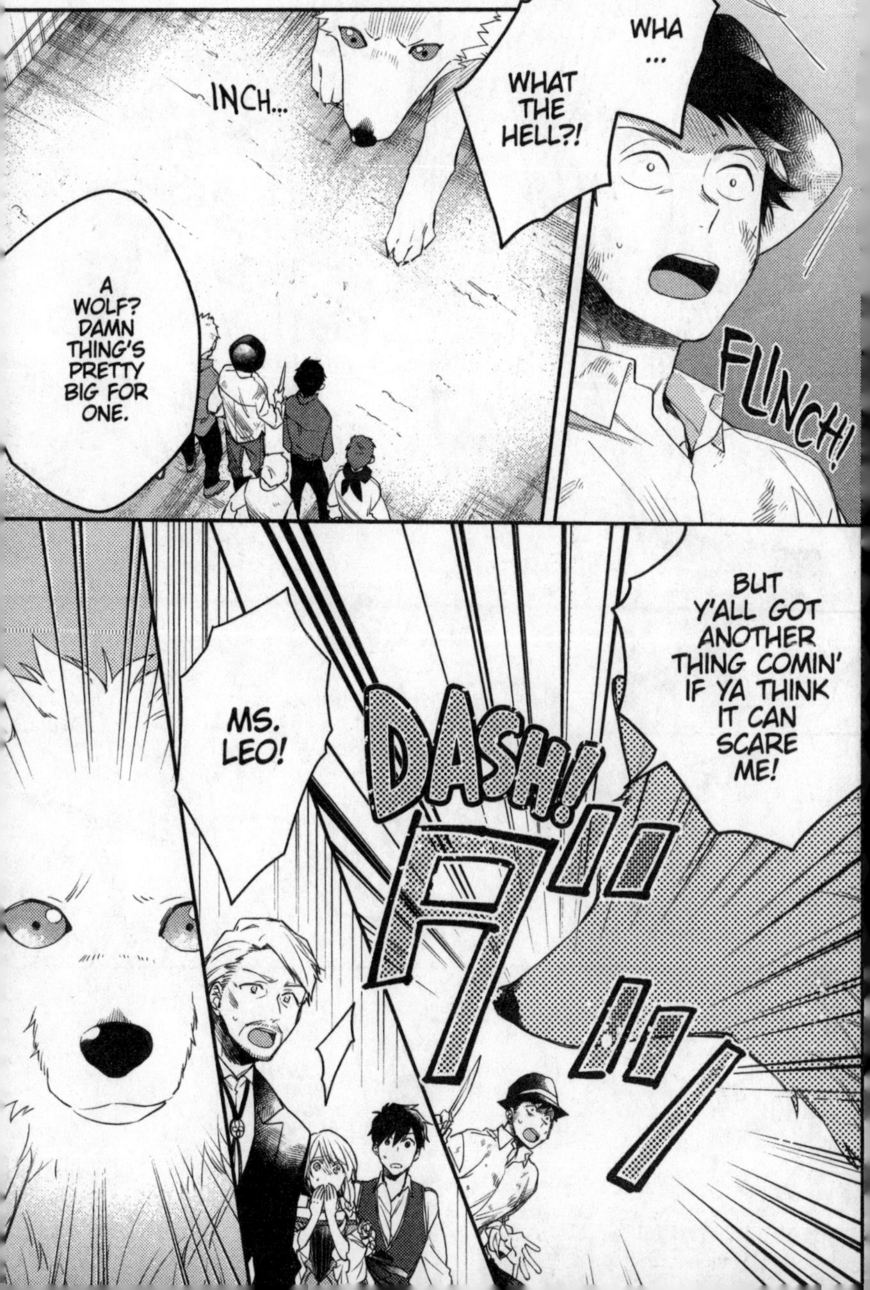
WHA ...
WHAT THE HELL?!
FLINCH!
INCH...
A WOLF? DAMN THING'S PRETTY BIG FOR ONE.
BUT Y'ALL GOT ANOTHER THING COMIN' IF YA THINK IT CAN SCARE ME!
DASH!
ダッ
MS. LEO!

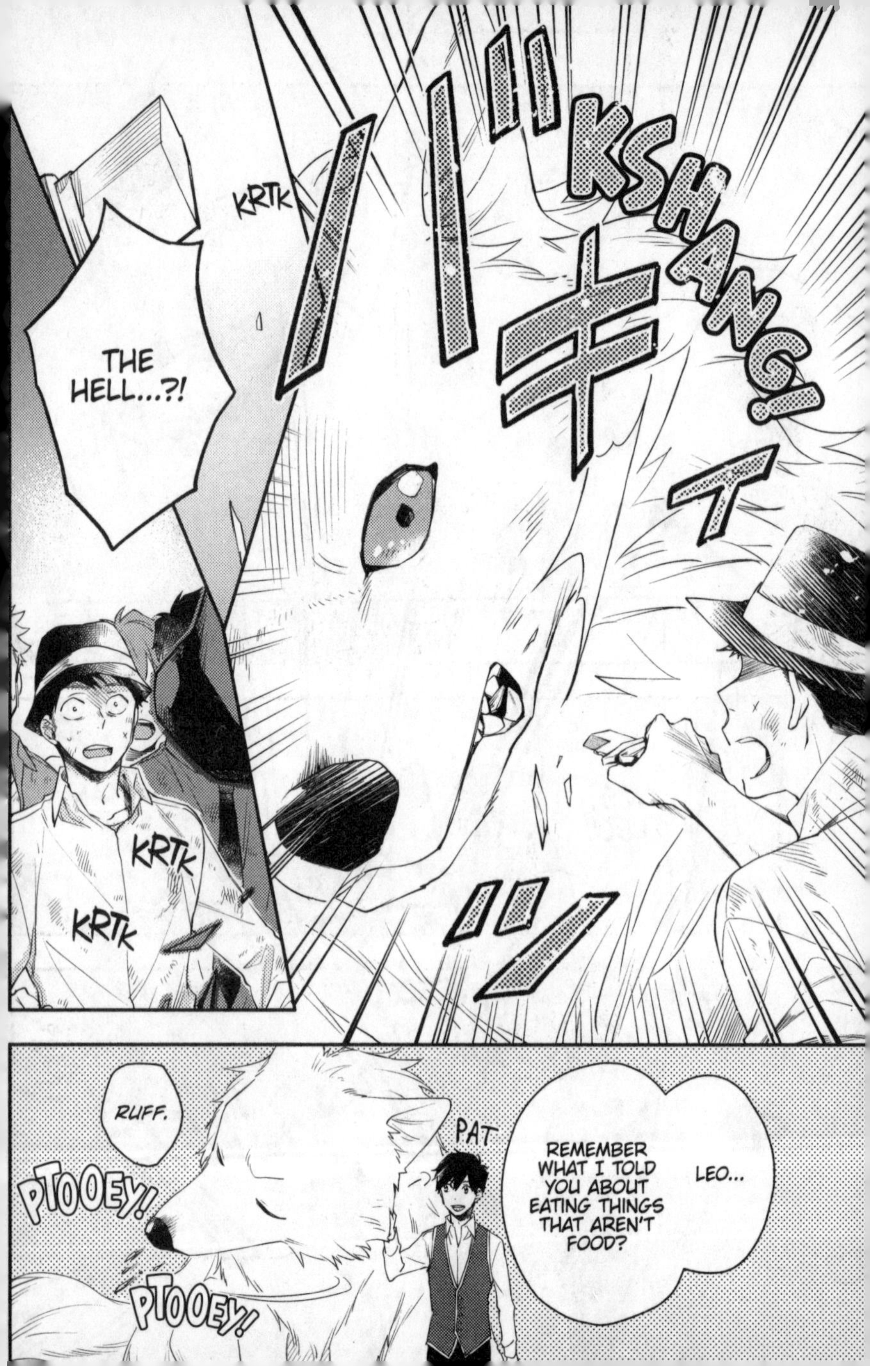
KSHANG!
KRTK
THE HELL...?!
KRTK
KRTK
LEO...
REMEMBER WHAT I TOLD YOU ABOUT EATING THINGS THAT AREN'T FOOD?
PAT
RUFF.
PTOOEY!
PTOOEY!

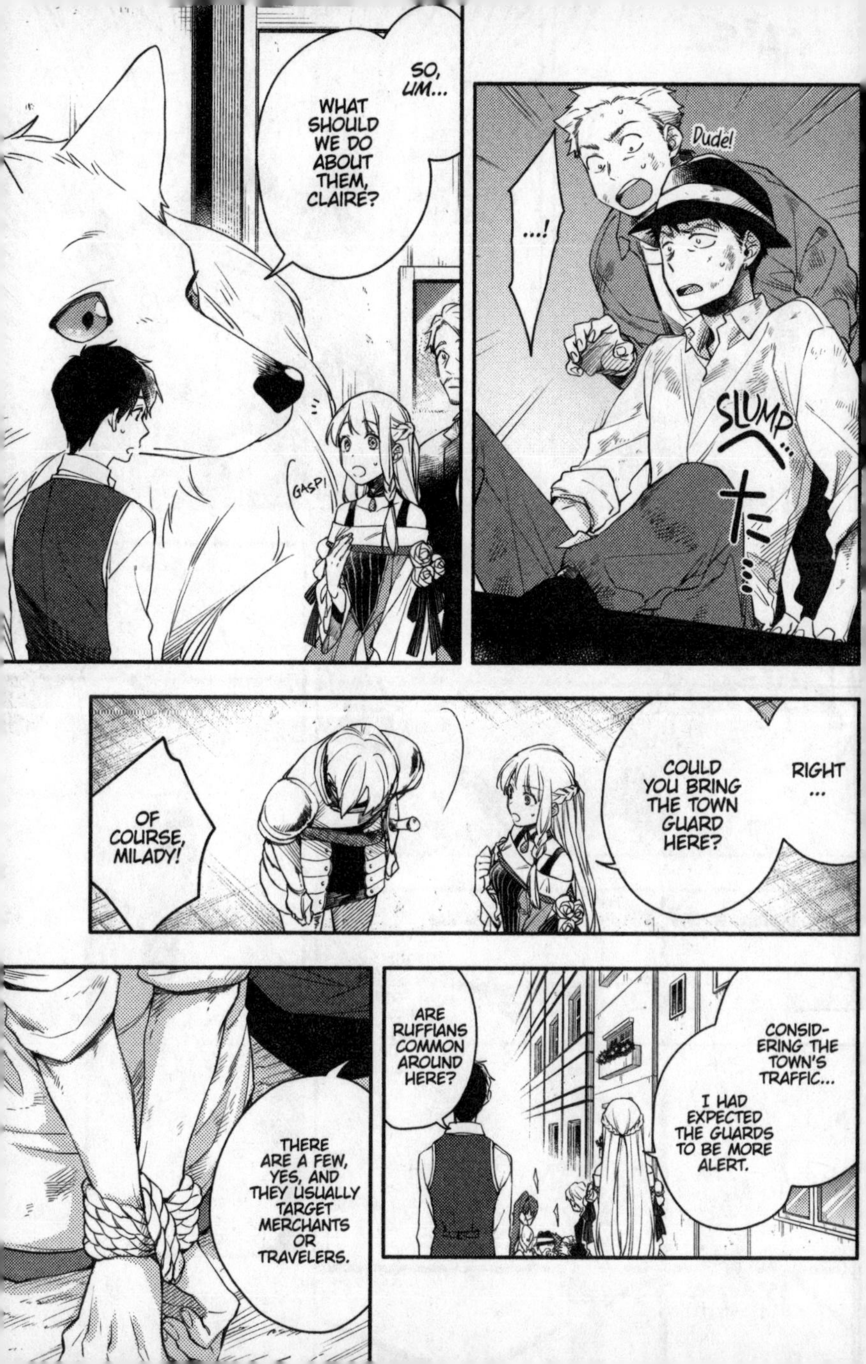
Dude!
...!
SLUMP...
SO, UM... WHAT SHOULD WE DO ABOUT THEM, CLAIRE?
GASP!
RIGHT ...
COULD YOU BRING THE TOWN GUARD HERE?
OF COURSE, MILADY!
CONSID-ERING THE TOWN'S TRAFFIC...
I HAD EXPECTED THE GUARDS TO BE MORE ALERT.
ARE RUFFIANS COMMON AROUND HERE?
THERE ARE A FEW, YES, AND THEY USUALLY TARGET MERCHANTS OR TRAVELERS.

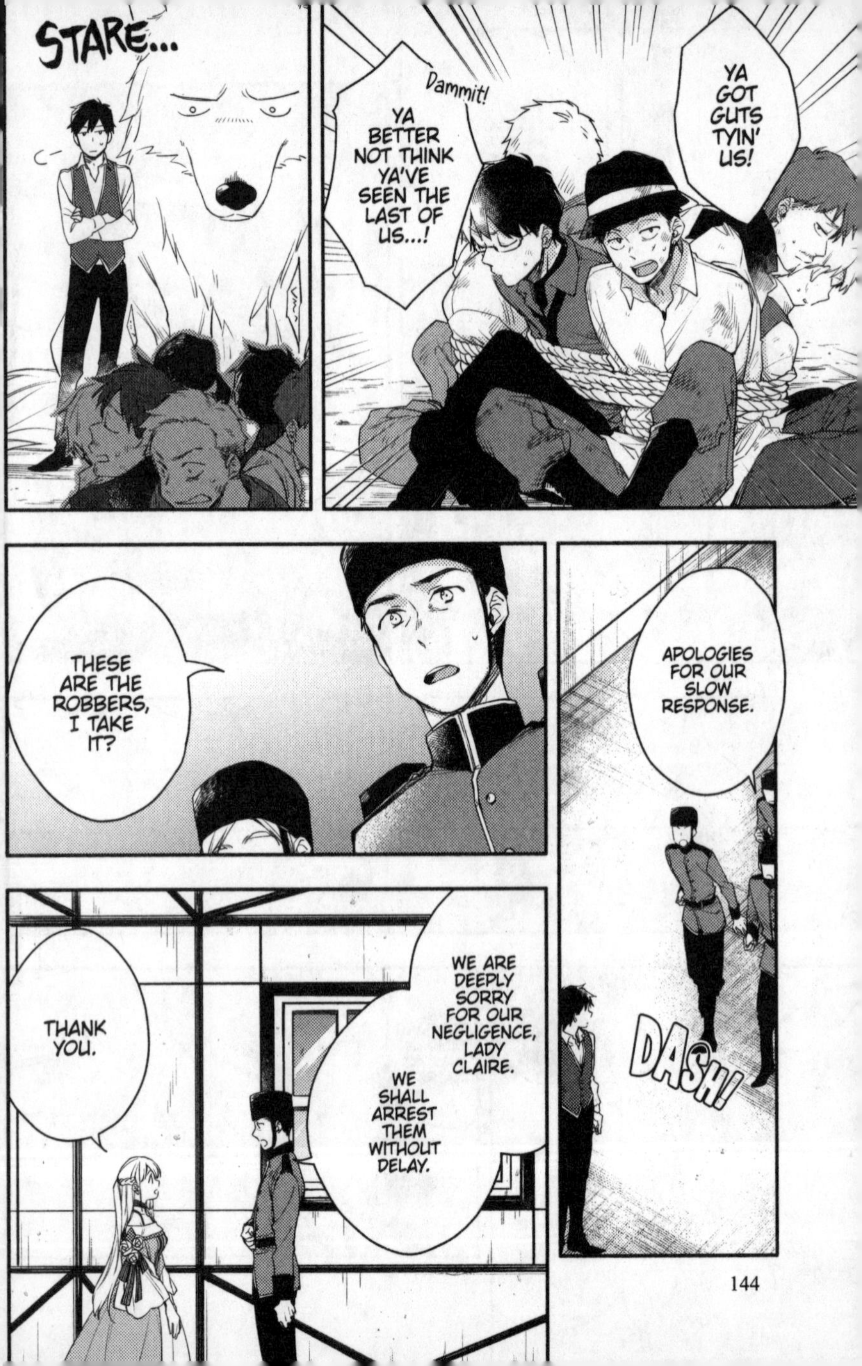
YA GOT GUTS TYIN' US!
Dammit!
YA BETTER NOT THINK YA'VE SEEN THE LAST OF US...!
STARE...
APOLOGIES FOR OUR SLOW RESPONSE.
DASH!
THESE ARE THE ROBBERS, I TAKE IT?
WE ARE DEEPLY SORRY FOR OUR NEGLIGENCE, LADY CLAIRE.
WE SHALL ARREST THEM WITHOUT DELAY.
THANK YOU.

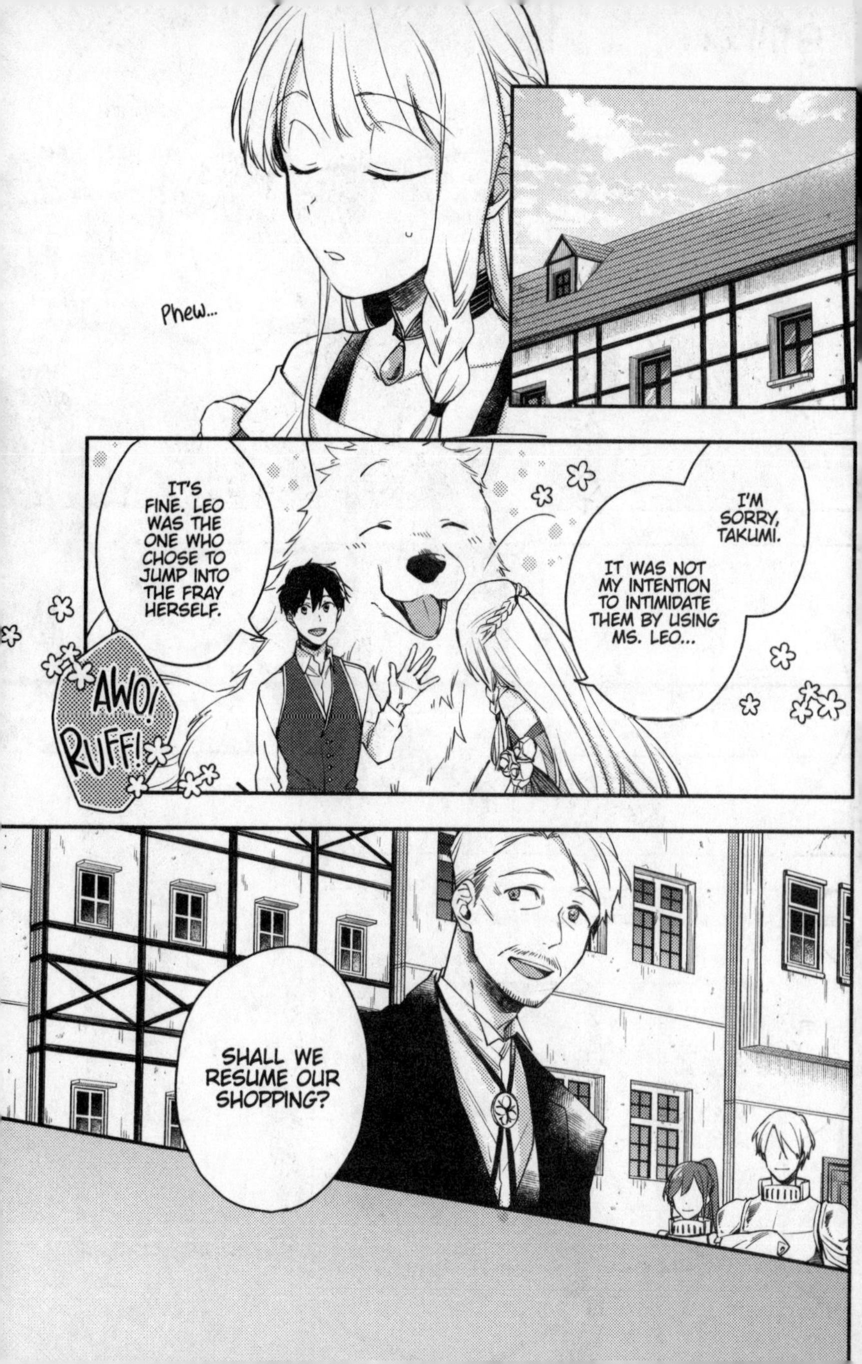
Phew...
I'M SORRY, TAKUMI.
IT WAS NOT MY INTENTION TO INTIMIDATE THEM BY USING MS. LEO...
IT'S FINE. LEO WAS THE ONE WHO CHOSE TO JUMP INTO THE FRAY HERSELF.
AWO! RUFF!
SHALL WE RESUME OUR SHOPPING?

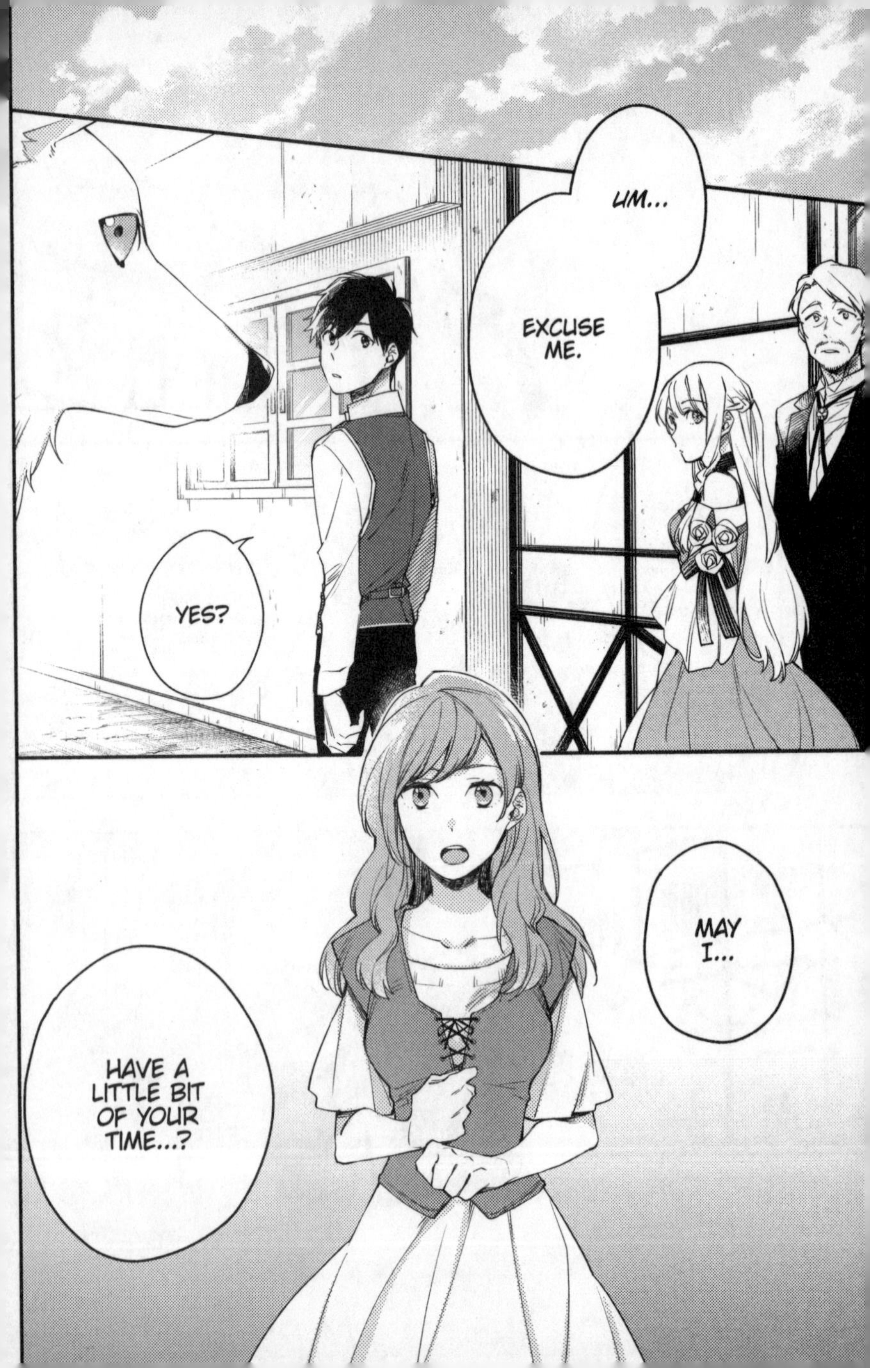
UM... EXCUSE ME.
YES?
MAY I...
HAVE A LITTLE BIT OF YOUR TIME...?

EVEN DOGS GO TO OTHER WORLDS

LIFE IN ANOTHER WORLD WITH MY BELOVED HOUND

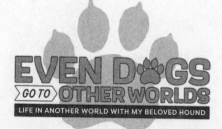

EVEN DOGS GO TO OTHER WORLDS

LIFE IN ANOTHER WORLD WITH MY BELOVED HOUND

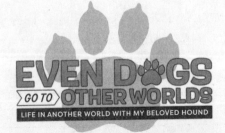

Short Story

The Day I Met My Reliable Partner

Ryuuou

Back when I was in college, I was heading home late from my part-time job.

It was raining cats and dogs. My umbrella did its best to keep me dry for the short walk from the supermarket to my apartment.

It's late. The supermarket should be handing out discounts about now. I hope there's some left. The rain probably kept other customers away, right? I have a lot to get. Please, please let there be something left.

I hurried. Luck was on my side. The store had discount signs plastered all over its windows.

If you didn't have time to cook, you needed those discounts to save money on meals.

I'd be extra lucky if *onigiri* was on sale. They were usually half off—if not more—and I wouldn't have to cook my own rice. I could save on rice and electricity! Not that I'm *that* cheap, but every little bit helps.

As I avoided a puddle and pondered my life as a poor student, I heard something.

whine... whine...

Hm? A noise...or was that a voice?

The loud roar of raindrops pounding against my umbrella couldn't drown out the voice calling to me.

I stopped without even meaning to, taking in the surroundings around me. Yet there was nothing but the sound of rainfall around me.

"Hmmm?"

Tilting my head, I wondered if the voice was just in my mind. Just as I was about to continue my walk to the supermarket...

whine... whine ... whine ...

This time it was loud and clear. I was certain I heard a voice.

"Doesn't sound like a person. Maybe a cat? Feels like an animal crying out...right around...there?"

I didn't know why, but it was almost as if that voice was calling out to me...like I'd be making a big mistake if I were to ignore it.

The voice was coming from behind a fence on the corner.

Well, no wonder I couldn't find it earlier. That corner was in a bit of a blind spot.

"I actually heard something...hang on."

whine... whine...

Closing in on the cry, I found an opened cardboard box with a small animal lying inside it.

When my eyes adjusted to the dim lighting, I found myself staring at a puppy, soaked from the rain.

"Did someone forget their puppy here...or did they just abandon it?"

whine... whine...

Seeing it whine helplessly, I couldn't help myself. I used my umbrella to cover it from the rain. However, my umbrella was little comfort. It was still whimpering expectantly.

It didn't seem like it was looking for its parents. Nobody else was here but me, either.

Perhaps in its weak state, capable of only minimal movement, it could think of nothing but barking in hopes that someone would save it from its predicament.

"What to do... Okay, first things first, dry the puppy off. It's not like I have all the time in the world to think of an elegant solution.

whine... whine...

"Easy, easy. I know I'm a stranger, but I'm not going to hurt you, okay? Whoa, you're pretty cold. Gotta take you back home fast."

If I were to leave the puppy, surely it wouldn't even have the strength to cry out when I returned. It looked *that* weak.

Dropping my umbrella, I picked up the puppy with both of my hands and cradled it. The puppy appeared to be so listless that stirring about seemed like a monumental effort.

So many things were racing through my mind. Who on earth could be so cruel as to leave the puppy there? Was there no one else who had the heart to help it? Were its parents nowhere around? What was the best thing to do for it when I stepped inside my home? But I squashed them all and focused on keeping the puppy safe and alive, first and foremost.

"Huff… huff… Hang in there! Just a little longer!"

whine…

I could barely feel the heat coming off of the puppy's rain-battered body. Its faint cries were the only thing telling me that it was still alive.

Dashing home, I kept talking to the puppy, hoping that it would continue responding to my encouragement instead of closing its eyes in resignation.

"Good, we're here… You're safe now, okay?"

whine…

Arriving on my doorstep, I carried the puppy with my left hand as I procured my keys with the right to unlock the door.

Though I wasn't sure of the best course of action, my instincts were screaming at me, telling me to bring some life back to the puppy. Driven by that feeling, I rushed toward my room.

It came at the expense of making the hallway wet, but I could deal with the cleanup later.

"I'm stumped. Liking cats and dogs is one thing, but nursing one back to health is beyond me."

I'd petted some animals, but I'd never actually kept one. I was at a loss due to my inexperience, fumbling around before I placed the puppy on the floor and searched for a towel or blanket.

The puppy took in the sights of the bright room, tucking its arms and curling down into a small ball. I took notice of its white fur, drenched from the rain we escaped earlier.

whine... whine...

In its feeble state, try as it might, the puppy could barely whimper and breathe. I spontaneously imagined reaching out to hug it after seeing the puppy try its best to cling to life, but that would only weaken it, so I held back that urge.

"Okay, for starters, gotta wipe you dry. Leaving you sopping wet like this will only worsen your condition. Upsy-daisy."

whine... whine...

"Good boy. Stay still for a bit longer, okay?"

I stacked some towels and laid the puppy on top of them. I used a dry towel to blanket the puppy's body and gently wipe it.

The puppy wailed, seemingly in protest of my action. I tried my best to placate it, telling it that I wouldn't take long.

I could feel the puppy squirming, trying to break free from my hold, but it lacked the strength to do so. From the looks of things, it might not even have the strength to stand on its own.

"Yeah, a towel alone won't be able to dry you off completely. A blow dryer's a bit on the loud side, though. Will it be too much for you? Oh, I should raise the room's temp. Hey, little guy, mind if I move you over here?"

whine...

Wiping the puppy wouldn't help much against the water that had seeped into its fur. With that in mind, I placed it on top of a blanket, and readied myself to carry it.

The moment I did so, I questioned whether I was actually carrying a living thing. Perhaps it was because some of the water had been removed, because the puppy felt far lighter than before.

I was dealing with a small puppy, no denying that. I was left wondering if its poor health wasn't just from the cold. It could be starving too.

Either way, getting it warmed up was the first step. I turned the heater on and switched the air conditioner to heat mode. It got warmer in a matter of minutes.

Back when I started living alone, the chilliness of springtime wasn't exactly endearing, so my uncle—who's also my legal guardian—presented me with a small kerosene heater.

I mostly used the apartment's built in heating or bundled up when it got cold. So the kerosene heater was fuelled up and unused, until tonight.

Using both at the same time ought to speed up the heating process. It was about as good as it could get for the hypothermic puppy.

Ah, I shouldn't keep the heater too close. Wouldn't want to expose the puppy to its heat directly, nor the kerosene-affected air.

"Okay, while we wait for the room to warm up, let's see what else I can do…"

I wrapped the puppy's body in a blanket in hopes that it would help raise its body heat. I supposed the next thing to do was to prepare some food to help the puppy regain its strength.

"Ack, I just realized I have no ingredients to work with."

All I had in my fridge were drinks, eggs, and condiments.

Yeah, come to think of it, I was supposed to go grocery shopping after work...

"Judging from its size, though, the puppy's practically a newborn. Consuming solid foods probably won't go well. Not to mention it's out of energy. Maybe this'll do?"

Putting aside my own meal for later, I started thinking on what I could serve the small pup.

Since I couldn't tell if it would be able to eat solid food, I took out an unopened milk carton.

Heating the milk would also help in restoring the puppy's body heat. I'd be killing two birds with one stone.

But a thought halted me. I distinctly remembered a random tidbit telling me how milk made for human consumption would have an adverse effect on dogs. *Hmmm...* The problem was that I didn't have milk for dogs, and I was worried about what would happen if I left the puppy to buy some.

"Why wasn't it allowed again? Was it the sugar content? Something about lactose, if my memory serves me correctly... Maybe I should dilute it with water, then."

I wasn't sure if I remembered that right, but since it was an emergency, I decided to give it a shot. I poured the milk into a pot then added some water into it afterward, hoping that it would work as a safety measure. Once everything was in, I turned on the stove.

I needed to buy dog stuff once leaving the puppy by itself became a viable option.

"Oh, took me a while to realize that I'm just as drenched as that dog. Man, the heat coming off the stove feels good."

My apartment was simple and didn't have anything fancy like an induction stove. I had a gas stove. I didn't notice I was soaked until the flames from the stove top radiated heat.

My apartment's heating system, the heater, and the stovetop all joined together to quickly warm me up.

Thinking back, I was so focused on keeping the puppy safe from the rain that I didn't think to use my umbrella.

"I still can't believe someone would abandon a puppy like that. It got lucky. If I hadn't been passing by…"

I'd like to think that if not me, someone else would have noticed, except I just didn't have it in me to believe in such an idealistic occurrence.

Even after I wiped the puppy and wrapped it in a blanket, I could still see it shivering. It made me think of how the puppy's small candle of life would've been snuffed out had I been a few minutes slower.

I'd go as far as to say it was a miracle that I heard its cries with how loud the raindrops were, like its wails were directed specifically at me.

whine… whine…

"Whoops. Gotta get the little guy drinking fast. *Hmmm…* I watered down the milk already, but maybe I should dilute it more?"

As much as I wanted to stay warm, the weakened puppy came first.

The milk started frothing, so I took a spoon and sampled it.

I could tell the cream and lactose were being separated and concentrated, and perhaps me thinning it down with water played a part, so I could barely taste its sweetness.

It was way too thin for my liking, but it seemed the right consistency for the puppy, so I spooned it onto a plate.

I turned off the stove. Washing the pot could wait until later, so I took the milk-filled plate to the puppy.

"*fwooo… fwooo…* Still a bit too hot, I think. Let's wait until it cools down a bit more, okay? *fwooo… fwooo…*"

whine…

The puppy's voice was still pretty faint, but it felt like there was a bit more oomph there. It probably wasn't as cold as before.

I half expected the puppy to be so tired that it'd close its eyes and lay down, but it was actually watching me cool down the milk.

The cries it was letting out didn't feel like the type that were seeking for help any longer. The twitching nose was perhaps a sign of its hunger taking over after picking up the aroma of the milk. Just my assumption, though.

"I think it's cooled off enough, maybe?"

Dipping my finger into the milk to get a feel for its temperature, I found that it was rather lukewarm, so I placed the plate in front of the puppy.

"Here you go. I think you're gonna perk up after drinking this."

whine… whine… whine…

"Oh, is it too fatigued? Doesn't seem like it can stand… What should I do?"

The puppy could only stare at the plate placed in front of it. It did seem like it was trying to move, but it could only continue to whine, as it was too tired to stand on its own.

I had the bright idea to search for a baby bottle until I realized that I didn't have one, not to mention it might not even be able to suckle, exhaustion plaguing its body.

At times like that, having a rubber pipette would be a lifesaver. Unfortunately, I was a single guy and a poor college student. I didn't have any special equipment.

"Let's see… how about you try licking it off me? Here you go, right at the tip of my finger. Lickety-lick…"

whine…

I dipped my finger into the plate of milk, then I let it hang near the puppy's nose, urging it to lap the milk off.

The puppy let out a soft whine, then sniffed my finger. Luckily, it chose to stick its tongue out.

I wouldn't say this was something to be embarrassed about, but it wasn't exactly something I was trying to show off to people, either… Imagine saying lickety-lick at my age…

Lost in my thoughts, I suddenly felt the puppy's tongue coming into contact with my extended finger.

"Nice, it's actually licking my finger. Thank goodness."

lick… lick… whine…

"Oh, licked my finger clean already? Round two it is."

After flicking its tongue a few times to completely lap off

the milk off my finger, the puppy proceeded to whimper as if demanding more, so I repeated the process.

It felt like the puppy was crying out for help earlier, so it was a bit jarring to see it transition to whimpering for more milk. But I guess it had been hungry to begin with.

Then again, I could be imagining things and it was vocalizing for the same reasons.

whine... whine...

"Phew, should be fine now. Ha ha ha, it's sleeping like a baby."

After several finger licking sessions, the puppy seemed at ease with its belly full, so it had closed its eyes to rest.

In the meantime, not only had the room gotten toastier, being wrapped in a blanket like that warmed the puppy to its core.

I might be exaggerating, but it felt like I could take a breather after looking at the puppy's slumbering state, since it was a pretty close call.

"I've always known cats and dogs can be cute, but I never expected them to be this adorable. Makes you wonder who on earth would abandon one like that."

Since I'd calmed down, I was seething at whoever did this to the puppy.

It would be one thing if the puppy was deep in the mountains. Heck, you couldn't even call it a stray. The puppy was inside a cardboard box when I found it. Ergo, it was abandoned, no questions about it.

Even if there were extenuating circumstances which led to this person no longer being able to care for it, they still could've reached out to foster care.

whine... whine...

"Sigh..."

Seeing the puppy sleep so blissfully, I couldn't help but inhale and let out a sigh to release my frustration.

It was hard staying angry when I saw the puppy's cute sleeping expression.

"Oh, I just realized, I'm also in dire need of food."

The moment my anger went away, I heard a growl far louder than the one that came from the puppy's belly.

I had taken the puppy home immediately after finding it, so I didn't exactly have the time for grocery shopping. To make things worse, I left the umbrella somewhere around the vicinity where I found the puppy, too.

I was cradling the puppy in an attempt to shield it from the rain, forgoing any other thoughts. It took until I got home for me to realize that I chucked my umbrella.

"I wasn't really thinking straight when I held that puppy, huh..."

"*Zzzz... Zzzz...*"

"It's sleeping so peacefully. I should make an effort to not wake it up when I buy my dinner. There's got to be *something* at the convenience store."

I glanced at the clock which let me know that it was already closing hours for the supermarket. Good thing I could rely on the good ol' twenty-four seven convenience store.

Sure, their stuff tended to be more expensive than the supermarket's— which was why I tried not to go there whenever possible—but I had little choice in the matter at that moment.

"But the puppy's going to make a fuss if it wakes up and notices I'm gone, isn't it?"

"Zzzz… Zzzz…"

It would only take around two to three minutes for a round-trip to the convenience store, but on the off-chance it woke up and started wailing, I'd feel so bad for it.

I had come to prefer seeing the puppy sleep without a care in the world.

"Oh, well, skipping dinner won't kill me. I'll just treat it as an impromptu diet."

You could hardly call me overweight, but by treating the situation as a method of dieting, it would be a bit easier to suppress my hunger. At least, I hoped so.

"Ngh… Looks like the sun has risen."

"Hrrr…"

"Sleeping like a log this time around, eh. I take it you're feeling much better already, then."

I could see the sunlight peeking through the curtains.

The puppy woke up several times throughout the night, and it was letting out faint barks as if it wanted more milk, so I let it drink via my finger again. I pretty much did this until the dead of night.

Staying home was apparently the correct decision.

My only issue was that when I searched for nearby vets, I discovered that none of them were open during the night.

It *was* rather late when I found the puppy, so it was understandable.

Anyway, I reheated the milk and watched the puppy's sleeping face It woke up and lapped the milk off of me. I watched it sleep again…rinse and repeat. Before I realized it, dawn had broken.

By the way, when the room was warm enough, I turned off the heater so only the air conditioner was putting in work. As much as I'd rather have used the heater, it would pollute the air.

"It's strange that I'm kind of sleepy now, considering that I wasn't drowsy whatsoever when I took care of the little guy all night."

I reckoned that was because I was trying to pay attention to the puppy's condition.

But I guess there was only so much my body could take before drowsiness pulled me in.

"*Oof,* I shouldn't sleep. Gotta take away this sleepiness. Washing my face should help."

whimper…

"A dog tilting its head? Wait, hang on for a bit, okay? I'll be back in a jiffy."

At some point, without me noticing, the puppy had woken up and was looking at me with awe while also tilting its head. I asked it to stay put for a bit to wash my face.

I also prepared a helping of milk while I was at it.

"Okay, what's next in our agenda? Well, I guess the vet's on top of the priority list."

Yelp! Arf, arf...

The puppy had somewhat perked up. It could even stand up. Ruffling its fur with the tip of my fingers, I started to plan my next course of action.

Since the warm milk did the puppy good, I tried serving it another helping. Unfortunately, the aroma alone wasn't enticing enough for it. The puppy would only consume the milk by lapping it off my finger.

I'd say the puppy had taken a liking to my digits.

The puppy clung to my finger using its forelegs, play-biting it as its teeth had yet to fully grow. Kind of ticklish, if you asked me.

The fact that it was still teething pretty much proved that the puppy was recently born.

The little pup appeared to have recovered, but after what I saw last night, it might have some sort of illness. Taking it to the vet was a must.

Choo!

"*Whoops,* it *is* pretty cold, isn't it? Okay, let's get you warm over there. *Uh,* you actually like it *here?*"

Arf!

Since the puppy sneezed rather loudly, I tucked it inside the blanket, but against all expectations, the puppy actually crawled out and climbed onto my lap. I was sitting cross-legged, so the space in-between probably seemed inviting.

The puppy seemed to be cozy, so I let it be and covered it with my blanket and used my hands for extra measure. The puppy settled down afterward.

"The puppy's getting attached to me but I guess that's better than being hated by it. Right, off to the vet we go. *Oof*."

I took my smartphone out, intending to search for the nearest vets. Just as I did that, my phone vibrated and rang out loud.

It was my morning alarm.

Oh yeah, I just realized that it was a weekday. Technically, I should have been going to campus.

"*Mmmhhh...* Can't just let the puppy stay here by itself, but it's not like I could expect someone to babysit it either. All right, skipping today's courses it is."

By no means could I be called an exemplary student, though I did pride myself in the fact that I held a perfect attendance record. A shame, but I wouldn't be able to forgive myself if I chose to maintain that over the puppy.

Since I'd made up my mind, I had to quickly make my moves. First off, I needed to contact the campus and inform my uncle on why I would be absent for the day.

I'd bet some heads would turn if I told them that it was because I was looking after a puppy. For what it's worth, I *was* sorry, uncle.

After that, I searched for nearby vets on the internet and contacted the available ones.

I told them of the puppy's condition. How lethargic it was

the night before, even though it seemed to be feeling relatively fine today. I also told them of how its teeth haven't fully developed. After that, I booked an appointment with them.

I'd already washed my face, and there was no need to spruce up for a trip to the vet, so I went as I was.

"But before that…"

I still had some time before the appointed time at the vet. I'd been trying to maintain some distance from the puppy, but maybe it was time for a change? I had to at least give *him* a name.

"*Hmmm…* On the thin side and had practically no energy the night before. Since I want you to become as strong as an ox and prance around, I think a name that conveys 'lion-hearted' will suit you better. Okay, how about Leo?! Do you like the sound of that?!"

Arf!

The name came to me in a flash when I was trying to think of a name befitting a male dog.

The puppy—I mean, Leo—barked in approval. It was safe to assume that he liked it.

"All right, Leo. Want to go on a short trip with me?"

Arf!

Seeing Leo's gusto-filled response felt nice, though it didn't feel like he was planning to let go of my feet anytime soon. This led to me carrying him, blanket and all, to the vet.

Then again, perhaps the blanket was perfect for the occasion, as it kept Leo warm while we were outside.

When we arrived at the clinic, the physician proceeded to examine Leo. I was advised on the importance of vaccines for both Leo's teeth and general health. While it did seem like a lot of trouble, I brushed off that thought and made another appointment while I was there.

Right then and there, they told me that Leo was a female Maltese. I somewhat regretted giving her a gallant name instead of a sweeter one.

It was only until after I told the vet the story of how I found Leo that I realized how lucky she had been. Had I noticed Leo even just a bit later, she might not be with us anymore.

We started for my apartment, and the landlord saw us just as we were about to enter it. I was afraid my landlord would raise hell for bringing a dog home without permission, but it worked out somehow.

My uncle was the one who picked out the room I'd been living in, so it was only then I discovered that if you wanted to keep a pet, you needed to discuss it with the landlord.

Fortunately, the landlord was fond of animals, and the room adjacent to mine was unoccupied, so I was granted the permission to keep Leo.

Moreover, not only was the landlord furious at the person who abandoned Leo, her eyes pretty much enchanted the landlord.

That being said, while you could definitely apply that to my uncle—who helped me out a ton—my landlord was no slouch either. I couldn't hold anything against either of them.

Sometime after I took in Leo, plenty of people extended their assistance. I couldn't find a foster care for Leo, so she was pretty much living with me.

"Oh? Interested in this, Leo?"

Arf!

"But I have to make our foods separately…"

Arf! Arf!

One such day, Leo wagged her tail and wiggled her butt at the sight of the sausages I included in my lunchbox, drooling over them.

It wasn't often Leo showed such a reaction, so I was tempted to feed some to her. However, my more rational side stopped me from recklessly handing human food to a dog.

Human cooking tends to be overly seasoned, making it unfit for dog consumption.

But seeing Leo looking at me with those puppy eyes was crumbling my will. Surely just a little bit wouldn't harm her, right?

"No more, got it? It'd be bad for your health, okay?"

Arf, arf… whine…

"Oh, come on, don't do this to me. That's it. No more extras, okay?"

That much would be fine. The sausage's length was only about as long as the tip of my pinky to its first joint. Once I served it to Leo, she immediately scarfed it.

The moment Leo finished it, she mewled, as if asking for seconds. Alas, that was the time where I had to harden my heart and finish the rest of the sausages myself.

After eating the remaining sausages, I showed my empty hands to indicate that there weren't any left over. Leo threw in the towel after that.

I decided to play with her after seeing the way she sulked.

It was interesting to know that Leo had a penchant for sausages, though. If my memory served me right, there was a convenience store by the vet we visited, and they sold animal feed.

What a strategic business location! With all the people who visited the vets, they must have had a lot of customers. I also heard that the owner adored dogs.

"I should make some time to browse that store tomorrow. There might be products that are to Leo's liking, and it would be nice if they sell sausages for dogs."

I wouldn't deny that I was kind of hoping for it, but I didn't actually expect them to sell the sausages I was looking for when I swung by the very next day.

Having made my purchase, I could already imagine Leo's elation as I walked home. The moment I served it to Leo, her ecstatic appearance told me everything.

Arf! Arf!

"Look at you, gobbling it up. You really like it, don't you? Ha ha ha!"

That day should've been marked as an anniversary of sorts, celebrating Leo's love for sausages.

Ruff! Ruff!

"Leo? *Oh,* right. I forgot that you've gotten big. Man, you look really majestic now."

Ruff?

"Nah, nothing big. Just had a dream where I revisited the day we met. It overwhelmed me a little bit."

When I thought I was being woken up by the barks that I'd become really familiar with, I saw a large Silver Fenrir's muzzle on top of my bed, staring at me while occasionally barking with a huskier voice.

After I took Leo in, my world became a bit busier. Looking back, though, I had no regrets whatsoever.

After Leo came to my life, I didn't feel lonely anymore. In fact, my days were filled with joy.

Thanks, Leo.

And I hope we continue to remain as the friends we were, but seeing just how great you were in action after we were thrust into this brand-new world, the one who will be needing help all the time is probably me.

"By the way, Leo, are you feeling okay after eating that many sausages? I wasn't really sure what kind of food they had here, and since your favorite food is sausages, I blurted it out to Claire without really thinking about it."

Ruff? Awo… Ruff!

"You think it's fine? Well, I guess you're no longer the same size you were, so extra salt intake probably won't be an issue, right? *Mhm,* let's go with that…"

EVEN DOGS GO TO OTHER WORLDS

LIFE IN ANOTHER WORLD WITH MY BELOVED HOUND

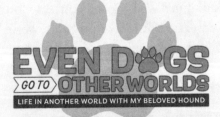